Principles of
FOREIGN POLICY

Principles of
FOREIGN POLICY

The Civil State in its World Setting

ROY E. JONES

St. Martin's Press · New York

First published in the United States of America in 1979.

ISBN 0–312–64561–9

Library of Congress Cataloging in Publication Data

Jones, Roy E.
    Principles of foreign policy.

    Bibliography: p.
    Includes index.
    1. State, The.   2. International relations.
I. Title.
JX4001.J65   341.26   79–9835
ISBN 0–312–64561–9

Contents

Acknowledgement

I am grateful to Professor J. E. Spence for his most helpful and
perceptive comments and criticisms.

R.E.J.

Introduction

This book is the record of an individual effort to resolve two linked problems that will be dauntingly familiar to anyone given to thinking about foreign policy in the liberal tradition. First, there is the intractable difficulty of bringing some sort of conceptual order to the daily mass of cross-national happenings that relentlessly deny the validity of received notions of the distinctive character of foreign policy. Second, there is the problem of relating a faith in constitutional government to an area of public affairs in which not only do domestic and foreign structures and issues constantly fuse but that also contains conflicts whose outcome could at any time be destruction of a societal order of magnitude. So this is both a search for intellectual order and an attempt to formulate a normative approach to matters ranging from the election of representatives to cross-national assemblies to invocations of thermonuclear holocaust.

CHAPTER 1

To Start with an Invention

An obvious way of formulating principles of foreign policy is to design a plausible model of the kind of world in which foreign policies exist. It should then be a simple matter to extract appropriate principles from such a model.[1]

A plausible foreign policy model

1. The constituent units of the world of foreign policies are sovereign national states, which possess varying resources of strength.

2. No national state can wholly trust another national state to remain bound by agreements or simply to observe ordinary canons of decent conduct because canons of decent conduct are not intrinsic to all national states and because deviant behaviour by one national state that affects other states may oblige these affected states to ignore obligations of a specific or of a general kind to further states, and so on through the whole system.

3. No universal institutions exist that can enforce either contracts or general rules, so a national state can only make itself secure by actual or threatened retaliation (in order to ward off the uncongenial moves of other states) or by the provision or the promise of rewards (in order to motivate congenial moves by other states). Enforcement in these senses is therefore a matter of subjective judgement as to the construction of supposedly broken contracts or rules by the enforcing or prospectively enforcing state. It is also a matter of the strength a national state can deploy in the international arena, so that attempted enforcement against a relatively weak state is much more likely than attempted enforcement against a relatively strong state.

4. Securing desired behaviour from other national states or making binding contracts with them therefore depends on power: that is, on economic and military strength; on the craft with which these resources are applied; and on the contingent circumstances in which favours may or may not be sought by other states.

5. Power is thus at the centre of all foreign policy operations and it is the external application of the resources of strength at the disposal of the national state.

6.   A national state may increase its strength both by its own exertions and by making cooperative arrangements with other national states. Cooperative strength is likely to have only limited external application because of the operational constraints that diversely placed partner states will impose on one another. And strength acquired cooperatively may be depleted very rapidly as a result of the sovereign withdrawal of partners. Extensive power in a disruptive or negative sense thus exists inside cooperative arrangements because an ally can threaten to desert at any particularly pregnant moment.

The principles of foreign policy that emerge from this model

1.   The national state must acquire as much individual strength as it can because it is only through the application, or threatened application, of strength that it can secure its foreign policy ends.

2.   A state's foreign policy goals must comprise those conditions of the international arena that secure it as much as possible from the unwelcome effects of power exerted by other states. It follows that the internal and external operations of the state are related in two essential ways: first, internal action is required to build up and maintain strength that may be exerted externally; and, second, the external deployment of power is required to ensure that the internal affairs of the state are not disturbed or determined by the foreign policy actions of other states.

3.   Strength that is acquired cooperatively is of limited application against third parties because it depends on diverse partners each of which may go its own way at any moment. The effectiveness of cooperative arrangements must therefore be founded on an accurate joint perception of the existence, or prospective existence, of common enemies.

4.   The number of partners in any joint enterprise must be kept to the minimum necessary to the successful pursuit of the common goal for three reasons: first, any benefits acquired by the cooperating group must be split among the partners, so the fewer there are the greater the possible share of benefits each of them may get; second, the greater the number of partners the more limited will be the circumstances in which joint strength will actually be applied; third, the more partners there are, the more opportunities there will be for individual disruption of cooperative ventures.

5.   The share of benefits that a national state can acquire for itself from joint ventures depends on the power it can exert on its partners, so the greater the strength it individually deploys the greater its chance of making disproportionate gains from partnerships. In any cooperative venture each state is concerned to be well placed when cooperation inevitably ceases.

6.   In exerting strength to obtain benefits within a partnership, a state is

constrained by the level of its relative dependence on its partners (the stronger the state the less this will usually be) and by the need to avoid causing them to destroy the partnership prematurely.

7.   If a state can secure greater returns at less cost from an alternative alliance, then it should speedily abandon those of its partners that it cannot take with it, or that, if taken, would reduce the benefits to itself from the new arrangement. Delay in matters of this kind increases the danger that allies likely to be harmed will move first to protect themselves from loss.

8.   A national state must be conscious of the fact that the motives to which it responds are the same as the motives to which other states respond. It should therefore beware of inattention to its own interests and of attributing to its international attachments a depth and permanence with which they can never actually be endowed.

9.   National states are relatively weak or relatively strong. An isolated weak state is in no position to obtain advantages from a strong state when their interests conflict. Similarly, within an alliance a strong state, being relatively independent, can secure greater benefits in terms of adaptations in the behaviour of allies than can a weak state. A weak state is best placed to obtain disproportionately large benefits when a strong state feels dependent on it. The policy of a small state must therefore be: first, to emphasise and exacerbate, short of damage to itself, those contingent circumstances that create an alliance of which it is a member; second, having done so, to obtain from its relatively strong ally maximum benefits by any available means; and, third, to be poised to transfer its attachments to a strong enemy in any circumstances where a greater dependence on its services is in prospect, always provided that this is not the dependence of a probable loser.

10.   In their mutual dealing, strong states should exchange influence over weak states as their interests dictate. However, under the terms of the model, they cannot incorporate weak states into their own territories since, in attempting to contain other nationalities, they would themselves cease to be national states.

Two major defects in the derivation of these principles

The deepest fault in these principles lies in the method whereby they are obtained. Given the model, the principles that follow from it are tautologies. They are simply further specifications of the model. A statesman in such a system would have no need of these principles because he would be acting along these lines anyway. These apparent principles define a world and they describe it too. They cannot also be prescriptions because they suggest nothing beyond what they define. A model does not propound principles, it contains principles. Altering this model (and variations come amply to mind) would not resolve any difficulties about the validity of principles drawn up in this way.

These principles are recommendations not to a particular state but to all states. Their conservatism is therefore complete. They are part of a defined system and their effect is the maintenance of that system. Change is simply the rearrangement of alliances and general adjustment to relative movements in the strength of states. The only fundamental transformation possible in this system is the annihilation of national states in miscalculated wars. But items in a model cannot miscalculate.

The unreality of the basic units of the model

The relevance of principles derived from a model is dependent on the empirical persuasiveness of the model in question as a generalised image of a specific area of public affairs. As such an image, the present model has a glaring initial defect. To establish the national state as its basic unit is wholly unreal if the national state is taken to mean a territorially defined population that coherently identifies itself as a single nation uniquely and organically joined to one particular state among the mutually recognising collectivity of states. What actual 'nation-state' meets this requirement? Not Spain, not Soviet Russia, not Great Britain, not Nigeria, not South Africa . . . yet these are widely held to be international actors. Almost every state contains a variety of groups claiming identity as nations. The organic nation-state is the ideal of nationalist movements and is seldom, if ever, realised.

And bland use of the term 'state' conceals a rich diversity of theory and practice. The state is a complex notion, full of contradictions. At the most elementary level of argument the state as a means for achieving grand social objectives (equality, proletarian dictatorship, wealth, national emancipation) is apt to conflict with the idea of the state as the condition of a legal order distinct from social movements. Within most western countries, if not within most western minds, there is a tension between these two views, each of which seems to imply a different kind of international role: one engaged and crusading, the other defensive and sceptical.

The actual variability of the state not depicted in the model

In the most simple practical sense the apparatus of the state differs widely in different traditions: in France the distinction between this apparatus and the rest of society is generally drawn with some exactitude, whereas in Britain the existence of hundreds of quasi-autonomous authorities and organisations, involving the services of large numbers of both paid and unpaid citizens, renders the same distinction much less precise.[2] More importantly, many actual states can hardly rank as states at all in terms of any clear and internally substantive definition of statehood. As an example, take this to be a proper definition of the state: *a territorially designated society whose members are equally subject to a body of law, with forms of legislative procedure and public administration that do not alter radically according to changes among the incumbents of public offices and in which legally ordered procedures are maintained for making such changes.* By this standard a large number of states in the underdeveloped world and elsewhere are not states at all. They may have an existence and a status in the language of diplomacy and, more evidently, in the rhetoric of public communications, but this is not the same as understanding them to be states in terms of any rich or longstanding conception of the nature of statehood.

States in the formal terms of diplomacy do not necessarily rank equally as actors in the international arena. Though Czechoslovakia and Hungary may have some characteristics of statehood in terms of this definition, their subservience to Soviet Russia means that in fact they may hardly rank with, say, Chile or Argentina as independent international actors even though these, by the same criteria, may be even less well qualified to be called states.

And, as a matter of practice, governments do not treat states as identical entities, differing only in their strength and alignments. A British government does not distinguish between the Soviet Union and the Netherlands thus: the Soviet Union is strong and hostile whereas the Netherlands is weak and friendly. The Netherlands is treated as a different kind of state from the Soviet Union.

The difficulties of sovereignty overlooked in the model

The term 'sovereignty' came into use at the same period as the term 'state' and is full of the latter's complexities. It denoted a desire to have in society the essential condition of order, which was deemed to be a determinate centre capable of clear decision and equipped with overwhelming power of enforcement. So sovereignty and the state could be conceived to be much the same thing and together they comprised a theory of public order. As such, sovereignty became subject to fundamental challenge about where it should lie—whether in a parliament, a nation, a king or in an ideological movement of some kind. And its very existence, let alone its desirability, could be questioned, so that federalism in the United States was devised as an alternative to the doctrine of sovereignty, placing law explicitly above government and setting separated authorities of government against one another in a system of checks and balances.

The variability of sovereignty is not much reduced if it is simply taken to mean the ability of a society to maintain an ordered existence for its members. A society may be both ordered and disordered within a short space of time (so that Germany was ordered immediately before the first world war and disordered immediately after the first world war) and it may be ordered and disordered at the same time at different places (so that the mainland of Britain may be ordered while Northern Ireland is disordered). Moreover, two ordered societies may be totally different in the kinds of order they maintain, so that though France and Soviet Russia may be ordered, they are ordered along such radically different lines that the doctrine of sovereignty must be deemed empty of substance if it is taken to refer equally to each of them.

Problems of sovereignty from an international standpoint

The model conveys that sovereignty has the same determinate internal meaning in all states and that this meaning is the key to the free, not to say vicious, way in which states act towards one another. The sovereign is master of itself both internally and externally.

(1) From the external standpoint sovereignty may be taken to denote a doctrine that the state, by its sovereign nature, can be bound by its own interests and by nothing else.

This doctrine may be disputed on a number of simple grounds. Items such as civilised conduct, natural law, the sanctity of agreements freely entered into, may all be claimed to have a standing at least as great as the state's interests because they provide the only long-term conditions in which interests may be obtained without incurring the intense foreign hostility that must ultimately create insecurity in their possession. In dire circumstances the state's interests may be traded off against these values, but this does not mean that they can be taken to be superior over them. Moreover, the state's interests do not exist as clear impersonal imperatives. They must be perceived and interpreted by fallible human beings. The doctrine of the absolute priority of reasons of state thus creates the danger of supreme claims to power being readily conceded to foolish or wicked statesmen. External sovereignty in this way becomes an invitation to internal tyranny. But sovereignty could also destroy the possibility of order in the international arena as well. The existence of large numbers of unconstrained sovereigns could result in an utterly disordered world environment. In this event the supreme value of internal order would be negated by the effects of international disorder. Given the catastrophic nature of possible wars, the present doctrine of sovereignty could result in the physical destruction of the state and of the internal order that is its justification. This doctrine thus contradicts itself.

(2) Alternatively, it may seem that the true mark of the sovereign state is that it can ignore international agreements and obligations and forms of law when impelled to do so by its own values rather than by its interests.

Though this view accepts that the sovereign is the servant of values and not their master, it suggests very little about the actual exercise of sovereignty. Presumably several values are involved. In concrete circumstances which is to be obeyed? Does the value of security (requiring, perhaps, alliance with a military dictatorship) override the value of liberty? And what is the standing of an arrangement made with a country that subsequently succumbs to tyranny? In a plural society these issues are argued about; the outcome is a line of action or inaction that may change as a result of further argument, a shift in the composition of government or an alteration in external circumstances. But the important things here are arguments and circumstances, not sovereignty.

The view that when values and specific international obligations conflict the latter may be ignored is an undistinguished one that requires no grandiose notion of sovereignty. Individuals may break agreements and obligations of all kinds in response to the dictates of values. And groups within a country are not uncommonly so moved by some cause as to ignore both the law and their own comfort and safety. Sovereignty from this viewpoint simply describes an aspect of the human condition in almost any conceivable circumstances. It is superfluous in another sense too. The capacity of a state (or of a group of some kind) to ignore specific commitments relates particularly to its strength. A state largely self-sustaining in terms of raw materials and industrial production is likely to be better placed to disregard international economic commitments than one that is not so well placed. But the important factor here is strength, not sovereignty.

(3) The capacity to go to war may seem to be the most clear external mark of the sovereign.

Of course any group may resort to violence. If the view here is that non-state violence is illegal while state violence is legal, two basic points must be made. First, a doctrine of natural law may justify individual or group violence in circumstances where actual law offends against natural justice; where, for example, the church is being persecuted. On the other hand, a state's resort to war is not necessarily legal. The right of the state to use international violence in furtherance of its disputes is circumscribed by many law-like limitations set out in the United Nations Charter and elsewhere. Though these prohibitions can be ignored it is still the case that there is a law of war and that a sovereign may break this law in going to war, just as a group or individual, in most circumstances, breaks a law in using violence.

That a state may go to war may be true but relatively unimportant compared with the question of when it should go to war or whether it should continue with a war. This kind of decision may be open to argument. Here again the argument is more important than sovereignty. Similarly, states do not ignore external circumstances, legal or otherwise, in making their decisions about belligerency. The United States was drawn into the first world war by, among other factors, German infringements of the law of the sea; but the illegal invasion of Hungary in 1956 by Soviet Russia did not lead the United States or any other country into war. In an age of thermonuclear weapons, going to war may be far riskier for first-rank states than for much weaker powers (in, say, the Middle East). So the tendency to chance war, to be apparently fully sovereign, may be inversely related to strength and even to statehood itself.

(4) Sovereignty may seem to denote the capability of the state to resort to

dictatorial rule, to create a sovereign, in order to survive a war or war-like crisis.

As a statement of fact—that a dictatorship is necessary to survive violent external crises—this is doubtful. In a dangerous situation there are likely to be important decisions to be made but no suspension of constitutional rule need be called for. Britain and the United States in the first world war can hardly be argued to have been ruled dictatorially. As a different sort of observation—that dictatorships are better able to survive wars and war-like crises—this theory of sovereignty does not stand up to examination in terms of second world war experience.

States as territorial units often survive wars in which they have been defeated. What sometimes fail to survive in these circumstances are regimes; but it may be highly desirable that some regimes should not survive. Doctrines justify actions. Internationally it is rarely the case that there are no wars or crises of other kinds. The existence of large numbers of thermonuclear weapons in constant readiness for use constitutes a permanent threat of the gravest imaginable kind. In such an environment the present doctrine of sovereignty as dictatorial response to danger may reasonably be held to constitute an open invitation to leaders to behave tyrannously since they can always claim the justification of a crisis in international affairs.

More significantly, this notion of sovereignty may be taken to refer to the capacity of a society, when its existence as a set of values and practices is at stake, to make hard decisions necessary to its continued existence even though these decisions may contradict the values and practices in question. This is certainly important. But at its core this view is a particular one, since it relates to some states only. For it accepts that there are values of far greater importance than sovereignty and that sovereignty, a practical necessity to ignore these values, should come into existence in only the most extreme circumstances. As a doctrine this really recommends the prudent avoidance of extreme external circumstances. It is a notion of no relevance to societies accustomed to arbitrary rule, because sovereignty in this sense can only be summoned up in constitutional states. Again sovereignty is a variable.

The model's portrayal of inter-state relations a gross over-simplification

The model maintains that the environment of one state is other identical states and that this environment is one in which there are no institutions with the authority to enforce either general rules or particular agreements.

Yet states, being concepts, cannot act. Governments act in the role of states and governments are far from identical. Indeed government is the greatest variable of all, subject to changes in terms of popular support and of internal composition and coherence from day to day. The relations between governments are in no way analogous to the mechanical actions and reactions of the states in the model: friendships, values, relative strength and authority are all taken into account in the daily conduct of these actual relations.

Territorial items other than states, say West Berlin or the Falkland Islands, may register importantly in international relations. Movements claiming many of the attributes of statehood may be of fundamental importance in particular international regions such as the Middle East or southern Africa. Governments may in some circumstances find themselves bargaining from positions of relative weakness with foreign-owned multinational companies. The UN Secretary-General, the Secretary-General of the IMF, the President of the European Commission and similar dignatories are often greeted and treated in a style much the same as that accorded leaders of more traditional status. Governments are repeatedly made aware of their turbulent existence within international systems remote from the inter-state model. The cross-national market in currencies has sometimes faced British and other governments with the quietus of their domestic policies. This market is composed of the actions and services of banks, of all kinds of national and multinational companies and organisations, of the decisions of the authorities of other states, some of which may be very small though very rich. It cannot be said to exist in some pure international medium since it is really a complex set of linkages between markets within countries and between liquid assets which may be deposited in large quantities outside their countries of origin.

Nor is the absence of institutions with the power of enforcement so markedly a distinguishing feature of the international arena as the model would seem to maintain. The notion that offices of state always confer internal power on their holders is a naive one: British governments, in many areas of apparently domestic economic policy, have not enforcing power but bargaining power. More generally, there is much force in the argument that the authority of a new law in any plural society lies in the political way in which it has evolved not in the way it may be enforced, because it could not be enforced were it promulgated in the absence of some kind of political consensus. Many agreements between elements in a plural society do not take the form of enforceable contracts but depend for their observance on the manner and circumstances in which they are made and operated. At the international level there are many institutions (the IMF, GATT, EEC) under whose auspices detailed agreements are made that are subsequently observed; in this process, just as is often the case at the domestic level, powers of enforcement are entirely secondary to the free way in which agreements are made. Yet there are cross-national courts (as in the EEC) that are charged with the care of cross-national rules and agreements. More commonly, detailed international enforcement is provided by the prospect of retaliatory action by aggrieved parties should infringements of agreements occur; but analogies to this enforcement process are not hard to find at the domestic level.

Following from this, it is plain that the relations between open plural societies, each internally familiar with the practice of political and economic bargaining and consensual agreement, are different in nature from the relations between plural states and closed states. But here again the problem of enforcement narrows down to the fact that in the latter category the number of agreements that can, or should, be made are relatively very few. It is the smallness of the area of possible agreement that is important, not the absence of international enforcement agencies. This goes to the roots of divergent notions of statehood and is not a simple matter of the nature of international institutions.

The vagaries of power

The principles contained in the model assert that the central variable of foreign policy is the differing strength of states, which is expressed in the varying intensities of power they exert over one another.

But even by the crudest standard power is in part a product of conditions other than national strength. Political and physical situations within the diplomatic arena may confer more scope for choice than does national strength. Egypt usually has greater freedom of foreign policy manoeuvre than, say, Finland, but this is not essentially the product of the superior national strength of Egypt. And the effect of military strength at the highest thermonuclear level is ambiguous; what it confers is the ability to offer threats of an order that might be wholly disastrous to all parties if carried out. In many circumstances this kind of strength may seem to constrain freedom of action; more strength may mean less power.

The role of military strength in foreign relations is related to its possible use. But in the relations between large numbers of countries there is no question of the possible use of violence in any foreseeable circumstances. The threat of force does not enter into the relations between the Scandinavian countries; but between countries of the Middle East the calculus of force is prominently at work. This indicates that fundamental distinctions have to be made between different international regions. Military strength is important in some but not in others. This variability is not created by strength itself. Power is always exerted in situations or systems that also contain values: my power in a boxing ring may be meagre; my power in a debating chamber may be resounding. Each of these environments is one in which different values are observed and in each case the kind of power in use is radically different. Power is not the same thing in different systems and in different circumstances. Governments and states operate in a variety of systems and power changes among these. The strength of an argument may be conceded in the Council of Europe; but argument unbacked by military strength is likely to be ineffective in bilateral diplomatic negotiations with the Soviet Union.

Not only is power fundamentally a variable in this way, so are the interests that power is used to pursue. The interests of French wine producers are important in Franco–Italian economic relations and are recognised to be so both by the governments principally concerned and by other Community governments; they have a legitimacy in cross-national relations that is not in any way linked to military power. Similarly, the number and variety of interests (commercial, industrial, cultural) involved in Anglo-American relations are vastly greater than are involved in Anglo-Soviet relations. So great is the order of difference here that one may conclude that these are different kinds of worlds in which power has entirely different meanings. To say that British and American governments respond to interests in their relations is a truism that conveys very little. It is the unmilitary way in which they respond to interests that matters and that marks these relations as being in a different category from Anglo-Soviet relations. And to suggest, as the model seems to, that a British government should realign itself if an American action harms its interests is meaningless because what is involved here is a complex range of linked interests and communications, official and otherwise, all in a constant condition of political change and adjustment.

Strength not in boxes

The model asserts that the state can only deploy its own military strength, developed by its own efforts, though this may be briefly aligned with that of inherently unreliable allies. This proposition fails to explain much cross-national defence activity. It makes little sense to describe the military situation of the German Federal Republic in this way. The GFR imports weapons; it develops others in association with other countries; numbers of Nato countries have forces, some armed with nuclear weapons, deployed on its territory. The defence resources of the GFR are different from the military strength of the GFR. The GFR's strength, economic or military, does not exist in a kind of national package, loosely piled with other national packages; it is part of a complex value-impregnated field of supply, planning and assorted governmental, military and unofficial relations and activities.

The model puts strength into national boxes assembled into stacks that are constantly being rearranged. Given the validity of this image, it follows that the individual state should arrange its alliances in such a way as to maximise prospective yields to itself and its partners; that is, alliances should be kept to the minimum size necessary to the attainment of joint objectives. This is a principle long observed by rational thieves. It rarely describes the cross-national commitments of governments. Large numbers of international associations (the GATT, the UN, the IMF) cannot in any way be described as alliances; nor do they pursue objectives in any exact sense, being more concerned to establish and nurture environments within which kinds of international relations may be conducted; nor do they strenuously exclude possible members. The most prominent of existing alliances, Nato, does not, for all its awkwardness, look like a clumsy stack of national boxes. It is in part held together by values. All kinds of linkages of a non-military character exist within it. It adjusts to numerous anomalies, not least the current associative status of France. It is more concerned with resisting the pursuit of uncongenial objectives by external powers than with pursuing objectives itself. Consequently the exact nature of the rewards it confers is open to argument. Whatever its rewards they do not accrue predominantly to its most powerful member, as the model insists they should. United States authorities repeatedly complain of 'free-riding' among their lesser partners whose military contributions are less than they might be. Yet these apparently weak and dependent allies are not easily bent to the policies of the United States, either within the alliance or outside it. And it seems odd that a strong state should urge weaker states to get stronger, because in the terms of the model this would inevitably have detrimental effects on its own power.

The plasticity of foreign policy

The model, and the principles contained in it, assumes there to be a distinct kind of activity that is properly described as foreign policy whose peculiarities derive from the unique arena of states within which it occurs. The term 'foreign policy' itself is full of the implication that there is a foreign environment to which one general kind of policy is appropriate. A moment's examination invalidates this. A British government may have policies towards arms control in Europe, involving the possibility of the redeployment of force by an alliance rather than by the state; towards the control of inflation, involving negotiation both with domestic interests and, not dissimilar in style, with foreign governments and international organisations whose attitude to the British need to borrow may be linked with the progress of economic negotiations at the domestic level; towards the development of the law of the sea, which may involve it in intricate negotiations in the European Community, in even wider negotiations under the auspices of the UN and in rancorous engagements with domestic fishing interests; towards a variety of high technology projects, civil and military, organised through cross-national consortia, which may mix diplomatic complexities at the inter-governmental level with equally perplexing problems of state intervention and industrial relations at the domestic level. And so on. To describe entanglements like these as issues of foreign policy tends to the conclusion that they all contain problems of the same kind, that they describe a distinct and singular category of affairs. But their only common feature would seem to be the unremarkable one that they involve foreigners as well as nationals.

In the not untypical British instance it is clearly the case that all public issues involving foreigners are not dealt with by the department of state formally charged with conducting foreign policy, the Foreign and Commonwealth Office. Virtually every government department, including the Home Office, conducts external relations and almost all ministers are active internationally.[3] Similarly, many quasi-governmental institutions (the Bank of

England, nationalised industries) operate in a cross-national context. Hosts of groups, firms and agencies (anti-apartheid campaigns, ICI, Amnesty International, conservation groups) have directly cross-national concerns. All kinds of professional organisations maintain close contacts with colleagues abroad. Can principles of foreign policy be made relevant to activities like these?

Conclusions

1.   The model created its own principles, which therefore applied only to itself.

2.   The abstract concepts arranged in the model could not accommodate the diversity of foreign policy practices.

3.   The model attempted to explain the foreign policies of all states; in doing so it committed itself to meaningless generality.

4.   The *a priori* arrangement of abstractions in a world model can never be expected to yield much that is of practical relevance. If we are to get near to the real problems of foreign policy we must locate ourselves inside the world, not make futile attempts to escape from it.

CHAPTER 2

Finding a Commitment

The abstract model that has just been abandoned proved deeply futile because it attempted to create an *a priori* world. Finding a tenable starting point for this enquiry in an actual social context is not difficult.

This enquiry the product of a specific setting

The present enquiry could not be stimulated by life in a world such as that portrayed in the model. In such a world there would be nothing to enquire about. Before one can be curious about the nature of something like foreign policy one must be aware of a puzzling reality. So this investigation can only take place in a social and cultural setting that is accepted to be complex. If this setting were simple, the nature of foreign policy would be given and it could not contain or generate enquiries like the present one. Similarly, this setting must be accepted to be changeful. If it were static, a given doctrine of foreign policy would last forever because we would be living in a world much the same as the model. And some sort of change has to be accepted to be interminable or we would again have to resume modelling. If a static future could be envisaged, the appropriate procedure would be to design an exact model to fit it. Yet puzzlement about foreign policy is created by the fact of change, so a model portraying a static future would have to be abstract because it would refer to an imagined world unlike any experienced.

Change must be a premiss of this enquiry. So must the undesigned nature of much change. If all change could be designed, stress between concepts and practices could never occur. Again, one would simply apply a model. But it is stress between concepts and practices that creates the sense of a need for principles. Not only are concepts challenged by practices, they are also challenged by other concepts. Arguments of both a general and a specific kind turn on actual problems of foreign policy. To enquire about foreign policy is not to wander in a silent desert; it is to enter a fertile tradition of discourse about foreign policy. The search for an ordered understanding of the nature of foreign policy arises from the existence of a discourse not from the acceptance of an orthodoxy. But a search that exists within a tradition of discourse cannot be inspired by a desire to bring that tradition to an end.

16

A commitment revealed by a process of elimination

An enquiry of the present kind presupposes a general commitment to the setting that brings it into existence. This conclusion can be reached by excluding other possibilities.

The first chapter's model contained principles of foreign policy that pretended to be appropriate to every state. Given the uniform nature of states depicted in the model there could be no other possibility. The outcome was policy unchanging in its effects on the character of international relations as a whole. The units in the model were therefore assumed to be committed to the maintenance of the international system depicted in it. Yet could a commitment really be felt by human beings to such a form of international life? The 'space' of the model's foreign policy arena contains nothing; it is simply the otherwise empty medium through which power is transmitted between states. There is nothing there to be committed to. In such a desolate world one could only be committed to the sovereign nation-state. And this would have to be a commitment shared by everyone; each individual would have to be equally committed to his own nation-state. In the model, national states are interchangeable within categories of strength, which is the only variable. Personal commitment cannot enter this model as an independent variable because if one were uncommitted to one's own state, and were not committed to another state, then one's commitment to the international system of states would be diminished to exactly the same degree and one would thus cease to be committed to its maintenance. For a similar reason values cannot be a variable. If each state's values were different from those of every other state, then among the totality of states there would be the most radical value divergences and at least two states would become so hostile to each other as to cease to be conservative towards an international system containing such extreme enemies. Alternatively, if the values of states differed irregularly it would follow that some pairs or groups of states would be more value-aligned than the generality of states. But this would introduce a fresh category into the system and those within this category could not be conservative towards the system they would have changed. The kind of commitment required for the maintenance of a world such as that created by the model is impossible.

Turning away from the model's requirement of exact commitment to one's own state to the possibility furthest removed from it—commitment to the whole world—is a course that soon strikes equally intractable problems. In practice it is impossible to sustain an exact commitment to the entirety of international society except in some mystical sense because it is bound to contain forms of living of which one knows nothing and practices and beliefs with which one has no sympathy. The profession of a commitment to the world as a human structure, to mankind, is common enough. But this is an abstraction. Mankind expresses itself through international trade, currency speculation, nuclear deterrence, war, drug traffic. A commitment to mankind is in fact a commitment to certain policies (to disarmament, free trade, national liberation or whatever) to which many among mankind may object. Similarly, a commitment to an acceptable condition of world affairs, to peace, boils down to a commitment to contentious policies for attaining or maintaining it. Embarrassingly, it may even lead to support for a *status quo* widely held to be unjust.

A direct path to a commitment

Let us accept the commonsense premiss that the actual international arena is partly characterised by systems of large-scale force deployment. What kind of personal commitment could exist towards the balance of power or towards nuclear deterrence? It could not reasonably be a commitment to the immediate use of massive violence since this would be a commitment to the probability of one's own extinction; it would have to be a commitment to the view that only through deterrence or balance of power can violent capabilities be internationally controlled. Accepting that systems like these do exist and do inhibit the use of large-scale violence, the commitment here boils down to a commitment to security based on the view that these systems are realistic ways of providing it. But security is not a substantive state of affairs. Security is the absence of a damaging state of affairs, of war. A commitment to security is thus empty of positive content. It becomes substantive only when associated with valued practices of some kind: with art, or cricket, or religion, or friendship, or philosophy, or making money. Given that the balance of power and nuclear deterrence are conflict systems, what fills security in one camp is unlikely to fill security in another. A commitment to security turns out to be a commitment to something other than security, to a kind of life practised in security, with all its attendant problems of foreign policy.

It would of course be impossible to worry about the nature of foreign policy if one did not believe there to be something valuable of an internal nature and something potentially dangerous external to it. Something must be at stake. Among the things at stake must be the context within which it is possible to puzzle about principles of foreign policy. Given this to be so, two necessary and related characteristics of life within this context follow: it proliferates layers of practical problems; it proliferates concepts that are open and changing. A premiss of concern about the nature of policy in this setting is that courses of acting and thinking of many varieties may be openly deliberated. One's concern in puzzling about the nature of foreign policy is principally with the ways in which complex practices may be conceptualised. But this concern is itself part of general deliberative processes. In deliberating one cannot also deny the validity of deliberation; this is an inevitable commitment. One cannot proceed (as one would with a model) as if one intended to bring deliberation to an end. Thinking about the nature of foreign policy in the context of complex practice and open concepts assumes the existence of a society providing the conditions of continual debate and legitimate challenge to official orthodoxies.

An autocrat may decide upon a course of action after having deliberated upon it, but his central concern is with the maintenance of the conditions of his own rule. His courses of action cannot be compared with other possible courses where these involve other ways of ruling nor can they be assessed independently of his will. His actions do not represent choice set in an endless political process, since there can be no other centres of authority or autonomy able to press or provide other possible futures or, through investigation and argument, reveal the error of selected policy. The limitations of autocratic policy are increased in the case of officially enforced ideological policy. If the fundamental nature of society as a whole is ideologically given, then so is the nature of rational policy. Choice cannot grow from a consideration of what is possible, since what is possible must also be rational and what is rational is officially defined in advance. In an authoritatively defined world there can be no policy experimentation that might create a different sort of world or reveal different forms of rational choice.

In a complex society with diffused authority and open concepts, in which individual knowledge of human needs, interests and activities is invariably incomplete, rationality is not obeying a big plan. It must include, though not necessarily wholly comprise, a continuous process of investigating the possible and the possible consequences of the possible. In part, rationality is the endless criticism and enquiry that revises objectives and investigates the nature of authoritative courses of action before and after their selection. It is a process within which different modes of thinking play upon one another. Principles of foreign policy formulated in this environment must aim to contribute to it, not replace it.

Conclusion

A search for principles of foreign policy thus comes into existence in a distinctive intellectual and practical setting, which is a necessary condition of its existence and to which it is committed. Our escape from abstraction is therefore complete. Discourse on issues of foreign policy is a familiar part of this setting. It seems that nothing has to be invented.

CHAPTER 3

Getting Down to Foreign Policy Issues

We can now, it seems, cease to attempt to formulate principles of foreign policy in advance of considering problems of foreign policy themselves. This enquiry can proceed to discuss different foreign policy issues without placing them in some coherent *a priori* model because it has been squarely committed to a discursive tradition that by its open nature is intrinsically inimical to the imposition of grand *a priori* designs on public or other affairs. It is because there is an actual variety of practical and conceptual problems of foreign policy that an enquiry such as this is undertaken. So we now survey seven different kinds of foreign policy issues with three purposes in mind: first to obtain some clear and direct sense of the matters with which we are engaged; second, to get an exact impression of the shape of foreign policy itself by approaching it from several different directions; third, to derive from foreign policy understood in this empirical way the form, or intimations of the form, that its fundamental principles take.

THE PROBLEM OF EXECUTIVE DOMINATION

The executive branch of government negotiates treaties with other executives. But treaties tend to have the effect of increasing the internal power of the executive by conferring ever greater status and responsibility on it. Treaties thus arranged may also commit a country to foreign alignments leading to war with possibly dire consequences for the internal enjoyment of individual liberty. They may draw a country into arrangements with autocratic, totalitarian or otherwise corrupt governments whose continuance in power may thus be supported. They may commit a country to engagements that it cannot muster the will to sustain and that create domestic dissension on a scale harmful to the internal order which it should be the duty of the executive to defend.

The executive in its foreign activities may deploy the threat of war and may actually go to war; since 1945 the United States, though often embroiled in violent engagements abroad, has not once gone to war in a formal constitutional declaratory way. War may have the effect of circumscribing the liberties of the individual through conscription, exposure to violent death or mutilation, by various forms of rationing, even by direction of labour. War seems permanently to extend the boundaries of executive power through the ratchet effect of the extension of executive controls inherent in organising a war effort. It confers on the executive and its military agents virtually dictatorial authority over large numbers of citizens who may be conscripted into the armed forces. And it could have the effect, through executive miscalculation, of complete societal destruction.

The diplomatic operations of the executive seem to encourage the habit of secrecy, for the following reasons: to conceal negotiating positions from foreign governments whose bargaining capabilities would be much strengthened by such knowledge; to preserve flexibility, which might otherwise be inhibited through the arousal of public opinion behind a fixed set of foreign policy demands; to conceal the course of one set of negotiations from a third party in the international arena that might see itself to be adversely affected thereby and that would therefore act in a way detrimental to the negotiations in question; to conceal military deployments from potential enemies; and to obscure the use of executive methods ordinarily held to be dishonourable yet that may seem necessary to the government concerned because of the distinctively imperative nature of life in the international arena. Yet secrecy entails a blurring of the boundaries of executive operations, particularly if its legitimacy becomes widely accepted. It may tempt an executive to behave unscrupulously domestically as well as internationally. It is likely to constitute a limitation on the activities of oppositions through its denial of the propriety of open and detailed investigation of government policies. It could conceal entry into harmful commitments unknown to citizens or the bulk of their representatives. And it is an encouragement to an executive to act foolishly or hastily in the absence of persistent and detailed discussion of policy alternatives.

Containing the treaty-making role of the executive

The traditional foreign policy role of the executive has thus seemed a perennial danger to free societies. A common constitutional way of attempting to counter the concentration of the treaty-making power in the executive is to consign the authority to ratify all treaties to a representative assembly. This has largely proved a weak constraint. Understandings and informal agreements between governments abound; a relatively small element of diplomatic effort is actually devoted to making treaties. Though rare in this sense, treaties are commonly sweeping in the duties and obligations they place on governments. The North Atlantic Treaty is a short and apparently simple document, yet it has led governments into engagements of a constant, intricate and potentially dangerous kind. Ratification may thus be a small element relative to the whole practice initiated by a treaty. Moreover, a government negotiating a treaty does so, as a rule, with the intention of securing ratification should its negotiations prove satisfactory to it. It is therefore likely to make its moves at the domestic level with this in mind; it arranges the scene within which ratification is enacted. More importantly, the negotiation of a treaty presents a legislature with a *fait accompli*, a signed treaty, which in its nature is a document that generally cannot be amended, only approved or rejected. Substituting ratification by referendum for ratification by representative assembly exaggerates this problem since the executive's role in a referendum is likely to be one of even greater dominance. Timing the campaign, phrasing the question to be put, releasing favourable information; by these means the executive is likely to obtain the outcome it requires.

General difficulties attend direct constitutional efforts to reduce the power of the executive in the negotiation of treaties. The more a government feels constrained in treaty negotiation, the more readily may it resort to understandings, secret or otherwise, of a less legalistic kind. An executive operating internationally in this way may confuse and alienate allied countries and involve itself in associations of an ill-defined and therefore potentially harmful nature. Broadly, constitutional provisions suffer from the apparent fact that the international arena as a whole is not the domain of legislation. Legislative or quasi-legislative bodies and procedures may therefore seem to be inappropriate to it. In its international setting a government primarily operates in relation to other governments and often these are of an authoritarian kind. So it may be held that there is a confusion of categories if domestic procedures are intermingled with international procedures. To deprive a government of authority in its external dealings does not add to the authority of a legislative assembly; it adds to the power of foreign governments not so encumbered and these are consequently able to move speedily to the detriment of constitutional states. Anyway, a legislative assembly dominant in external relations might prove to be dangerously uncertain in its actions, subject to emotional shifts of opinion, to twists of policy occasioned by shifting political coalitions and to the repeated distractions of electioneering. A further difficulty attaches to legislatures that proceed by way of specialist foreign affairs committees. If such a committee contains members representing constituencies with large ethnic groups, as is likely, it will be unable to approach international disputes in a disinterested spirit when the loyalties of these groups are roused.

Taking war out of the hands of the executive

Containing the dangers of the war-making authority of the executive may take the apparently fundamental form of attempting to banish war from the international arena altogether. There may seem to be two possible ways of doing this. First, treaties banning war, such as the Kellog–Briand Pact, may be negotiated. But signatories of such documents may cheat from the start; major states may refuse to sign or fail to ratify; and states that have signed and ratified may change their governments and then cheat or abrogate. Second, attempts to remove the threat of war from international society may be made through the creation of world organisations like the United Nations. The primary difficulty here is the logical one that an international organisation with this purpose must guarantee peace before states give up their war-making capabilities. But no international organisation, actual or projected, can guarantee peace *until* states give up their war-making capabilities. If it were conceivable that an international organisation could itself acquire so overwhelming a war-making capability as to solve this conundrum by rendering the military strength of states comparatively insignificant, then a centre of power would have been created that could dominate the world and might have to. Given the international rarity of parliamentarianism, a centre of this sort could hardly be other than unstable and even, periodically, tyrannically prone to violent outbursts.

Another apparently fundamental solution may seem to be the explicit banishment of the war-making power from the state's foreign policy. Again there are two possibilities. First there is the total abandonment of the state's military strength. This would have the additional merit of removing from internal relations the presence of armed forces of any kind. These have long been argued to constitute a threat to civil society; in their own ranks they subject citizens to military discipline, which is particularly felt to be an imposition when a form of conscription is necessary to the maintenance of the required level of strength; they offer the prospect of the violent overthrow of civil authority; and even in more stable circumstances they may be held to place too great a physical power at the disposal of governments. Yet the abandonment of military strength removes from the state the possibility of legitimate resistance to external enemies and of the legitimate control of internal disorders and emergencies of many dire kinds. It also reduces to negligible proportions its weight as an ally of other states. In fact a state so placed would hardly be a state, and in most practical circumstances is likely to be a subject territory enduring the presence of alien armed forces. Second, the removal of the war-making power from external relations may seem to be consequent upon the espousal of a policy of strict neutrality. But this course is unlikely to be wholly pacifist because neutrality is a definite policy requiring a capability for independent decision. Neutral states therefore commonly maintain relatively large armed forces, often with major conscript elements, so the traditional internal hazards of armed forces are not avoided by neutrality. At minimum a neutral policy is one of refusing to go to war except by way of resistance to direct attack. If by statehood is meant the sovereign capability of a society to direct itself to its own goals, neutrality should be open to all states. But its actual adoption is related to a number of practical factors: to international political situation (so that neutrality has been a possible policy for Ireland but not for Poland); to international geographical situation (Switzerland and Sweden have not been in direct line of fire in recent European wars whereas Belgium has been, so that neutrality in the latter's case has proved a futile policy); to the acquiescence of a first-rank power (Soviet Russia agrees to the neutrality of Finland provided it is not abandoned in favour of alignment with an uncongenial power or powers, so that neutrality in this case is not to be confused with freedom of choice); to the agreement of two first-rankers (the contemporary first-rank powers require and guarantee the neutrality of Austria, which, though it allows Austrian governments to associate themselves generally with the rest of western Europe, is again not to be equated with freedom of choice). In a number of cases, therefore, neutrality does not represent a policy chosen from feasible alternatives. In such cases the reduction of the power of the executive is external and not internal and is a function of the power of foreign executives. Regardless of whether neutrality is a choice or a necessity, no necessary relationship exists between it and a domestically docile executive; it can reasonably be argued that Yugoslavian neutrality depends on the existence of a strong central executive able to deal severely with internal dissension.

If the war-making power cannot be abolished, its removal from executive hands may seem to be assured by the simple constitutional requirement that war proceed only from a clear legislative declaration. But formidable difficulties also attach to formal provisions of this kind. An executive may have to respond to an attack; if war exists, declarations are irrelevant. Or a speedy response may be essential to prevent an incident becoming a war; but obtaining a formal legislative declaration may be laborious. On the other hand, a formal declaration may transform a relatively trivial incident into a major war unnecessarily; historically not all wars have been unpopular and an executive could be thrust into war by an aroused assembly. But if an executive has the normal authority to direct armed forces to particular locations, it necessarily has the power to place them in situations where they may have very little alternative but to fight. An executive deploying armed forces in a blocking role (to prevent the shipping of Soviet missiles to Cuba is an obvious example) would of course be severely disadvantaged if it were known in advance that it had no authority to allow them to open fire. Mutual defence treaties would also lose much of their stabilising effect were it known in advance that the immediate effectiveness of their military guarantees would be subject to the outcome of a possibly lengthy debate. The essence of the policy of nuclear deterrence lies in conveying threats that are believed to be real; undermining these threats weakens deterrence and, by thus encouraging boldness in adversaries, increases the possibility of major crises. A distinction should probably be drawn between the situations of states of different capabilities: a first-rank state with a variety of foreign involvements may be argued to require greater flexibility in deploying force than a relatively small state with only regional commitments. The prevalence of undeclared wars is indicative of the widely varying forms of international violence. This variety exists and it may be argued to be desirable since it offers many opportunities for holding war below catastrophic levels. And an undeclared war is probably an easier war to get out of than a declared war. Compromise, or outright retreat and withdrawal, is likely to be easier the less complete the commitment.

Against secrecy

Suggestions to deal with the hazards of executive secrecy to a free society take three broad forms. The first of these relates to the reform of the international arena, where the cause of secrecy seems to lie. If all the actions of states on the international stage were revealed to public view, then domestic secrecy on the part of one government would be both impossible and pointless. But open diplomacy at the United Nations and elsewhere, though it may perform several useful functions, commonly takes the form of sweeping declarations of malice or hypocritical displays of self-righteousness that are the antithesis of productive diplomacy. If this were the only kind of diplomacy allowed, a deterioration, not an improvement, in the quality of international relations would follow. However, if the international arena contains states, secrecy cannot be abolished. At least some states may be secretly absorbed in planning harm to others and it may be difficult to be certain about which are and which are not so engaged; nor can scheming of this kind be prevented. The conduct of foreign relations by a constitutional state cannot therefore be entirely open since every state, constitutional or otherwise, must keep a watchful eye on this aspect of the behaviour of other states, whether they are actually occupied in this way or not. Additionally, a government subject to open and active constitutional opposition is unlikely to be eager to dispense information tending towards the downfall of itself and its foreign policies. Contact with authoritarian and corrupt governments is particularly likely to contain some material of this kind. Yet authoritarian governments are a fact of international life and to force the severance of discreet relations with them may be argued to remove possibilities, however remote, of moderating their behaviour.

At the domestic level it is often contended that the proper antidote to the secretive tendencies of the executive is to be found in the continual investigations of a powerful legislative foreign affairs committee made up of expert members. One difficulty here is that practically any issue of government policy can have cross-national aspects; a really expert committee would therefore have to include virtually every member of the legislature. A problem already mentioned is that if the members of such a committee represent constituencies containing strong ethnic groups then foreign policy can be unduly influenced by the emotional sympathies of minorities insensitive to traditional national interests. A committee with sweeping powers to examine otherwise secret matters might have a dubious effect on the everyday conduct of diplomacy for other reasons. Material useful to possible enemies might be revealed and, just as important, material embarrassing to allied governments might also suffer the same fate, to the lasting damage of traditional friendships. In general terms, the stronger a legislature becomes, the more divided, and therefore ineffective, the direction of foreign policy is likely to be.

A second domestic possibility is that the representative assembly, either in whole or in part, should become a party to executive secrecy. But secrecy is contrary to the nature of an assembly if it contains, as it should, loquacious deputies of widely separated views. A legislative committee entering too intimately into executive work becomes, in a sense, a branch of the executive; but the point of a representative assembly is that it should be constantly concerned to extend its freedom to criticise the executive. In practice, legislative secrecy on anything other than a clearly defined matter of military importance is unlikely to be achieved. If an assembly were to concede that foreign relations in general should be conducted secretly, it would in effect accept an executive gag on almost all its activities because every government department operates externally in some way.

Conclusions

1.   Arguments about the control of the internal machinery of foreign policy-making run in many directions and are rarely determinate.

2.   There is scope for a variety of practices. Though, for instance, complete executive secrecy may be undesirable, complete and open legislative dominance in foreign policy may seem at least impracticable. Foreign policy practice may therefore tolerably include a variety of forms of legislative participation. But this is a commonsense observation, not a principle of foreign policy. Presumably a principle would indicate in what circumstances legislative involvement is desirable and in what circumstances it is not.

3.   Foreign relations deeply penetrate the domestic environment. But a characteristic of the international arena is the possibility of war between states and war is not a feature of the domestic relations of a civil society. Attempts to contain the war-making power within constitutional procedures cannot be entirely successful because war is not a constitutional kind of activity. It does not follow that foreign policy as a whole is an extra-constitutional activity. It would seem that at least one fundamental distinction has to be drawn within foreign policy itself: in what circumstances does it include the threat of war and in what circumstances does it not?

4.   In all constitutional debates questions of structure and questions of policy tend to be interwoven. A mistaken policy is often taken to be the result of a faulty policy-making structure. If diplomacy conducted secretly is

deemed to have contributed to the outbreak of a misconceived war, then secret diplomacy may be widely held to be the cause of all misconceived wars. If an executive enters into a foreign commitment without full legislative consultation and approval, and if this commitment turns out to have been miscalculated, then compulsory legislative involvement may be seen to be the guarantee against future miscalculated external involvements. The error of this sort of reasoning is obvious.[4] A structure is not a policy: a changed structure does not necessarily provide security against inappropriate policy. It seems that principles of foreign policy should resolve this conundrum by containing prescriptions relevant to both structures and policies.

THE RELATIONSHIP BETWEEN FOREIGN POLICY AND INTERNATIONAL ORGANISATIONS

The 'space' between states in the international arena is far from empty. Large numbers of international organisations constitute much of the environment of foreign policy and in some cases they enter into the internal structure of policy-making. Governments have created international organisations for an assortment of reasons:[5]

to set the relations between all states within a context of quasi-parliamentary process (as in the case of the League of Nations);

to provide world security through an international concentration of force to be used according to supposedly agreed criteria (the UN Security Council);

to provide the conditions of mutual defence among partial groupings of states commanding sufficient force to deter or repel potential adversaries (Nato);

to make acceptable to lesser powers the overall dominance of larger powers (as was an intention of the UN Charter, which places a duty on the generality of UN members to support the decisions of the Security Council with its permanent core of five large states);

to make or to appear to make acceptable to affected lesser powers the specific dominance of a larger power (the Soviet Union uses or attempts to use the Warsaw Pact and Comecon in this way);

to obtain influence over a first-rank power's policies (thus Britain played a central role in the creation of the IMF and of Nato partly to acquire influence over the course of United States economic and defence policies);

to facilitate cross-national cooperation in the performance of specific operations that cannot by their nature be efficiently undertaken by individual states (as in the case of the Universal Postal Union and many other functional organisations);

to provide the conditions of obtaining agreed constraints on national policies with the intention of increasing the welfare of all members (the GATT);

to legitimate external intervention in internal affairs (the European Community);

to mobilise resources for the provision of international economic services (the World Bank group of institutions);

to create an association expressive of a common situation and outlook (the Council of Europe);

to press a specific economic interest on non-members (the OPEC).

Governments join organisations they have not created in order:

to obtain material advantages otherwise apparently denied them (as in the case of British entry to the European Community);

to achieve the status conferred by membership (as in the case of the entry of new states into the UN);

to obtain a purchase upon specific areas of cross-national policy-making (Britain and the European Community again).

International organisations may:

be specific in competence (the GATT, the Universal Postal Union);

be general in competence (the UN);

stress the notion of the equality of states (the UN General Assembly);

operate, or attempt to operate, some form of weighted voting designed to reflect differences in the size and resources of member states (the UN Security Council, the IMF Board, the Council of the European Community);

be largely inter-governmental in membership (the UN, the GATT);

involve parliamentarians (Nato, WEU);

involve non-governmental groups (European Community, the ILO);

contain a directly elected element (the European Community);

contain an active and influential permanent staff (the IMF, the European Community);

be relatively informal (group of Twenty) or relatively formal and constitutional (the European Community);

be unofficial (Amnesty International).

International organisations impose costs on governments in terms of:

direct financial contributions (as in virtually all cases);

constraints on policy options, sometimes in matters of a sensitive internal nature (the European Community, the GATT);

the liability of governments to organisational discipline and even judicial process (the European Community, the Council of Europe);

internal constitutional change (the European Community);

complex penetration of important instruments of policy (as in the case of Nato and the armed forces of its less powerful members);

hostility among non-members (OPEC);

vexatious criticism by other members (the UN).

Surrounding and penetrating all international organisations is the older international institution of diplomacy, which:

is almost always government controlled;
can operate secretly;
can bring national power to bear without rigidity or posturing;
is flexible as to bilateral and multilateral contacts;
is not strictly bound by organisational procedures;
is sensitive to questions of power and status;
is unspecific and flexible among issues, though its agents are unlikely to possess technical expertise in many fields.

The replacement of foreign policy by international organisations

There are a number of possible attitudes to the relationship between foreign policy and international organisation. It may be contended, first, that international organisations should replace foreign policy altogether. In all areas of practical governmental effort (in the maintenance of economic stability, the achievement of international security, the protection of the environment) there is no such thing as purely domestic concern or purely domestic governmental capability. In areas like these the capabilities of governments to get to grips with problems are partly a product of the level of effectiveness achieved by international organisations because the problems themselves are not exclusively national. Nor are these problems of the kind peculiar to the competence of traditional diplomacy: the provision of credit to countries in balance of payments deficit and the organisation of major cross-national industrial and military projects are highly technical matters with which specialist government departments and agencies, not generalist foreign ministries, continually grapple. The substance of governmental efforts lies in the practical issues that affect the lives of citizens. Effective government in these areas is a product of cross-national coordination and adjustment. It may therefore seem to be the primary purpose of foreign policy to establish on a sound basis the appropriate international and cross-national organisations. Having done so, there would remain nothing of a fundamental nature for foreign policy as such to do. Governments could then get down to dealing in an effectively organised manner with the practical problems that are their crucial concern and responsibility.

(1) But tolerably effective government cannot be reduced to mundane questions of organisation, whether it be national or cross-national; nor is government simply a matter of rationally selecting correct policies at any level. The social and legal conditions of the existence of government are ultimately more important. There has to be the possibility of ordered government before one can speculate about what government should be doing. So far, the conditions of government, where they exist, have been

largely established on foundations delimited by state frontiers. These frontiers have been located in a variety of ways: by wars, by the dynastic and territorial ambitions of rulers and by their need to acquire wealth to support their peculiar enterprises, by religious and other movements, by fortuitous geographical circumstances. Given the historical conditions of rule, irrational and insecure though they often are, it is unlikely that any particular government could draw more than a minor element of its authority from international organisations. To be effective governments must be authoritative and to be authoritative they must link themselves with societies that are historically given. Any government that is attentive to the sources of its domestic authority may seem to benefit from resisting policy pressures emanating from beyond national boundaries or even from ignoring them altogether. Though it may be desirable that foreign policy should establish cross-national organisations to contribute to the effectiveness of government, success in this field is unlikely to do away with foreign policy. Frictions between national societies that seem to define the authority of governments can occur inside and outside organisations. And in some instances these frictions may be exacerbated by organisations; governments operating in different kinds of internal conditions cannot be expected to respond in the same way or at the same speed to the problems that assail them, even when these are widely and deeply shared.

(2) The concerns of governments range beyond attempts to maintain balance of payments equilibrium at congenial exchange rates and suchlike. Most traditionally, governments are periodically intensely concerned with defence. It is certainly the case that the search for defence effectiveness has inspired the creation of a number of cross-national organisations, Nato being the foremost western example. The search for economies in defence has also created many interdependencies and complementarities in the deployment of military forces and in their supply. Yet, whatever its achievements in terms of joint defence provision, organisation in this field does not seem to do away with the defence policies of states. Many constitutional states do not belong to defence organisations of any kind. First-rank powers have national defence capabilities that are substantially unaffected by organisations and they continue to have foreign policies. And militarily weak governments organisationally linked to the constitutional first-ranker, the United States, continue to attempt to exercise influence on its foreign policies. As well, any first-ranker opposed by a military organisation will have an interest in the depletion of its unity and its effectiveness. Policies playing on the interests of individual members will evoke individual policies. Organisation does not appear to abolish defence policies; it complicates them.

(3) International organisations do not fit into some neat interlocking pattern of world relations. There may be conflicts among organisations: the universalist principles of the GATT and the potential for exclusivity of the European Community are full of actual and prospective tensions. The more

an organisation attempts to serve the interests of its members, the more likely are collective conflicts with non-members: in matters of agricultural policy, relations between the European Community and the United States are often in conflict. Within organisations stresses occur between groups of states: between rich and poor countries in the IMF for example. Problems of these kinds are problems of foreign policy as much as problems of organisations.

(4) Members of international organisations do not, simply because of shared membership, bring to bear common norms of political action or common expectations of organisational effectiveness. Divergencies within organisations may reflect basic social, material and ideological divergencies outside organisations. What exists outside organisations is likely to be of more substantial importance than what occurs inside. What happens outside the UN General Assembly is rarely deeply affected by what happens inside it; and what is outside is certainly important to foreign policy.

(5) Issues cannot always be contained within organisationally neat boundaries. United States governments have been prone to stress West German defence dependence on Nato as a means of pressing particular kinds of economic policies on West German governments, particularly in connection with international monetary relations, which in turn are supposed to fall within the competence of the IMF. Bilateral relations between France and Iran centring on mutual trade in oil and armaments have been intermingled with Iranian pressure for favoured treatment in European Community trade. Examples such as these seem to suggest that organisations are at least as likely to be incorporated into individual foreign policies as they are to absorb individual foreign policies into themselves.

Foreign policy as international constitution-building

Another reformist line of argument would admit that the issues upon which governments divide are never likely to go away. But this may seem to be the fundamental reason for reform rather than a permanent block to it. Foreign policy should seek to create organised settings within which conflicts of interest could be worked through in constitutional, non-violent ways. The key problem of foreign policy as it stands is its propensity to large-scale harmfulness. Remove this by means of constitutional structures and foreign policy becomes politicised. Foreign policy problems do not go away but they do cease to be special kinds of problems.

(1) This view may seem to idealise constitutions. Constitutions are plentiful, constitutionalism a rarity. Amid the plethora of modern constitutions few have retained their authority for any lengthy period and many have collapsed to the accompaniment of violence. Even the maintenance of the federal constitution of the United States has a bloody history. Most existing constitutions, almost invariably liberal in form, are substantially ignored, coexisting with arbitrary rule and even terror. The creation of a

constitution is often an illusory achievement. A constitution must be supported by social habits and beliefs that cannot themselves be established by a highsounding legal formula. Tolerance, for example, can never be legislated, but it is both a foundation and an effect of the practice of constitutional rule. The traditional habits of international relations include a good measure of intolerance and incipient violence. The Covenant of the League of Nations, probably the greatest single effort to reform international relations along constitutional lines, did not have such an impact on statecraft as to replace foreign policy by an institutionalised political process. And it is often argued that the Covenant was deeply harmful in that its constitutional ideas distracted attention from the severe realities of the use of national power, which required, but did not get, determined action from the constitutional states.

(2) One of the difficulties of international life is its plurality of constitutional forms: at one level there are documents like the UN Charter, the Treaty of Rome, the GATT, the Articles of Agreement of the IMF and the like; at another there are state constitutions such as those of the United States and the German Federal Republic, which can also affect the course of international relations. To this plurality, itself apparently generative of stress, must be added constant uncertainty as to the authority of constitutions of each kind. Relations with a government to which a national constitution means little are unlikely to be domesticated simply by that government's membership of the UN. Moreover, in their foreign dealings, governments, even those of a constitutional kind, can always claim *force majeure* in evading their obligations. And where constitutional sanctions are principally normative in character, as they usually are at the international level, there is ample scope for hypocritical evasions by the governments of closed societies, emphatically but selectively committed to the traditional diplomatic principles of state sovereignty and non-interference in domestic affairs.

(3) If foreign policy is to place international relations on a constitutional footing, then its first duty must be to establish the conditions of constitutionalism in world society. There are two fundamental problems. First, it is far from clear what the conditions of constitutionalism are: what specific conditions create toleration? Second, constitutionalism represents a set of political practices and convictions to which numbers of powerful governments are overtly hostile: converting them to a new outlook would in itself be a highly active and crusading foreign policy, possibly violent and probably futile

(4) Among small groups of countries, typically those of the European Community, constitution-building may contain relatively fewer difficulties than it does at the universal level. But the more formidable such regional edifices as the Community grow, the closer, it may seem, they approximate to states. The addition of large newcomers to the international arena of states is unlikely to reduce the hazards with which foreign policy traditionally

grapples or to render constitution-making in a world setting any easier.

Foreign policy as the master of international organisations

International organisations, being the creations of states, should also, it may seem, be their creatures. In general, international organisation is a provider of useful and specific benefits. When it makes otherwise extraneous or disagreeable demands it should be ignored. The disruption of an international organisation, or simply quiet disregard of its rules, are entirely legitimate means whereby a government may further its purposes. The dominant instrument of the state is traditional diplomacy organised and directed by government.

(1) Any generalisation, not least this one, seems to run into immediate difficulties because of the rich diversity of organisations it must attempt to encompass. An organisation like Nato establishes close cross-national communications at a number of levels (governmental, parliamentary, bureaucratic, military and scientific) about a complex problem, namely defence. To describe this set of communications and influences simply as an instrument of several national defence policies is inadequate in two general ways. First, the existence of Nato influences the military dispositions of its members, the kinds of weapons they produce or acquire, the formations they deploy, the contingencies for which they prepare. The links generated by this organisation are not such as can be readily severed at an individual government's whim. Though France under de Gaulle's presidency left Nato, it remains in many ways integrated into the Nato network of consultation and communication. Second, for some powers, such as the German Federal Republic, Nato is an intrinsic part of national defence policy and not something added on to it.

(2) In practice, governments rarely leave organisations. Remaining inside an organisation inevitably entails some measure of acquiescence in organisational norms, if only because total isolation within an organisation is psychologically uncomfortable. Attempts to use an organisation become, perhaps in small measure, participation in an organisation. In this kind of way it can happen that an unconstitutional government becomes extremely legalistic in its construction of an international constitution like the UN Charter. To argue that the UN constitutes an important instrument of state policies would be to argue that the UN is a highly effective organisation, which it is not. But if almost all states remain members of the UN when, because of its weakness, it is unlikely to achieve much for any one of them, it would seem to follow that their membership must be explained in other ways.

(3) International organisations vary greatly in the constraints they lay upon governments. As a rule, the UN is relatively undemanding, whereas the European Community is relatively demanding; and the former is more a

setting of a kind of diplomacy, whereas the latter is more a setting of an administratively detailed kind of government. Generalities about the instrumentality of international organisations as a whole are meaningless. World society, if it may be so described, is made up of a variety of international and cross-national systems of differing organisational possibilities. Differences among organisations reflect differences among the systems to which they attach. The notion of instrumentality itself has a variety of connotations. Each of its participating elements sees a number of purposes in the European Community: to encourage economies of scale; to form a new centre of world power, economic and otherwise; to provide markets for the products of poor countries on preferential terms; and many more. Most of these purposes would hardly occur to the members of the UN in relation to that organisation. The assumption that international organisations, individually or as a whole, can be instruments of some exact purpose for each state would seem to ignore deep differences in the nature of states and of their settings.

(4) There are limits to the kinds of associations that can be abandoned. A British government could leave the IMF, but, in almost any circumstances, Britain cannot leave the international monetary system. A British government could leave the GATT, but Britain cannot leave world trade. The French government has left Nato, but France cannot leave the European arena of military danger.

(5) The notion that traditional diplomacy is somehow the fundamental instrument of foreign policy does not bear examination. Traditional diplomacy can be untraditional: it can become committed to novel organisations such as those of the European Community. In itself the diplomatic function in many circumstances means little more than servicing other departments of state in their substantive cross-national engagements, to many of which it can make little direct contribution. There is nothing fundamental about traditional diplomacy because in itself it has no fundamental substance. It is a means whereby a government may express itself in terms of the problems and institutions that engage its attention. In this way international organisations have become a part of the substance of diplomatic relations, just as the European diplomatic community of the nineteenth century was part of the substance of diplomacy in the nineteenth century. The international society of the later part of the twentieth century, though retaining many vestiges of nineteenth-century practice, is one that also expresses itself in and through a variety of international organisations.

Conclusions

1. Generalisations about the relationship between international organisation and foreign policy seem doomed to collapse among the complexities of international structures and practices. Yet this is an area in which principles

of foreign policy must generalise.

2.   The place of international organisation in the foreign relations of states seems to depend very much on the nature of the states concerned. A requirement of generalisations in this area would thus seem to be that they should be related to generalisations about statehood.

3.   International organisation can penetrate the domestic community in many ways. It can involve parliamentarians, directly elected and otherwise; it is apt to constrain executive options and it may even expose governments to the possibility of judicial proceedings; bargains struck cross-nationally can have a directly legal effect on companies and citizens, as in the case of the European Community; and so on. A practical difficulty in all this seems to lie in determining, in diverse matters, whether a boundary should be drawn beyond which international organisation should not go in penetrating the mechanisms of the domestic political process.

4.   There is a second kind of boundary issue. The presence of unconstitutional states in the Universal Postal Union is a matter of little note; but could such states ever be accommodated in any organisation bearing on the dispositions of western military forces or having a direct place in western legislative or judicial processes?

5.   Yet the divergent nature of governments is a fact of some international organisations. What status can be accorded a vote in the UN General Assembly when only a minority of those votes represent the views of constitutional governments? Often it is suggested that the IMF should have greater capabilities to control world supplies of credit and to operate monetary policies in a way favourable to poor countries; but to what degree should unconstitutional countries be admitted to the constitutional running of the IMF?

FOREIGN POLICY AS THE PURSUIT OF NATIONAL INTEREST

The term 'foreign policy' implies that a consistent design or strategy appropriate to the national state can and should motivate its leaders in their foreign dealings. If the source of the authority of the statesman is the state it may seem reasonable that service to the interest of the state should be his primary duty. Knowledge of the requirements of a state should thus both explain its foreign policy and provide a guide to instruct its statesmen.

National interest as the geographical determinants of foreign policy

If the national interest is a practical imperative of statecraft it should be possible to specify its particular sources and objectives. The geographical circumstances of the state would seem to offer the most exact explanation of its true concerns. A state whose agriculture cannot feed its population must be concerned with the expansion of trade. A small landlocked state must keep a close eye on the continental balance of power. A maritime state must be anxious to maintain freedom of sea communications. A state whose access to the sea is impeded by ice over much of the year will be interested in acquiring ports free from this impediment. A continental first-rank state will be watchful of efforts to subvert surrounding client states. In ways like these the longstanding existence of the state in given geographical circumstances seems to establish specific concerns that together comprise an interest that no statesman can neglect.

(1) But the state as a geographical entity is markedly unstable. The domestic territory of the United States has expanded from the eastern seaboard of North America to the middle of the Pacific in two hundred years. In Europe, many states (Sweden, Poland and Austria are obvious examples) have changed their shapes in the last hundred years. Germany has altered radically both in shape and in the forms of its statehood. Resources of population, industry and even raw materials can change over short periods as well.

(2) The international concerns of the state are as much the product of the activities of other states as of geographical circumstances. During much of the period of British naval dominance the interest of American governments in the world balance of seapower could afford to be less than compelling because the British navy constituted no kind of threat to the continental expansion of the United States. Currently, British anxieties about its naval weakness can be less intense than they would be were not American naval forces so large. To say that Britain as a maritime state is interested in naval strength is true but uninteresting: a great deal hangs on the nature of the world naval balance, which changes, and upon the relative capability of Britain to make and maintain ships, which also changes.

(3) Furthermore, geography in itself gives no sure indication as to how a state responds to its physical circumstances. Finland, Denmark, Austria and Yugoslavia, being small states in close proximity to a first-class continental state must be acutely aware of the balance of forces in Europe. But their responses to it have been dissimilar. It may follow from this apparent variety that the European balance of military strength has peculiarities of its own that override purely geographical problems. But it may also be that even in the most pressing geographical situation there is room for choice.

(4) Space is also a variable when related to weaponry. Britain's sea moat has shrunk to negligible defensive proportions during the twentieth century as a result of armaments developments. These expensive changes in military technology, coupled with the relative decline in Britain's economic strength, have quickly transformed her from a world naval power into a regional power with a long-term continental commitment.

(5) In an age when governments can claim widespread attention at the UN and elsewhere even a small state's active engagements cannot be wholly defined by the narrow confines of physical situation. Small landlocked states may, for example, take a vocal interest in the codification of the law of the sea and may make strong and plausible claims to a share in any proceeds forthcoming from the exploitation of mineral resources lying beneath international waters.

National interest as defence

If the primary duty of the state is to defend its citizens then the first principle of foreign policy may seem to be the duty to maintain national security. The service of this supreme interest requires foreign policy to deploy and align the state's military capabilities in such a way as to maximise its safety. In this pursuit, alliances may be broken and reconstructed as circumstances require. The statesman's fundamental obligation to the defence of the state is not to be transcended by sentiment.

(1) Descriptively, this statement is unconvincing. The actual use to which an army is put may defy clear description in terms of such apparently precise foreign policy objectives. In part, British forces in Northern Ireland have been involved in a dispute about whether their role is domestic or foreign. On the other hand, small states such as the Irish Republic that contributed forces to the UN operation in the Congo can hardly be argued to have done so in furtherance of their own defence.

(2) In the thermonuclear age there is no convincing defence of population from major attack by a first-rank power. Involvement in the military relations between the first-rank states means involvement in a no-defence system. The essence of the policy of deterrence is to threaten retaliation should an attack occur. But this is not defence from the consequences of attack. No state can defend its people from major attack and only a first-rank power can retaliate in kind should such an assault occur. In these circumstances the meaning of the military forces, nuclear and otherwise, acquired by lesser powers must often be something more complicated than is covered by the notion of an instrument of state foreign policy designed to achieve national safety.

(3) And, in practice, defence by means of an alliance is not a conceptually simple matter of acquiring, or swapping, partners on the basis of elementary calculations about their potential contributions to national strength. The acquisition of allies in advance of a possible thermonuclear conflict may in fact be the acquisition of increased risks of annihilation, not the converse. The United States does not need the strength of Denmark to bolster its own forces in their pursuit of its national defence; all that Denmark contributes to the United States in this sense is an extension of obligations that could draw her into, not keep her out of, large-scale war.

(4) A root difficulty of the present doctrine of national interest lies in the

concepts of defence and security it incorporates. If defence is taken to mean the physical preservation from violence of the statesman's countrymen, it follows that all military actions are counterproductive because resistance to attack is a sure way of getting people killed. Surrender is the only policy likely to defend the lives of the maximum number of citizens. Yet this policy is rarely adopted by statesmen. Defence is usually conceived to mean more than the preservation of life in human bodies. The values defence is claimed to preserve are likely to be various (liberty, self-government, a religion) and far from clear. But in many cases they can hardly be described as national; neither liberty nor self-government nor most religions are exclusively national possessions. But if values are not national, at what point should they be defended; at the perimeter of the homeland, or wherever they are threatened, or somewhere in between?

(5) Security is the absence of fear of attack. It is the freedom to do other things without the distraction of this fear. The relationship between the pursuit of defence and the achievement of security cannot be a simple one. The creation of a defence community like Nato is in one sense a manifestation of security because most of these defence partners do not fear one another. But their joining together increases, as well as diminishes, fear. Peripheral members must fear that they may be abandoned; that, if not abandoned, they may become nuclear battlegrounds; or that, with the same consequence, they may be drawn into first-rank quarrels extraneous to their immediate concerns. Similarly, a first-rank power will fear that it may over-extend its commitments to the extent of being drawn to attempt the defence of the indefensible; that a peripheral incident may develop into a central war; and that, with the same consequence, it may be drawn into the extraneous quarrels of minor allies. First-rankers, subject to these kinds of fears and to the costs of developing modern weaponry, necessarily have much in common. They may therefore make mutual efforts to contain costs and dangers. In this way a diplomatic community of sorts is created between first-rankers. This community of adversaries is concerned with the establishment of security; whereas a community of Nato-like allies is concerned with defence because of its hazardous international environment; but now it may seem that safety requires emphasis on the former at the expense, if need be, of the latter.

(6) Security is a state of mind conditioned by the form of order in the international arena. At the higher levels of international conflict the policy of defence creates the situation of mutual nuclear deterrence. This situation is associated with vigorous competition in the acquisition of highly advanced means of delivering massive attacks. The pursuit of technical advantage creates the possibility that one competitor might actually achieve a clear superiority. But this superiority could not be expected to last. So a party with an advantage may be tempted to use it before it is lost or overtaken. This effect of defence policies can hardly be expected to be conducive to a secure state of mind. So it may seem that defence and security cannot both be

in the national interest because the first is the negation of the second.

National interest as the pursuit of wealth

The fortunes of most elected governments are closely related to the levels of prosperity enjoyed or endured by their constituents. Few such governments do not overtly hold the material welfare of their citizens to stand high among their policy objectives. If governments have such a duty it would seem to follow that the national interest requires them to follow foreign economic policies best suited to their performance of it.

(1) But the proper role of government in the promotion of material advancement is not a matter upon which there is much settled agreement. Men's individual efforts to improve their lot in a free environment may be held to provide the essential human motivation that increases total wealth. From this viewpoint, the proper foreign economic policy of any particular government should be that of minimising the economic role of all governments in international trade through the promotion of the free movement of goods, services, expertise and capital in a monetary setting of floating exchange rates. Blandly declaring that governments have, or should have, a sense of economic responsibility implies nothing whatever about the nature of the particular foreign policies they may, or should, adopt. The national economic interest has seemed to require states to attempt to achieve material self-sufficiency through foreign conquest. In economics, as in all other matters, the notion of national interest leaves out what is most important; namely, the arguments about what should and should not be attempted.

(2) Foreign economic policies in fact often serve non-economic goals. Thus the creation of the European Community was attended by many official and unofficial hopes that it would increase the integrative substance of western European life and thus obliterate the national hostilities that had previously marred it. Similarly, a particular foreign aid programme may be undertaken to secure strategic facilities or simply to prevent another power from establishing an exclusive patronage. Economic policy, internal as well as external, is constantly being put to the service of non-economic objectives. In these circumstances it makes no sense to suggest that economic foreign policies are inspired solely by the national interest in material gain.

(3) Specific foreign economic policies are almost invariably the subject of domestic sectional dispute. An overseas policy favourable to one sector of the home economy (say agriculture) may be vigorously opposed by another sector (food processing and retailing interests perhaps). Though industry in general may favour the maximisation of foreign markets through the mutual reduction of national tariffs, particular sectors of industry (textile manufacturers not uncommonly) may be apt to complain of unfair competition and demand protection. A policy of support for one sector of the economy (the

British fishing industry) may even lead to conflict with a strategically important ally (Iceland). More generally, in periods of unemployment and balance of payments deficit many representative voices will call for the reduction of imports through direct national controls on trade; but opposing views will stress, first, the need to avoid possible limitations on exports as a result of retaliatory discrimination by other countries and, second, the necessity of promoting domestic efficiency through exposure to overseas competition. Virtually no actual economic policy in a plural society can claim to be in the national interest in the sense that it benefits everyone and harms no one.

(4) Except in siege conditions there is no clear distinction between foreign economic policy and domestic economic policy. The domestic economy is deeply penetrated by cross-national shifts and trends. A change in domestic economic conditions, such as a general rise in wage rates, is likely to affect foreigners because of its effects on demand for imports and for the foreign currencies necessary to their purchase. If an American government acts to raise interest rates in the United States, a British government cannot as a rule do other than allow interest rates in Britain to rise higher, unless it is able to cope with the removal of funds from London to New York and a probable decline in sterling exchange rates. Within the western international economy each government knows that its scope for independent economic action is limited and that the actions of other governments are likely to affect its own options. These governments also know that domestic prosperity is going to be difficult to achieve if the overall economy is depressed. In these circumstances there is little rational alternative to a high level of inter-governmental contact. Substantial cross-national support is likely to be available to a member of this circle experiencing economic difficulties, though the authorities of a receiving country are likely to be expected to be attentive to the views of other authorities about the appropriateness of their policies. In this setting, a government is both a domestic and an international authority and the exclusively national interest is little more than a rhetorical symbol.

Values the core of the national interest

Practical policies, it may seem, shift with shifting circumstances. The national interest is, or should be, the stable core of the national community. It is the lasting values that make this community a unity and that confer on all its institutions their distinctive national character. The national interest unifies state and society, their past and future. It both guides and legitimates those actions of the statesman that are inspired by this ultimate source of his authority.

(1) All the terms of this doctrine are indefinite. It gives no indication as to what actually should be done, only that most things that are done may be claimed to be in the national interest. This version of the national interest

is available for use as a kind of tribal rallying cry by statesmen under stress. Or it may be used in an attempt to arrest argument or enquiry. It seems to provide the form of a claim to metaphysical truth. A statesman possessed by a sense of knowledge of the national interest may feel entirely justified in ignoring ordinary argument, common sense and perhaps ordinary rules of moral and legal conduct too. But if metaphysical content is denied the term, its use adds nothing to the merits or demerits of a specific line of authoritative action: if, say, joining an international organisation is held to be desirable for the several particular benefits likely to accrue, then nothing is added to the force of an argument built on these points by the claim that such a course is in the national interest. This usage is either an attempt to evoke a response of support that should be evoked by the points themselves or it is an effort to conceal their weakness in empty but highsounding verbiage.

(2) This conception of the national interest may seem to refer to the nature of the motivating force of self-consciously nationalist groups. But it is usually the case that nationalists comprise less than the total of citizens within a state or territory and they may be a very small minority. The national interest in this sense is what is demanded by a nationalist group. This may or may not be desirable, but there is no reason to suppose that it is inherently of superior worth to what is demanded by other groups.

(3) The national interest may be used to signal that a summing-up has taken place; that arguments turning on a particular issue have been considered, constraints calculated and a course of conduct selected. This course is then declared to be in the national interest. In itself, this usage does not claim to add anything to arguments but simply announces that a decisive outcome of arguments has been reached. It cannot be an outcome that is uncontentious, since contending arguments have been considered. Nor does this usage convey anything in general about the nature of the arguments involved except that the set supporting the course taken or proposed is deemed superior to the rest. Nor, more importantly in the present context, does it indicate the sources of telling arguments. They need not necessarily spring from within the territorial state but may originate in some transnational community, as is often the case in questions of economic policy. The national interest used as a signal of decision has no additional empirical content.

(4) In its international dealings a government may use the term to convey that it has reached a point in negotiations beyond which no further compromise is possible. But the reasons for this stand will be various and often far from eternal. There may, for example, be an election in the offing and a government leader may wish to cosset an important group in his party. Different governments of the same country may thus have different national interests; and the same government may have different national interests before and after an election.

Conclusions

1.   National interest figures prominently in the rhetoric of statesmen. But it is a notion that on examination appears to be without specific empirical reference. It simply seems to denote anything that is held to be desirable in particular circumstances.

2.   Interests of an exact kind are invariably generated in and by a larger social context; the interests of bankers could not exist if there were no specialised function of banking. Interests are also invariably associated with general modes of expression in a larger setting: with public argument, news-paper advertisement, representation to ministers, demonstrations. Com-paring the national interest with other kinds of interests immediately creates three difficulties. To what group or function does the national interest attach? In what larger context is it produced? And by what particular method and style of articulation can the national interest be distinguished from all other kinds of interests? It is certainly not the case that the national interest is peculiar to foreign policy since it is a term that figures prominently in domestic politics. Relations across traditional international frontiers cannot be resolved into a coherent and relentless promotion of the national interest; all kinds of unofficial as well as official interests are pursued cross-nationally within the western circle of states. And this kind of interest activity is markedly different from that which occurs in relations between relatively closed societies such as Soviet Russia and China. International society as a whole cannot be taken to be a coherent context of interests. Consequently no single generalisation about interests and foreign policy can be expected to hold.

3.   It may be contended that the distinctive character of the national interest is that its international pursuit may lead to legitimate large-scale violence in the form of war. Two points must be made about such a claim. First, if the pursuit of the national interest in itself confers legitimacy on violence, then almost any group using force may reasonably employ this claim to be legiti-mate. The view that legitimacy is conferred only by the generality of states upon the violent furtherance of their national interests by its own membership does not bear examination. States do not confer legitimacy on all the wars of other states. Waging 'aggressive war' has been widely conceded to be illegal. And some of the violent actions of non-state groups, such as guerilla actions by nationalist movements in southern Africa, have been widely held to be legitimate by states. Second, it is rare for governments to make war for the explicit purpose of securing an interest. They almost invariably claim to be supporting general principles: international order, collective security, self-determination, even peace.

4.   An understanding of the relationship of interests to foreign policy must

incorporate an understanding of the proper role of the state in relation to the promotion of specific goals. One seems thus inevitably drawn to view the state as a value if one wishes to establish a significant link between it and interests. If the state is simply a bundle of interests then statehood as a particular notion collapses.

WAR AND FOREIGN POLICY

Repeatedly this enquiry has been confronted by war as the distinguishing mark of the external environment in which foreign policy operates. If war is an institution largely peculiar to the relations between states, then its connection with war must be a central concern of foreign policy.

In post-medieval Europe the right of the state to go to war was substantially unquestioned. Given this right, all states had to be prepared for possible trials of strength. But the prominence of war as an institution of international relations could create hazards for a civil society. An effective military force is of necessity rigorously structured and may therefore be particularly critical of the style and content of political government. So the military capability for rapid violent intervention may seem to constitute a standing threat to civil authority. On the other hand, the existence of undisciplined forces creates the twin dangers of anarchy within civil society and of defencelessness before the potential violence of international society. These dangers have been long appreciated; added to them is the problem created by the arousal of popular passions sometimes associated with international war. These excitements may encourage the military in ruthlessly destructive policies without regard to the priority of political goals and constraints.

The war-making right of the state has rarely been taken to mean that any war undertaken by a state is therefore right. In the present century the attempt to limit legitimate war has created the formal obligation accepted by all UN members to refrain from starting a war in furtherance of an international dispute. More radically, a form of war has become a duty of members of the world community in the formal sense that the UN Charter pledges its signatories to support a call to action from the Security Council.[6] This means that the inherent right of the state to make war now legally refers only to national or collective self-defence. But in practice the cause of defence is a catholic one: to attack may be to defend; and to deter is always to threaten to attack.

Efforts to regulate entry into war have been paralleled by efforts to regulate military conduct in war. Again, in the present century many prohibitions (against maltreating prisoners, taking hostages, using indiscriminately harmful weapons) have been given legal form in international agreements. But large numbers of currently deployed armaments would by their nature transgress the more important customs and laws of war if used. A thermonuclear weapon targeted on a foreign city makes hostages of its civilian inhabitants: if launched in execution of a policy of nuclear deterrence it slaughters them because of an offensive action by their government in some other theatre that, living or dead, they cannot alter.

The pacifist response

The pacifist solution to the problems of military capability seems to be a comprehensive and consistent one. Given the total abandonment of all military establishments and weapons, moral and practical difficulties of relations between armies and civil societies disappear as do those relating to the initiation and conduct of foreign wars.

(1) But for good reasons no state has adopted a wholly pacifist policy. If all states became pacifist at the same time there would still be the formidable danger of a strong state giving up pacificism, rearming and thus dominating its neighbours. On the other hand, a solitary pacifist state in an otherwise non-pacifist world would have to depend on assistance from armed states when attacked or threatened with attack. If this dependence were a policy there could be no moral quality in pacifism: it would simply be a selfish diversion of public expenditure from building up military strength into more pleasing uses. And a state taking this position would always be unsure that support of sufficient weight would be forthcoming when required. This uncertainty would be of no importance if pacifism were a condition of national indifference to conquest. Yet if this indifference were actually sustainable through any crisis, the measure of popular support for the political community of the state in question would almost certainly be so low as to render it incapable of effective government in peace or war. Alternatively, if the prospect of conquest aroused a widespread will to resist, then pacifism would not be a sustainable policy.

(2) Because of these difficulties, pacificism tends to press its adherents towards a highly reformist outlook on world society as a whole. If there were a world government there would be no need for national defence. But to succeed in obviating defence a world government would require armed strength to enforce its allocations. It could not be a pacifist government. In the same kind of way a world association of states operating the principle of collective security against the possibility of armed aggression needs armed forces to deter potential wrong-doers and to subdue them should this kind of deterrence fail. Collective security is not pacifist. One is therefore driven to conclude that the pacifist position is essentially a personal one, public only in the hope of the pacifist that his private example will generally modify men's destructive propensities. Simply to oppose a particular use, or threat of the use, of military strength is not of course pacifism, which is a total not a partial stand. As a personal policy, pacifism suffers from a major defect.

The pacifist refuses military service because he believes the intrusion of violence or the threat of violence into otherwise peaceful relations to be wrong. But if this is so, how can a determination to deter states prone to the use of violence also be wrong? Military strength deployed to prevent the resort to violence or the active use of the threat of violence by an aggressively disposed state would appear to meet the pacifist moral requirement of resistance to the use of force.[7]

Force as an intrinsic part of foreign policy

The incorporation of military strength into foreign policy need not be the mark of an authoritarian government. Radical domestic policies would even seem to require sustained attention to the maintenance of national defence in order to protect experimentation with new internal social arrangements from external military disruption. This kind of conception of the role of force accepts the existence of the potentiality for war in international relations, but it also includes a clear preference for peace over war and for small wars over big wars. Keeping the domestic population alive is a necessary, though not a sufficient, condition for investigating the possibilities of improving civil society. So to maintain a military establishment is not necessarily to maintain a war-like foreign policy. Apart from its inherent unpleasantness, war is also to be avoided because it is a form of collective activity in which emotions tend to run high and in which, therefore, the difficulties of acting rationally are more than usually acute. Additionally, war is an enterprise in which contingent unknowns can be major determinants of outcomes: battles are notoriously prone to go wrong. Rationality, the concern only to undertake actions instrumental to specific and realisable results, therefore requires the avoidance of all battles other than essential battles, and these should be arranged so as to achieve desired outcomes with the minimum of loss. Government policy must determine when war is no longer avoidable. It becomes so as a consequence of deteriorating inter-state relations over a particular issue. The desired outcome of such a war is thus contained in its beginning: victory is the establishment of conditions in which peaceful relations may be resumed, and at any particular point in a conflict these conditions should be amenable to exact definition. If they are rational they should be achievable without disproportionate loss. They should therefore be such as might be expected to become acceptable to an opponent and, in practice, they should rigorously control the actual use of force. War, then, is simply an impasse in the political relations between states that one side attempts to break by military action. The resolution of such an impasse in inter-state relations is the only rational point of war, which in itself is nothing more than the continuation of political relations through an impasse. Once the impasse has been resolved by means, as it were, of violent 'negotiations', then non-violent relations can be renewed. So a possibility of war is a part of quarrels between states. And these quarrels are conducted by governments, not by military hierarchies.[8]

(1) An immediate objection to this doctrine springs from direct observation of inter-governmental practices. The quarrels between states do not all contain the possibility of war. European Community discussions on agricultural pricing, heated though they may often be, do not include threats of war. In a field such as this, war cannot be a continuation of politics (a) because war could not secure a desired support price, and (b) because war must be excluded from their relations before states can form the kinds of associations in which matters of this sort may be discussed. So not all foreign policy fields contain the possibility of war. The fields that do appear to contain the possibility of war are determined by the actions and policies of governments. The proposition that war is a continuation of policy is therefore a tautology since the possibility of war defines the kind of policy of which war can be the continuation. True, the policy field containing the possibility of war seems to exist mainly within the network of international relations. But it does not coincide with this network. And no tautology can explain the nature of the boundary between relations that do contain the possibility of war and relations that do not. Simply to pronounce that on one side of this boundary war or the threat of war is an intrinsic part of policy whereas on the other side of the boundary it is not, explains nothing. How is the boundary created in the first place?

(2) Difficulties of a different category are created by the nature of many contemporary weapons, which range in destructive capability up to massive inter-continental missiles armed with multiple thermonuclear warheads. The deployment of weapons, if it is to be rational, must be related to their possible use. But the only possible use to which many weapons of this order can be put is destruction on a societal scale. It is difficult to see how this kind of military operation could be interpreted as the breaking of an impasse in a set of diplomatic relations that would thereafter be peacefully resumed. Thereafter very little could be resumed. As indicated above, thermonuclear violence of this order also transgresses traditional and formal rules of war. It certainly entails the destruction of non-combatants on a scale that cannot be interpreted as an instrumental necessity of operations to bring a military force to defeat.

(3) In practice, a military force is not always a national instrument of policy. British forces currently deployed in Europe could not in any reasonably foreseeable international circumstances be put to continental use by a British government acting alone. Nor, in a sense, are they wholly British forces, since much of their essential equipment is either purchased abroad or produced collaboratively by Britain and other countries. Additionally, the contingencies for which they prepare are defined in terms of Nato connections. If, as a matter of fact, a military force cannot be an instrument of exclusively national policy in the theatre from which threats to the existence

of the state emanate, then it can only be an instrument (if it is an instrument at all) of some admixture of national and international policy. This is a different kind of circumstance from that traditionally associated with the combined use of national forces in temporary military alliances between states. An army that may be used in association with a number of possible allies is different from an army that can be used *only* in association with a particular set of allies.

(4) Governments deploy military force at the sub-national level, as British governments have in Northern Ireland. Here the dictum that force should only be used as a continuation of policy is a truism because no government in this situation, when questioned about its use of force, can fail to set forth a policy of some kind. The problem that now becomes pressing is whether military force used internally has anything to do with the use of force in the supposed service of foreign policy at the international level. If not, then a case has been made for regarding the foreign policy arena as different in kind from the national arena. But in the present example the distinction is an odd one: at the international level military force is not an instrument of government policy whereas at the internal level it is.

Foreign policy as the regulation of force

War, actual or possible, may seem to be a wholly distinctive preoccupation. Killing other people is different from all other kinds of contact with them. Violence is nevertheless an undeniable if uncongenial feature of international relations. Given these premisses, foreign policy should encompass violence or potential for violence but violence should not be incorporated into the deepest nature of foreign policy. In this way foreign policy becomes a means of constraining war. So a major object of foreign policy is not to deploy war but to control war, to reduce its role in international affairs. Since the means of doing harm in international society are widely dispersed, a state wishing to control war, or the effects of threats of war, must have military strength of its own. But deploying the military to control the international system's propensity to violence is different from deploying the military to further a specific interest abroad. No problems of a metaphysical kind relating to the sovereignty of the state are created by allocating national forces to a cross-national defence organisation or in entering into joint supply arrangements. The purpose of force in the present conception of its role is the prevention of the possible use of violence by states that see this as a means of obtaining their interests and extending their power. Force is only included in foreign policy when it is confronted by a state that is prone to obtain its ends by the use, or the threatened use, of military strength. The threat of the use of war is not the distinguishing mark of international society as a whole but only of a part of it. A peaceful state entering the potentially violent sector of international relations does so for three reasons: first, because it has no choice; second, in order to contain the potential harmfulness to international society emanating from this particular part of it; and, third, to prevent the deployment of military strength from being, or being seen to be, the most rewarding form of international action.

(1) But when this general viewpoint is brought to specifics, defects soon appear in it. Entering into the relationship of nuclear deterrence cannot readily be equated with controlling the potentially violent factor in international relations. Deterrence, so far anyway, has been associated with a costly deployment of weapons having the capability to destroy human societies. It is not easy to see this as the restriction of violence within narrow confines since it seems to threaten violence of an absolute order.

(2) A military capability cannot in practice be isolated from foreign policy as a whole. If a state possesses massive military strength it cannot, whatever the wishes of its government, keep this a secret. The scale of a state's strength is known and colours the viewpoints of foreigners regardless of whether they are directly threatened by it. The numerous statesmen who visit Washington do so because they believe the United States to be a first-class power and thus worth cultivating. Likewise, the standing of the American Secretary of State in the Middle East or in southern Africa rests in large part on the strength of the United States. The United States is a first-class power largely because of the scale of her military capability. The European Community is not a first-class power largely because it has no military capability at all.

(3) Similarly, a state that uses its military strength to defend other states thereby acquires an influence over them in non-military areas. War-making potential cannot, it seems, be isolated from influence of other kinds. The influence that American governments carry with West German governments in matters of economic policy, though seldom oppressive, is in part a product of the apparent dependence of the Federal Republic upon the American commitment to her defence.

Conclusions

1. A central difficulty in arriving at a settled view about the place of force in foreign policy lies in its close connection with beliefs about the role of force in international society. In traditional theorising about the state from a purely internal standpoint there is no logical problem in dealing with violence. The state can be assumed to possess a legitimate enforcing capability sufficient to maintain internal order. Theory may then address itself to the circumstances in which citizens have the right of revolt against the authorities of the state. As a rule this right may only be exercised when major defects appear in the state because of tyrannous or grossly incompetent government. It is not a right that derives from the existence of the state as such. The notion of the state is traditionally a normative one, so the internal use of force (by, say, an oppressed population) may be seen as morally necessary to the restoration

of the state from the debased condition to which it has been brought by wicked rulers. This kind of theory is not a justification of war against the state but of war to make the state truly what it should be, in which rightful condition there exists not a duty of violence but a duty to abstain from violence. In connecting foreign policy with the use of force, much seems to depend on the view taken of the international arena. Here there seems to be no right to take arms against a tyrannous ruler as such. Indeed, this arena is one that accommodates tyrannous rulers fairly readily. So a solution to the problem of the place of force in foreign policy would seem to depend, first, on whether a just state can have a distinctively just foreign policy; second, on whether a just order can exist in international relations; and, third, on whether a just international order can be furthered or defended by the deployment of force.

2. The destructive potential of many modern weapons is of a societal order. Their instrumentality to any foreign policy is therefore questionable because their use could annihilate foreign policy. Yet they exist and policy must comprehend them.

3. War manifestly has no role in many cross-national issues and institutions. So at least one fundamental distinction must be made 'inside' foreign policy between issues and institutions related to the use of force and issues and institutions unrelated to the use of force. This distinction may be so deep that entirely different conceptions of foreign policy apply on each side of it.

MORALITY AND FOREIGN POLICY

Instances of the amoral or apparently immoral character of many foreign policy actions are not hard to come by. In an international regime of fixed exchange rates, it may seem to be the duty of an otherwise truthful finance minister planning a currency devaluation to deny categorically that a devaluation is in prospect. An otherwise just and constitutional state may be obliged to ally itself with a state whose government's customary behaviour is manifestly unconstitutional and unjust. In time of war decent statesmen may sanction military operations such as area bombing that cause mass casualties among non-combatants; and in time of peace they may order the development and deployment of massive thermonuclear weapons that would inevitably have indiscriminate effects if used. States generally may feel obliged to remain inactive while one of their number behaves with manifest injustice towards another: western European states were largely passive in 1956 when Soviet Russia invaded Hungary. States have ignored rules laid down by international agreement, as did Britain in invading Egypt in 1956 in disregard of the general terms of the UN Charter and of specific principles enunciated by the Security Council. Actions and inactions such as these affront ordinary habits of personal moral conduct. The central issue of foreign policy may thus seem to be presented by its peculiar relationship with moral principles.

The priority of order over morality

The international arena is not without rules. By and large these emphasise the (not untroubled) maintenance of the system of states throughout constant fluctuations in the distribution of strength within it. The effect of such rules may seem to be that a measure of order is achieved in potentially the most disorderly of all societies. These rules are not concerned with any lofty morality. To accept them is simply to accept the priority of order. True, this is an order that contains much that is morally reprehensible in the domestic conduct of governments. But it is because the world contains much that is undesirable that the order of multiple statehood has priority in it. The mutual recognition by states of their different identities protects much that is desirable. The international system of states, if its rules are observed by both the just and the unjust, may reasonably be claimed to maximise the safety of what is moral in the world's governments among a great deal that is immoral.

(1) This view suffers from a number of historical defects. The rules of the system of states traditionally included rules of imperialism, whereby some people were not members of states but of territories or estates and could not claim the protection of statehood for their own forms of living, moral or immoral as they might be. Nor did small states enjoy equality of status in the system, being often subject to the purposes of larger states. The contemporary international system, particularly as it manifests itself in eastern Europe, contains many vestiges of rules that contradict any pure notions of a system of mutually recognising independent states. The achievement of such a 'pure' system has for long constituted a widely desired reform of international society; it does not describe it.

(2) An outcome of the first world war was a proliferation of states. This was accompanied by an attempt to create an international order based on the equality of all states in terms of their right to independence. In fact the League of Nations, subject to the principle of collective security (whereby the whole community of states supposedly committed itself to defend from external attack any of its members regardless of their individual size or geographical position or mode of government), made little positive impact on the outcome of most international crises in which the fate of small or big states was at stake. It is often argued that during the period between the world wars the League simply distracted liberal governments from attention to the balance of power and the harshly real policies demanded by it. Yet the traditional balance of power included war in its mechanisms of adjustment to change. War could not itself be called a form of order. If no principle or

structure but sovereign statehood exists to manifest both the will to change and the will to resist change, then war is inevitable if change is inevitable. In the thermonuclear age this may seem a poor principle because of war's potential for obliterating states both large and small. If war is not itself a form of international order, and if it cannot be shown to maintain the existence of states, then an order that includes states but excludes war must be based on some other principle than crude sovereign statehood.

(3) In fact, numerous efforts to introduce values into the international system have been undertaken: legalistically, in documents like the Kellog Pact for the Renunciation of War or the European Convention on Human Rights; and ideologically, in doctrines of self-determination or social revolution. And in practice neither governments nor individuals consistently confine their interest in what they consider to be justice to their own domestic situations: British governments may entertain foreign dignatories known to flout individual rights, but they commonly do so to the accompaniment of public and parliamentary protests. Though formally bound by the domestic jurisdiction clause of the Charter (Article 2, paragraph 7), the members of the UN repeatedly utter moral judgements on one another's internal affairs. Order does not seem to be given total precedence over morality.

Morality as an irrelevance to foreign policy

It may seem that there can be no such thing as international morality, that is, a morality intrinsic to international society, because this is a contingent collectivity that is not founded on any common values. To adjudge an action in the international arena to be a mistake or to be stupid may be entirely appropriate, but, from the present viewpoint, to condemn such an action as immoral is meaningless. Morality can only be used as a criterion of authoritative conduct within the value-based order established for its own citizens by the state. External conduct can be matched against no morality appropriate to all the participants in the world arena, which, as a whole, is a stateless one. The only criterion applicable to any particular foreign policy is thus one of service to the state from which it emanates.

(1) But this is itself a moralistic doctrine. It proposes a criterion, service to the state, that recognises no superior or countervailing principle and that can therefore be stretched to justify any international action. The statesman can be drawn to see himself as the state and all his acts to be those of the state. The unlimited justification of the behaviour of statesmen that this kind of doctrine provides comprises a criterion that is likely to accentuate international society's propensity to disorder. The apparent foundation of this criterion, the internal order of the state, is thus rendered precarious by the external horrors that can be its consequence. Furthermore, a doctrine that can be used to justify virtually any external action of the statesman is unlikely to encourage him in domestic moral humility. A doctrine that supports

external ruthlessness is also likely to be used to justify tyrannous internal behaviour, because this, too, can be claimed to be essential to the service of the external position of the state. Again the criterion deemed appropriate to foreign relations adds to the hazards of the internal order from which it is supposed to spring.

(2) As a matter of fact, foreign policy may be shared by several states, in which case it presumably serves an order that is international, not national. More importantly, statecraft operates in cross-national institutions in which all kinds of national and international actions can be deliberated in the absence of sharp moral conflicts. In other words, cross-national communities (the Atlantic community, the European Community) can come into existence. It follows that either the state is not necessary to a moral order in public affairs, or, more probably, that the state is not a simple territorial entity but a complex concept amenable to non-territorial interpretation.

Necessity as the rule of international action

International life may seem to be conditioned by necessity, not morality. Moral judgement does not bear on wholly necessary action or inaction. If an act is one that has no alternatives, its moral status is irrelevant. Necessary action is exactly dictated by circumstances: if a house is burning down, those of its occupants wishing to survive must exit by the nearest available route.

But international circumstances short of direct military attack do not reach this pitch of directly compelling urgency. Severe international crises manifest themselves as agonising choices. By definition a crisis cannot be a no-choice situation. British and French support for Czechoslovakia in 1938 might have been a more efficacious, let alone a more moral, policy than that which necessity was deemed to require. Necessity is more often an excuse than an explanation of international action.

Foreign policy as trusteeship

The statesman may be taken to be a trustee. Thus the finance minister is responsible for the stability of his country's currency and this duty takes priority over moral scruples about personal conduct. Ordinary moral rules of truthfulness or generosity cannot be applied to the trustee if they require him to neglect the terms of his trust, which invariably require him to secure the interests of those for whom he acts.

This is too simple. A trustee is bound not to give away the assets with whose care he is entrusted; in other words, he may not be generous with other people's money. But the rule that restrains his generosity is not one that requires the abandonment of virtue: he may not cheat, steal, lie or murder in order to multiply trust properties. Anyway, the trusteeship analogue of statecraft is an inappropriate one. The statesman does not act principally for minors or the infirm of mind. Nor is it at all clear with what assets he is entrusted. One such asset may be the honour of his fellow citizens, which can hardly be cherished by turpitudinous behaviour abroad. And his constituents may be widely divided about what is both morally and materially at stake in particular issues of foreign policy; some may hold the statesman to have moral responsibilities to citizens of other countries as well as his own. There may be a case for a suspension of ordinary moral rules when dealing with a blackguard for whom moral rules are meaningless. Some blackguards may be active in international affairs. But they do not dominate all the relations of statesmen. A meeting of statesmen from the Scandinavian countries is not a pit of iniquity and no suspension of morality is appropriate to it.

Reform as the moral object of foreign policy

The moral dilemmas of international statesmanship may be felt so keenly that the reform of states and of international society as a whole may seem to be the sole solution of otherwise hopeless problems. Given that the internal order of the state can be one in which moral conduct on the part of statesmen is to be assumed, it seems to follow that if the internal arrangements of all states were reformed to such a standard then international society itself would be changed and moral norms would be as applicable internationally as they can now be internally.

(1) One of the essential difficulties of life in international society lies in the widely differing views contained in it as to what constitutes an appropriate internal order. If agreement on this matter is unlikely, the only method of achieving uniformity within states is through conquest or the threat of conquest. But enterprises of this sort render international society more disorderly and amoral, not less so. And an imposed internal order, however ethical its individual acts of government may be, is likely to be felt by those most affected to be in its nature immoral. If consent is a necessary condition of moral rule, imperialism can never be moral. When it is resisted its maintenance may require acts of brutality matching anything occurring in an unreformed international arena.

(2) It is by no means evident that states appearing to possess internal forms of government of a similar kind enjoy relations free from mutual distrust and threats of violence. Relations among socialist states such as Soviet Russia, China and Yugoslavia have hardly been noteworthy for their placidity. Violent foreign engagements, undertaken in the face of moral dissent among their circle, are not unfamiliar aspects of the foreign policies of liberal democratic countries either; Britain's invasion of Egypt in 1956 is a clear example.

A world state as the foundation of moral order

Given this feature of the plurality of states (that even similarity of ideology and governmental structure apparently provides no guarantee of foreign policy harmony), the institution of a world state may seem to be the only way forward to a universal society in which ordinary moral criteria are applicable to the conduct of statesmen.

(1) As a foreign policy recommendation this suffers from the fundamental defect that no government is likely to hand over vital functions, particularly defence, to a world authority unless it is sure that all other governments are proceeding likewise at a similar pace. But if each government could be sure of this, such a degree of trust would exist among all governments as to obviate the need for a world state in the first place. Similarly, the capacity of states for massive violence cannot be made to disappear; a world state would have to face the possibility of rearmament by former national states capable of developing weapons of a scale sufficient to deter any authority, universal or otherwise.

(2) A world state, were it to fail to ensure the conditions of moral states-manship, would provide the conditions of tyrannous statesmanship on an unexampled scale. The central fact of world society is its extreme variety. The plurality of states both expresses and controls this variety, though it may do so imperfectly. Yet there are no grounds whatever for believing that in these respects the inappropriateness of a world state to world society would not be immeasurably greater.

The moral problem of scale

The international statesman operates on the largest conceivable scale. Observance of a general moral rule, a form of utilitarianism say, may seem to be invalidated both by the possible scale of the unintended results of doctrinally determined action and by the variety of values embedded in international society. The universal diversity of welfare functions, for example, is of such a magnitude as to make a utilitarian calculus impossibly complex and, in practical terms, worthless.

But not all statesmen are benign dictators. In the context of the present enquiry none are. Moral decision is not the iron application of a rule to a problem. Internally, an authoritative decision is largely the product of a process of deliberation and adjustment, about both the nature of the problem and its possible solutions, which makes the outcome a broadly acceptable one having a chance of success in a complex society. An international decision about, say, tariff reductions may be much the same. The process of decision, which is likely to be more laborious internationally than it is domestically, may include discussion of possibly appropriate moral considerations. The nature and difficulty of these considerations are part of the process, implicitly if not explicitly, and are not extraneous to it. The process itself is partly moral and may be much the same at home and abroad.

Statecraft as trade-off

If the moral justification of some of the actions of statesmen is difficult, and if the fundamental reform of international society is impossible, then the last resort may seem to be an outlook that emphasises the practicable. The statesman is at the centre of many opposing demands and influences. He is likely to have to contend with a difficult and various domestic community and externally he must negotiate with both friendly and hostile governments. The kinds of issues confronting him will vary from the parochial (drains, roads and trains) to the universal (deterrence, arms control, war); and many will fall neither wholly in the international nor wholly in the national categories (exchange rate regulation, tariffs, inflation). The groups, individuals and institutions with which he must deal will differ widely in their interests and the scope of their authority (constituents, political parties, parliaments, local government authorities, trade unions, national corporations, international organisations, multinational companies, foreign statesmen). The policy objectives thrust upon him may contain strong antitheses (full employment–no inflation, welfare services–balanced budgets, defence–reduced military expenditure, international cooperation–parochial interests). In this setting, general principles ('never treat men as means to other ends', 'maximise utility') are useless as coherent guides. The statesman must be practical. He must trade off what is desirable here against what is relatively less desirable here; what is moral against what is necessary; achievement on one front against loss on another; pursuit of specific national gains against costs to foreign goodwill; risks to defence against benefits to welfare services.

(1) However, the trade-off approach gives no guide as to what may not be traded off against what. Just as a statesman may explain all his actions in terms of exigency, so he may always claim that the benefits of his selected policy outweigh the benefits forgone in an abandoned policy. But can a benefit to welfare really be set against a loss of safety? Or an improvement in safety be set against a loss of liberty? And is every value – liberty, morality, the rule of law – tradeable? The trade-off principle equates the statesman with the kind of entrepreneur whose function is to provide a market bringing buyers and sellers together at prices that reflect the state of supply and demand for the items exchanged, and whose personal interest in these proceedings is confined to his percentage of the turnover. Though this analogy may carry conviction in a number of cases, it is usually necessary that the statesman, for the sake of his career if not from personal predilection, should identify himself with some values and some specific policy objectives.

(2) The trade-off principle, if it is to have any operational exactitude, requires deals to be made in terms of quantifiable objects: so many schools

against so many miles of new roads. But the statesman habitually expends much labour on unquantifiables: on support, confidence, his own personality. Guns are quantifiable, but security is not; one can have a gun but does it yield security? The goodwill of a foreign statesman may be cultivated with banquets and processions: but do so many banquets and processions yield so much goodwill?

(3) More importantly, most domestic markets function within the bounds of general rules relating to contract, misrepresentation and ethical practice. In the same sort of way, a 'trading' statesman in the domestic 'market' is constrained by ordinary law and by constitutional process, to which must be added the attentions of constantly prying critics. It is these conditions that are morally important and they do not exist in the international arena taken as a whole. But they do exist in parts of it.

(4) One area of international affairs requires no trading analogy because trade on a large scale is intrinsic to it. But the complex system of institutions, negotiations and agreements that has grown out of western economic relations does not constitute an international bearpit. By the indifferent standards of traditional diplomatic conduct it might reasonably be held to be morally admirable. The threat of war is absent from it; it is open to arguments and suggestions from a wide variety of private and official sources; from time to time engaged governments and cross-national institutions provide generous support for unlucky or incompetent members; the internal economic policies of governments are subjected to both interested and disinterested external observation and criticism; its affairs are open to pressure from poor countries and it makes some provisions to meet their needs; no government is forced to be a member of it yet no government is anxious to leave it. The moral assumptions of this sector of international relations must be different from those of the sector dominated by thermonuclear weapons. An analogy based on the former is unlikely to apply convincingly to the latter.

Conclusions

1. Morality would seem to reside in the conditions of activities, and these conditions differ widely in international relations.

2. A condition of the conduct of statecraft must be the nature of the state. It would thus seem to follow that relations between moral states may be expected to be moral, whereas relations between immoral states may be expected to be immoral. But what is a moral state?

3. Though the moral status of relations between moral states may not present a special problem, the relations between moral states and immoral states must do so, since a relationship is apt to contain qualities contributed by the parties to it. Foreign relations with an immoral state may thus be expected to contain immoral elements. Principles of foreign policy should

presumably offer a resolution of the problem of how a moral state should handle these elements and how far it should go in absorbing them into the substance of its foreign policy.

INTERVENTION

Almost all the land surface of the world is now apportioned to what are, in the language of diplomacy, independent states. Many foreign policy operations that are intended to move affairs abroad in a preferred direction may therefore be called interventions. This term traditionally refers to two sorts of activities: first, intervention by a state or states in the internal affairs of another state; and, second, intervention by a state in an international dispute to which it is not a principal party.

Intervention in the internal affairs of another country may have the objective of maintaining a congenial leadership in power; of replacing an uncongenial leadership; of encouraging or resisting social and political changes of a structural kind; of forestalling or resisting the interventionary activities of another state or states; of encouraging an existing leadership to pursue specific policies of an agreeable kind. To achieve such goals means like these may be used: bribes to individual leaders or to leading groups; economic assistance (gifts, cheap loans, preferential trading arrangements) or economic punishment (cessation of loans or gifts, an embargo on trade); clandestine violence; overt violence in the form of direct military operations on land; overt violence in the form of aerial or naval bombardment; military assistance in terms of supply and advice; the provision of safe bases for irregular forces engaged, or about to engage, in internal war; diplomatic pressure; entry into treaty guarantees to support a particular settlement of an internal dispute by some such device as partition.

Intervention in a regional international dispute may have the objective of influencing the outcome in favour of one of the parties; of countering the interventionary efforts of another state; of influencing the outcome in favour of stability; of protecting a directly endangered interest; of enhancing the intervening state's general standing and influence in the region concerned. To achieve such ends means like these may be used: economic assistance; military assistance in terms of supply and advice; clandestine military operations; open and direct military operations and threats thereof; diplomatic conciliation and provision of good offices; support for diplomatic conciliation and good offices provided by another outside power or by an international organisation; declarations and recommendations, multilateral and otherwise, to the parties directly engaged; participation in or support for interdispositionary action to separate parties to a violent dispute; entry into guarantees to provide security to parties to a dispute.

The capability to intervene

Direct intervention in internal conflicts may demand the use of substantial military strength over a long period. The existence of this capability and the cost of its use are likely to be subject to many misgivings and uncertainties, particularly when the nature of victory is elusive or subject to wide disagreement. The power of an indigenous participant in a domestic conflict is likely to be suspect; if it were very strong there could be no internal conflict in the first place. Supporting a losing side is almost certain to be an extended form of political and material embarrassment.

Diplomatic meddling in internal disputes that is unsupported by a more direct interventionary capability may be futile, misleading or plain dishonest. Guarantees of a partitioning frontier or of a constitution designed to placate internal dissidence that turn out to be without substance when put to the test are likely to encourage the parties directly engaged to adopt extreme goals. Total solutions may seem attractive to embattled parties when partial solutions have no substantive backing.

Prudent interventionary activity in disputes of both an internal and an international kind is likely to be designed to allow for quick withdrawal in case of difficulty. In some cases this withdrawal capability may be useful in bringing about changes in the policies of parties that are being supported. But, on the other hand, emphasis on a quick withdrawal capability is apt to reduce the effectiveness of diplomatic pressures founded on the prospect of intervention. Prospectively unreliable partners or policemen are likely to be treated with a good deal of scepticism.

The effectiveness of intervention

A course of action is effective if it attains a clearly conceived particular objective at anticipated cost. The more exact the objective, the more readily may the prospective effectiveness of available means to its attainment be judged. General objectives ('order' or 'the peace of the world') may seem to contribute little to immediate problems of determining the effectiveness of a prospective interventionary action. But unrelated to general ends immediate objectives may turn out to be contradictory and futile; what can be the point of effectively supporting a particular leadership that then sows the seeds of its own destruction by erratic and oppressive behaviour? So the pursuit of effectiveness in intervention raises four basic problems: first, the selection of immediate objectives (the support of this potential leadership rather than that, for example); second, the selection of clear general objectives (stability in a particular country or international region rather than justice in a particular country or region); third, the establishment of a clear relationship in operational terms between immediate objectives and general objectives; fourth, the selection of means appropriate to the attainment of immediate objectives.

In the most simple of imaginable circumstances these problems would be difficult enough. In practice, intervention in a domestic conflict will be additionally complicated by the almost certain involvement of more than one outside power. The interests of regional powers will be engaged by disturbances inside one of their neighbours, so intervention by one regional state in the affairs of another will provoke the involvement of other regional states. In the same sort of way, actual or prospective intervention in domestic conflict by a first-class power will arouse the concern and suspicion of another first-class power. Regional international disputes, besides being international in nature, will also claim the attention of first-class powers, which, by definition, have worldwide concerns. All interventions raise problems of widespread international reaction. The decision to intervene and the selection of appropriate means and objectives all take place in a very large environment, which is likely to add innumerable complications to the considerations that must be weighed.

In the pursuit of effectiveness an effort must be made to relate immediate particular objectives to long-term general ends: but on what basis is the convincing selection of long-term ends possible? Can rational choices be made at this elevated level? Traditionally, long-term policy possibilities tend to take forms such as these: (a) the achievement of what appear to be specific and lasting national interests like 'freedom of passage through the Suez Canal'; (b) the achievement of 'power' or 'prestige' in a country or in an international region, so that 'influence' over future events there may be exercised in a variety of eventualities; (c) the long-term denial to another outside party of this 'power' and 'influence'; (d) the establishment of lasting internal regimes of a particular sort; (e) the establishment of stable international regional orders of a particular sort.

A number of familiar difficulties cluster around these kinds of objectives. None appears to have any inherent claim to superior rationality that could give it priority over the others. Yet these objectives are replete with the possibility of policy conflict: action in pursuit of a specific long-term interest, say easy access to vital raw materials, may conflict directly with prudent policies aiming to support a certain regional order. This kind of problem can only be resolved in two ways: first, by the acceptance of value-premises establishing rules of priority among both ends and means, but of course intervention of both kinds is likely to be a manifestation of the existence of differing values in the first place; second, by ordering long-term goals by reference to longer long-term goals, but this procedures slips into an infinite regression.

Apparently precise and categorical interests (such as the maintenance of freedom of passage through the Suez Canal) often turn out to be dispensable. In the long run, structural adjustments are made to their loss and what were thought to be necessities cease to be so. If specific interests are variable, their status as proper objectives of long-term strategies becomes questionable.

If specific interests cannot substantiate such strategies, then general interests must fill this role. But general interests are vague, value-saturated and conflicting, and cannot easily be accommodated in a supposedly rational calculus.

Experience would seem to support the proposition that largescale social values and arrangements cannot be eternal. Population turnover through reproduction and death, among many other factors, militates against the lengthy maintenance of specific social structures. A benefit for one generation turns into an oppression for the next. Yet many long-term interventionary objectives seem to contain the assumption that a static state of affairs is achievable; that a region can become 'stable', or that 'power' and 'influence' in a country can be obtained as if they were durable articles subject to once-and-for-all purchase.

To the mutual contradictions among objectives must be added intrinsic self-contradictions within many objectives. To maintain a congenial regime in office by interventionary action may be the one certain method of ensuring its decline and fall. To use force to maintain regional stability may be a sure way of creating instability.

Ethics of intervention

The practical problems of intervention are likely to be exacerbated by moral uncertainties. Intervention through involvement in a regional international war may make a small war big, then make it bigger still by drawing in other external parties; it may make a short war long; it may encourage unrealism and exaggerated ambitions in governments receiving large-scale aid; it may commit the intervening power to the support of governments of repellent values. Intervention of this international kind raises the spectre of entanglement in a distant war that is domestically unpopular. Yet purely diplomatic intervention to secure a peaceful and moral settlement to a dispute is unlikely to be effective in bringing about adjustments in war aims without some kind of deeper extra-diplomatic commitment.

Intervention in the form of involvement in a domestic conflict may make small-scale violence large-scale; may make short-term violence long-term perhaps by delaying the defeat of the weaker internal party; may encourage unrealism on the part of a leadership receiving aid; may commit the intervening power to the imposition, or seeming imposition, of an unjust regime upon a country that does not support it; may cause a counterproductive nationalist reaction among an indigenous population and thus make a strong internal party receiving assistance weak, or a weak internal party weaker; may (through the support of, or participation in, military operations against covert opponents) cause counterproductive harm to an otherwise inactive population. Intervention in domestic violence also opens the prospect of entanglement in a war that becomes progressively unjust because of the involvement itself. It is a kind of war that is prone to require military operations to be undertaken among partially armed domestic populations, and in such situations the legal and traditional rules of military action become difficult to apply. Yet, again, diplomatic intervention to secure a peaceful settlement is unlikely to be effective if it is unsupported by a deeper extra-diplomatic engagement.

Intervention of almost all non-diplomatic kinds in both internal and international conflicts risks appearing to be taking the power of decision out of indigenous hands and thereby to be infringing rights of choice and self-direction. At the opposite level of difficulty, intervention in both categories is often undertaken in the cause of world order. Logically, the world should decide what world order is. But the world organisation, the United Nations, is usually unable to intervene itself, partly because it is unable to muster the means to do so, but more importantly because its members are unable to agree in most concrete circumstances on what constitutes the proper form of world order.

The nature of intervention

Intervention is a term so freely used in relation to such diverse circumstances that it is difficult to ascribe any precise and useful meaning to it. In a sense, all actions originating in one country that have effects within another are interventions. Restricting the term to refer to external government involvement in conflicts of a violent or potentially violent kind excludes, for example, support for a government that might otherwise collapse relatively non-violently under the weight of its internal problems. But including this kind of case in the category of intervention leads also to the inclusion of all the ordinary ways in which western statesmen assist one another during periods of economic difficulty.

If intervention is restricted to the category of violent action it becomes difficult to sustain the distinction between intervention in domestic affairs and intervention in regional international conflicts. As has been indicated, a situation within a country that makes foreign intervention in its internal affairs likely is almost certainly going to concern and involve several neighbouring countries at the regional level. So operationally the internal–external distinction is unlikely to hold. Likewise, intervention in regional international conflict merges into the category of traditional international violence. All wars start somewhere and where they start may reasonably be called a region. In the presence of this concept-defying formlessness one may feel inclined to take refuge in a tautology: intervention may thus be deemed to be action that is widely felt to be interventionary or becomes widely felt to be interventionary. But nothing follows from a tautology in the way of principles of policy. Direct contemplation of experience without benefit of exact conceptual apparatus suggests simply that intervention is a matter in which states should exercise extreme caution. The need for extreme caution suggests emphasis on the use of flexible instruments of policy. Indirect assistance that can be modulated quickly and without embarrassment would seem almost invariably preferable to direct military commitment on land. But commonsense points like these convey nothing about the point and legitimacy, or otherwise, of intervention. Modulated intervention looks like intervention without serious conviction.

Conclusions

1. Intervention is not an exact concept and interventionary action, actual or projected, is replete with complexities and dangers. This is obvious and it does not advance understanding. Principles of foreign policy should presumably discover in intervention's complications some relatively simple pattern of explanation or prescription.

2. Intervention by one state in the affairs of another state raises fundamental questions about the nature of statehood. A theory or view of the state that applies equally to all states could never, seemingly, justify one state's attempts to take over the functions of another state.

3. The long-term objectives of intervention merge into unordered vagueness. Yet it is from such objectives that the point and purpose of intervention must derive. Principles of foreign policy that aim to refer to practical operations should offer some way of establishing a priority ordering of general objectives.

SOME ECONOMIC PROBLEMS OF FOREIGN POLICY

This enquiry emerges from, and is committed to, pluralist social experience. Many of the preoccupations of the governments of open states are economic in nature. Open states are joined by many cross-national linkages that influence the tenor of economic life in each of them. When a United States government operates a domestic tight money policy, interest rates are likely to rise in a number of other countries; a run out of sterling is matched by a run into another western currency or currencies; and so on. A western international economy exists in three basic senses: first, international trade among western developed countries is by far the largest component of the total of world trade; second, western money markets are closely associated and financial movements among them can be massive and swift; third, movements of direct and indirect investment and of managerial and technical expertise are markedly greater among the western countries than between them and the rest of the world. But the western international economy is not made up of identical units. The European Community is proportionately a greater importer of goods and materials than the United States; Japan is more heavily dependent on imports of sources of energy than Britain; direct government involvement in economic operations is greater in Britain than it is in Japan or in the United States. Despite these differences, consumer tastes in the system as a whole often converge and this, combined with international efforts to reduce official barriers to trade, creates large cross-national markets that are in many cases exploited through cross-national modes of production and distribution.

The western economy generates and contains far more wealth than the rest of the world put together. The trade of underdeveloped countries with it is greater than their trade with one another and much greater than their trade with the eastern bloc or with China. And the eastern bloc's imports from the western economy contain a far higher element of relatively essential foodstuffs and capital goods than is found among the West's imports from the East, so that economic depression in the West, which leads to cuts in effective demand for relative inessentials, tends to cause Soviet balance of payments deficits.

For a country such as Britain, whose production of goods is heavily dependent on imports and whose currency is widely used, the international economy cannot be clearly separated from the domestic economy because the level of domestic activity and the effectiveness of domestic economic policies is heavily dependent on overall levels of economic activity and on policies adopted by governments elsewhere in the system. This level of interdependence is not a constant throughout the system. The wealth of the international economy is unevenly distributed. The most obvious assymetry is caused by the wealth of the United States, which is about equal to that of the rest of the western countries put together. National economic strength is a traditional resource of governments. The larger the proportion of domestic trade to international trade in a country's generation of wealth, then the less vulnerable it is to economic pressures exerted against it from abroad. The larger a government's domestic economy, the more autonomous it is in its pursuit of domestic economic objectives and the more formidable is likely to be its capability to influence the economic policies of foreign governments not so well placed. The more efficient a national economy, the greater is likely to be its resistance to inflationary pressures in the international economy at large. The intimately linked but variable nature of the western economy engenders a miscellany of conceptions of foreign economic policies appropriate to its members.

International economic government as a policy objective

If interdependence is the fundamental fact of economic existence for western countries, then the rational objectives of foreign economic policy may seem to be the construction and operation of a cross-national organisation authoritatively equipped with policy instruments sufficient to the task of regulating the whole economic environment, which currently engages the partial and inadequate efforts of national governments.

(1) This straightforward prescription loses much of its appeal on examination. Currently the international economy is regulated largely by the actions of its national governments, which constantly subject one another to argument, advice and pressure. International organisations, prominently the IMF, join in this continuous debate and subject the domestic situations and policies of governments to close investigation and comment. As well, particularly in the case of the IMF, they may possess modest economic capabilities of their own in the form of credit facilities and the like. Before governments would surrender all their own regulatory powers to a prospectively mighty international economic organisation they would have to be sure that their votes and voices under the new arrangements would be such as to cause no diminution in their effectiveness in attempting to secure whatever they might conceive to be their economic interests. Rigid and sometimes complicated voting arrangements are already a feature of many international economic organisations. This is one of the many constraints that usually make them slow-moving bodies. Prominent among others are quarrels among governments and their not uncommon propensity to ignore international organisations regardless of their voting arrangements. Structural infelicities like these could not be made to disappear by a new organisation. They are not wholly the product of pig-headedness but are substantially the international effects of the diverse social and economic conditions under which the governments of the economic arena labour in their domestic political domains. The imposition of common conditions of government throughout this arena would require a ruthless world tyranny not an international economic organisation.

(2) The western international economy can be broadly divided into two parts: the international system of economic relations; and the confused apparatus of governments and international organisations that investigate it, debate it and attempt to regulate parts of it. It is a matter of contemporary fact that authorities, groups and individuals of all kinds actively differ over the degree, if any, to which governments should intervene in economic relations. A world economic organisation with authority over national governments would have to be founded on a common view of the proper solution to this problem at the highest level. But such an agreement, supposing it to be possible, would be harmful for two reasons. First, this is an area of widely differing government experience and social habit among different countries. A general solution would therefore stand a high probability of being wrong somewhere. Not only would this sort of agreement be a denial of the value of cautious experiment both towards intervention and away from it at the national level, it would also be a denial of the central relevance to political practice of historic social differences between countries.

Second, the governmental arrangements of the international economy as they stand are founded on a broad acceptance of the central place of a diversity of views in almost all areas of policy. To proceed on the basis of a massive orthodoxy would be to destroy what is of greatest value in the present world for the sombre security of a future world designed to simplify the tasks of government.

(3) Existing international organisations, economic and otherwise, do not fit into a neatly interlocking pattern. Presumably they would have to be replaced by a single coherent world organisation. But the tolerable degree of contemporary tension between, say, the activities of the European Community and the principles of the GATT is not something that is artificially concocted; it reflects the differing natures of these two enterprises. If the activities and ideas upon which different organisations are based were to continue to influence affairs after their abolition, then the tensions between them would simply reappear in another probably more destructive guise. Acknowledged tensions between different organisations may stimulate compromise, whereas tensions within one massive organisation committed to coordinating the inherently diverse are likely to make for a state of paralysis if not organisational breakdown.

(4) Existing international economic organisations may have very wide memberships. Many governments outside the western developed circle are members of the IMF. A single authoritative organisation able to run the western economy could not include in its governing body the representatives of unconstitutional countries outside that system. But what possible long-term interest could be served by creating a rigid barrier between developed and many underdeveloped countries in this or any other field? If western governments represent open societies then closing frontiers between themselves and the rest of the world would be as much a contradiction as closing frontiers between one another.

The promotion of the national economy as a source of power

From a realist standpoint the national economy of the state may seem to be its primary power resource from which all the state's material capabilities spring. It may therefore seem that a government has the duty to develop its national economy as the essential condition of maintaining the state's self-directing capabilities, of providing it with the means of pursuing its interests and of protecting itself in the international arena.

(1) But in practice it is far from self-evident that governments generally give the development of their national economies this kind of priority. They often undertake interventions in the economy to promote non-economic distributional and directional goals: they act to maintain employment in declining and inefficient industries, to alleviate regional disparities in wealth, to manage what they take to be natural monopolies, to create state mono-

polies for social as much as for economic reasons. These kinds of actions are not centrally directed towards the maximum development of the economy. Though governments usually declare themselves to favour economic growth they also favour other goals that may tend to constrain it. And it can even happen that a government may look askance at the whole prospect of economic development as something destructive of traditional religious or other values. Nor is economic strength often seen as a means of enhancing the power of the state in terms of any crude military calculus. Currently the governments of the two largest non-American national economies in the western system, those of Japan and the German Federal Republic, maintain military forces well below a level that their wealth could readily sustain. In most pluralist democratic countries, regardless of national income levels, there is a tendency for defence expenditure to be eroded by constant electoral pressure on governments to make provision for increased national allocations for social expenditure or for personal consumption.

(2) Few governments or individuals have a clear notion of what economic power is. A growing economy generally permits a government to undertake extra public expenditure more freely than it might otherwise. Provided immoderate inflation is avoided, the greater the public and private spending an elected government encourages the greater may seem to be its chances of remaining in office. For this reason, if for no other, elected governments prefer growing economies to static economies. But it by no means follows that governments of wealthy countries always have an easy domestic time, nor does any clear connection exist between governments having an easy domestic time and their international power. Governments of countries with persistent balance of payments deficits must as a rule raise international credit, expose themselves to international criticism and endure the pressures of currency depreciation; whereas governments of countries in balance of payments surplus may be providers of credit and are likely to be able to prevent uncomfortable levels of currency appreciation. What this amounts to is that a 'deficit government' is likely to be embarrassed abroad and constrained at home, while a 'surplus government' is unlikely to feel the prick of such indignities. This may be claimed to demonstrate that some governments perform their economic functions with indifferent competence and suffer in consequence; it does not demonstrate that they are indifferent economic managers because they pursue international power or because international power has been denied them. Britain and Finland have been in deep balance of payments difficulties when France and Austria have not; but no sound general conclusion about the pursuit of international power by these countries can be based on this fact.

(3) It must be true that the international military power of the United States is related to the size of its economy. Poor countries cannot build and maintain large fleets of inter-continental missiles. But it does not follow that the size of a state's economy is the measure of its military power. The Soviet

Union maintains an arsenal of much the same size as that of the United States on the basis of a smaller national income. It is probably true that in periods of relative peace societies with freely elected governments are likely to have difficulty in maintaining military forces of levels similar to those of authoritarian societies unless they are considerably wealthier. But for any given level of population it is usually the case that they are wealthier. Can it therefore be said that the power of a country depends on the level of free choice its citizens enjoy?

(4) Much of the western international economy coincides in geographical terms with an area whose overall defence is broadly guaranteed by the United States. In terms of the categories that determine that an economy is a power resource of a government this is an anomaly. Proportionately to her wealth the United States is not a great trading nation. It might be argued that in the past the international system she defends has been a drain on the United States since she has had to provide assistance to many of its members. American governments, though clearly highly influential, do not rule this economic system, being engaged quite often in debates about the precise nature of what is going on in it and about whether anything can or should be done by one or more of its governments. It might seem to follow that the United States is a military resource of this system, not that this system is a military resource of the United States. Yet this international economy is clearly an asset of some kind since it creates trade, provides direct investment and credit, inspires technical advance and propagates scientific and managerial expertise. These are benefits of the system as a whole and do not constitute an exclusive resource of any particular government. The structure of authority in this system is a strongly pluralist one that rarely produces a coherent policy about anything. Among its more prominent member governments are those of Switzerland and Sweden; yet these heavily armed countries are outside its formal defence arrangements and pursue individual policies both internally and externally.

(5) The view that the national economy is a national power resource is as much a doctrine as a description. It equates international power with domestic economic autarky. A government bent on increasing its power that accepts this doctrine must attempt to acquire direct control over an economy sufficiently large to supply all its national needs without recourse to international trade. The pursuit of this goal will almost certainly bring it into conflict with other countries as it attempts to extend its authority over what it considers to be vital materials and services. The attempt to achieve power now becomes the necessity of using power in its most crudely violent form in order to achieve autarky. In the consequent war the relative sizes of the economic resources that each side can mobilise will be a major determinant of the outcome. Taken to this conclusion the doctrine of autarky traditionally fulfils itself: the more completely autarkic a war economy is, the more likely is its victory. Yet it is a strange doctrine that predicts defeat for the country that

it urges to initiate war: a government that starts a war in pursuit of autarky is likely to lose to a set of governments that already have the autarky it wants.

(6) The abandonment of the goal of national autarky through foreign domination in favour of the expansion of trade may have the effect of rapidly increasing national income, as the postwar examples of Japan and the German Federal Republic seem to demonstrate. But increases in national income by this means do not bear any elementary relationship to increases in the power of governments. In communities growing richer, governments are likely to increase public expenditure; but this course can lead governments into all kinds of social and economic entanglements that may have the effect of decreasing their scope for swift and decisive authoritative action. Exposure to an international economy is also unlikely to confer command in external matters since other governments will not easily yield to direct threats and pressures to which they are able to retaliate. So increased national wealth does not necessarily mean more government power; it may mean more complicated government.

The economic containment of the United States

The essential problem of the international economy may seem to be that it contains a disturbing concentration of wealth in the United States, whose governments consequently enjoy a measure of autonomy that may make for irresponsibility. Not only do economic trends and changes in the United States widely influence and, sometimes, disturb the other members of the system; American governments are able to ignore the rest of the system in framing their domestic economic policies or in pursuing external objectives (such as protecting an insecure regime in south Vietnam) that may turn out to have widespread international economic repercussions. The proper economic objective of non-American western states may therefore seem to be to create concentrations of independent economic activity of sufficient strength to insulate them from deleterious influences emanating from the United States and confer on their authorities sufficient economic capabilities to enable them to bring pressure to bear on American governments.

(1) But governments never in fact try to foster economic growth in order to counter the economic strength of the United States. Their inspiration, if they have any, usually lies much closer to home. Their effectiveness depends on many conditions, not least on domestic social attitudes to the creation of wealth, which are not the product of anti-Americanism. Foreign policy operations (entry to the European Community or tariff negotiations in the GATT) may be conceived as instrumental to the attainment of some measure of economic growth. But it is seldom that economic growth is conceived as an instrument of foreign policy.

(2) Policy prescriptions such as the one under consideration start from uncertain premisses. Most prominent among these is the assumption that

economic power can only be controlled and deployed by contending national economic authorities, actual or potential. This approaches closely to a kind of balance of power doctrine of international economics. From this standpoint the western international economy is an arena of separate national governments of varying strength in much the same way as nineteenth-century Europe was an arena of states subject to no general authority other than that of the balancing process that seemed to be the inevitable outcome of their mutual struggles. The crudity of this analogy is confounded by the extremely complex cross-national language in which the affairs of the western international economy are conducted; by the many kinds of parties, official and unofficial, that are involved in its business; and by the numerous ways in which economic authorities relate to one another. An alternative premiss might thus be that the western international economy is so complex, so indistinctly enclosed, so full of change and of potential for change that no centralised form of rule at either national or international levels is appropriate to it. But a pluralist form of rule is not the same thing as a power struggle between states.

(3) This prescription is also outdated in a deep sense. During the second world war and in the early postwar years the economic predominance of the United States was a matter of unchallengeable fact. In this period the United States played a major role in founding a number of international economic institutions, the most notable being the IMF and the GATT. The early IMF system of fixed exchange rates was founded on the strength of the dollar in the sense that this was the *numéraire* against which other currencies were measured. In the GATT the United States took the lead in many negotiations to reduce national constraints on international trade. In both cases it can reasonably be argued that the United States obtained disproportionately large benefits from these new institutions. Her economic efficiency was so much greater than that of most other countries that she did very well in the increased business activity that ensued; and much did ensue. However, American postwar balance of payments surpluses did not persist; other centres of economic strength did in fact develop, particularly in the ex-enemy countries. Then liberalisation of trade ceased to work markedly to the American advantage and her leadership in the GATT began to fade. As her balance of payments deficits grew she found that her currency could not be readily devalued because it was the *numéraire* of the old IMF system. The United States consequently played the leading role in the abandonment of this system. The upshot of these developments in the 1970s was that the world was left with important international institutions in which no economically advanced state was taking the leading part. The key problem here was not building centres of power to counter the United States but finding a way of operating these and other international institutions without strong American leadership.

(4) The proposal that wealth should be created to contain the United

States has no particular relevance to existing states because these usually attempt to increase their wealth anyway. But this prescription seems to go further than this. It seems to recommend the construction of new state-like entities able to live on equal terms with the United States; and the only existing programme that qualifies to receive this advice is that of the European Community. The Brussels organisation, and all the apparatus of multilateral policy-making associated with it, crosses state boundaries at numerous levels. But it does so principally in the form of a series of processes that are subject to continual change and that cannot be described in terms of a highly formalised structure analogous to a traditional state. Economically the Community is a customs union within which efforts are made to harmonise policies in particular limited areas; but it does not have a central bank or finance ministry and its efforts to move towards a common European currency have been signally hesitant. In trade policy it attempts to move as an entity; in monetary policy it is often in open disarray. It has a court of justice, but the legislative capability of its parliament is unimpressive. Its foreign ministers meet regularly, but it does not deploy its own military forces. For the military weight of their defences many of its members are expressly dependent on the United States, yet European Community boundaries are not coterminous with those of Nato in Europe. And so on. To transform the Community into a highly structured traditional state is a course beset by three fundamentally intractable problems. First, the laborious and uncertain nature of the Community's policy-making processes is the manifestation of wide economic, administrative, legal and political diversities within it; an attempt to fit all these inherently disjointed mechanisms coherently together would have destructive not constructive results. Second, the traditional sovereign power is responsible for its own defence; so a major new European state would remove the United States as the major provider of western European defence capabilities. But this is just the conclusion that many existing Community partners wish to avoid. Third, such a state would create a worse imbalance in western Europe than the supposed transatlantic imbalance it would seek to redress; this new first-rank European power, besides fuelling Soviet suspicions of the outside world, would be flanked to the north and south by a number of much smaller states in no position to withstand its influence.

Relieving world poverty

The truly serious problem of the world economy may seem to lie not in minor frictions within the western developed part of it but in the immense disparities of wealth between this rich part and the larger poor part. Closing this gap should thus be the major imperative of economic foreign policy.

(1) If it recommends direct transfers of wealth in the form of immense gifts from the relatively rich to the relatively poor, this kind of proposal

meets the invariable obstacle of limited human altruism. The level of taxation that British people will readily endure to relieve housing problems in British cities appears to be modest; the level of additional taxation they would endure to relieve housing problems in Indian cities is certainly negligible.

(2) A longstanding economic doctrine would hold that in terms of direct foreign policy operations poverty itself is not a substantive problem. In any geographical context, national or international, the most productive use of resources is the consequence of free economic activity. Where alternative uses of effort and investment are always available, the self-interest of those directly engaged will as a rule ensure that productive factors are committed to uses yielding higher rates of return than are likely to be forthcoming elsewhere. This decentralised process of economic choice-making ensures that limited productive resources are as a whole used in the most efficient possible way. Governmental interference in this market process must divert resources from uses where returns are relatively high to uses where returns are relatively low. Given the limited availability of productive factors, official interference in the market always results in less wealth being created in total than would otherwise be the case. The goal of maximising world wealth is therefore best obtained by allowing free movement of goods and resources, rather than by governmental attempts to make crudely direct wealth transfers, even were these possible on any substantial scale.

(3) This free market view of the problem of world poverty is a persuasive one, but there are a large number of objections to it, of which only a selection need be mentioned here:

Though total wealth may best be increased by the market mechanism, it by no means follows that this wealth is best distributed by the market. The present issue is one of distribution. Nineteenth-century free trade worked to the British advantage because Britain was ahead of the field industrially. The same is the case for the developed world as a whole now.

Even if free trade were to the benefit of rich and poor alike, there would still remain the problem of obtaining it by foreign policy action. A characteristic of a free trading system is that a party that cheats, provided its partners do not cheat, will benefit to a greater degree than it would if all parties including itself played the game. For this reason it can be argued that free trade can only work where at least some of the parties are sufficiently strong to be able to bring severe pressure to bear on a state that is attempting to obtain an unfair advantage by directly or indirectly impeding imports. The system must thus contain economically strong states committed to free trade and able to retaliate against policies such as this. But as a whole the world's poorer countries are by definition weak and unable to retaliate formidably against selfish actions by others.

Free foreign investment in poor countries tends to flow towards extractive commodity-producing uses and this tends to create economies dependent on the production and sale of a small range of primary products. These commodities are particularly subject to rapid and extreme shifts in demand according to the phases of the trade cycle in developed countries. The consequence of this sort of economic development is not so much an increase in wealth as an increase in the dependence of the poor on the rich.

Free movement of goods and resources is far from being common practice among developed countries anyway. British governments periodically make strenuous efforts to discourage the export of capital. And the collective propensity of the richer countries to admit cheap manufactures from poor countries is not outstanding. So it would seem that free trade is not so much a practice as a theory that is used when it is to the advantage of the rich and ignored when it is not.

It is arguable that a system of free trade can only exist when erected on the foundation of a common political system and a common security system such as those provided by the British empire and the British navy in the nineteenth century. The common characteristic of almost all poor countries today is their freedom from direct governmental domination from abroad. Whatever its advantages, this condition creates nervousness among potential foreign investors whether they be governments, firms or individuals. Fear of expropriation cannot coexist with a system of free movement of investment and expertise.

(4) Yet abstract arguments about free trade can be held to be essentially beside the point. The underdeveloped world is not a simple entity. Most obviously the oil-producing states that joined together in the OPEC cartel rapidly became richer. There have been high rates of growth in Brazil, South Korea and elsewhere. Commodity producers other than the OPEC have joined together to improve their trading positions and to obtain concessions from the industrialised countries. Gatherings such as UNCTAD have repeatedly brought the plight of the very poor to the attention of the rich. In response to this sort of pressure the IMF has auctioned gold reserves and used the proceeds to help the poor. The IMF has also developed its own credit-creating facility, which has been used for similar purposes. The central issues in all this are not whether to give special help to developing countries but how to give it; and not whether to respond to the demands of the poor, and those growing less poor, but how to incorporate them into the institutional management of the international economy.

(5) Arguments about aid inevitably include arguments about the nature of poverty. If poverty is a product of a particular kind of traditional social structure, the issue of economic assistance is a secondary matter since aid can achieve nothing unaccompanied by appropriate changes in indigenous social habits and values. But how is it possible or legitimate for external parties to act to upset established forms of life in poor countries?

Conclusions

1.   International economic issues among open constitutional states cannot be clearly divorced from domestic economic issues. Not only are the two arenas deeply interconnected in practice, but economic doctrines about one run into economic doctrines about the other. It seems to follow that in economic matters at least there can be no principles of foreign policy that apply only to external affairs.

2.   The view that the western international economic system should be given the formal authoritative structure of a traditional state is neither a practical nor a desirable one. But this means that these economic relations should continue to take place under and between a miscellany of national, cross-national and international authorities that do not comprise a state but that do not comprise a classical balance of power system of sovereign states either. Here there is something that is not a state; but it is also not a non-state. Principles of foreign policy must address themselves to an indistinctly delimited setting that appears to defy political classification.

3.   Many important issues occur in the relations between the western international economy and the rest of the world, particularly the poorer part of it. Principles of foreign policy should presumably be concerned with such issues. But principles in this category must make recommendations about the affairs of an international system rather than about the affairs of particular states. Foreign policy would thus seem to be capable of springing from entities other than territorial states.

GENERAL CONCLUSIONS

We set out to examine the foregoing foreign policy issues with the hope of finding therein some intimation of the form that principles of foreign policy might take and to get some concrete impression of the general structure of foreign policy itself. We have now gone far enough to be able to frame some generalisations from the effects of these endeavours.

1.   It is plainly absurd to imagine that one can somehow get directly to the problems of foreign policy without the intercession of concepts.[9] The form that problems themselves take (executive secrecy; war and morality; poverty and intervention) are shaped by concepts. Rejecting the abstract *a priori* world of the first chapter does not enable one to step directly into a wholly empirical world free from conceptual problems. The empirical world and all its problems are encapsulated in concepts.

2.   The concepts that are incorporated into one's perception of issues of foreign policy are largely inherited. There is nothing immediately unfamiliar

about the concepts of power, the state, national interest, or of foreign policy itself. The first chapter's model was not a pure invention but an agglomeration of concepts crudely abstracted from nineteenth-century experience. But what did not emerge from the procedure of the first chapter and does emerge from that of the present chapter is the way in which largely inherited concepts become variables when used in the exposition of actual problems of foreign policy. Abstraction renders static what is in practice changeable.

3.   Not least among practical variables is the distinction between what is internal and what is external, what is domestic and what is foreign. Yet a clear notion of the nature of this distinction would seem to be a necessary condition of an understanding of what foreign policy actually is. Though the foregoing discussions do not go far towards offering a general solution of this problem, they do suggest that as a matter of practice the internal–external distinction varies according to the kinds of issues in which it occurs; its place in the issue of war is different from its place in the issue of international monetary reform. Given this to be so, it would seem to follow that at a deep level foreign policy itself is a variable. It can have entirely different kinds of meanings. But it follows that principles of foreign policy must spring from sources outside foreign policy to account for the variability of foreign policy.

4.   In this way principles of foreign policy cannot avoid referring to, or containing, theories about internal relations as well as about external relations. A hard-and-fast conviction about the impermeability of state boundaries, like that contained in the first chapter's model, enables one to speculate about the relations between states irrespective of the nature of political relations within states. Indeed it is only on this premiss that a wholly distinct mode of international action, productive of its own kind of theorising, can be held to exist. If this premiss is destroyed, an understanding of internal relations becomes an intrinsic part of an understanding of external relations.[10]

5.   Not only this. The contemporary diffusion of domestic relations beyond national boundaries means that the interior–exterior distinction has to be made from the domestic side. An extension of internal relations (rather than a change in the nature of internal relations) cannot be caused by a change in exterior relations if these are held to be essentially different from internal relations. A shift in a state's external circumstances can allow a foreign extension of its domestic relations to take place; but a shift in international circumstances cannot be the cause of such a change if the nature of these external relations is taken to be wholly distinct from the nature of internal relations. An example makes this fundamental point clear. The possible impending hegemony of Soviet Russia in Europe might be held to have caused an alliance to be formed between Britain and the Netherlands and others. But the impending hegemony of Soviet Russia could not be held to have been the cause of the spread of domestic forms of relations across national

boundaries among this group. An effect like this must at root derive from the nature of the forms of domestic relations themselves since it must be this that enables such a diffusion to take place. It cannot derive directly from the possible hegemony of Soviet Russia because the hegemonial relationship is wholly unconnected with the legal and political nature of these forms of domestic relations.

6. A point to emerge forcefully from the foregoing issues is that they are full of general policy preferences (free trade, the priority of the national interest, executive secrecy and suchlike) that are all elements in longstanding arguments. What often present themselves in the guise of principles turn out on examination to be contentious doctrines. It follows that a requirement of foreign policy principles is that they should distinguish themselves from doctrines. And though the conclusions reached in the foregoing discussions of issues did not reveal principles of foreign policy, they did reveal the conditions that such principles must fulfil.

CHAPTER 4

Excursions Among Definitions of Principles of Foreign Policy

At the beginning of the first chapter principles of foreign policy were clearly defined. They were general rules guiding the actions of sovereign national states in the world depicted by a model. This definition was also an exact description of the ways in which such states would act in this setting. This description was also a set of specifications of the form of the model. These specifications also comprised a definition of principles of foreign policy. . . . In order to escape from these empty tautologies we abandoned invention to consider a varied selection of actual issues of foreign policy, partly in order to get a sense of the general nature of foreign policy itself. Having encountered some of the practical and conceptual forms that foreign policy issues take, it may now seem that we can return to defining in general terms what principles of foreign policy may realistically be taken to be. Equipped with such a definition the task of actually specifying operational principles should be a relatively easy one.

A Lexicography of Principles of Foreign Policy[11]

As a first step it is a simple matter to set out the several possible meanings of each of the three words 'principles', 'policy' and 'foreign'.

Principles

A principle or a set of principles may be taken to mean the correct procedure for successfully undertaking a specified task. Thus the principles of gardening would be general guidelines relating to the propensities of different soils, to drainage, plant propagation and the like, which must be followed by gardeners aiming to expend their labour efficiently.

Slightly differently, principles may refer to the general mode of a particular practice. Thus principles of seamanship may be those insights upon which the soundness of a practical approach to seamanship is based. In this usage, principles are not simply technicalities; they include points of personal character and understanding that cannot be conveyed in a manual of rules.

A discovery or set of discoveries. The principles of perspective are the rules devised by men for conveying a sense of three-dimensional space in images drawn on a two-dimensional surface.

The correct representation of a particular setting or subject. Thus the principles of geology include an evolutionary account of the earth's form in terms of its material components and of the forces acting upon them. Without an understanding of this picture a prospective practitioner of this science cannot be called a geologist.

Principles mark the quality of those rules that are ethically appropriate to a kind of activity. Thus the principles of law or accountancy may be taken to exclude rules for the perpetration of fraud.

Standards of conduct whose observance is a mark of virtue. A man of principles is one whose actions are not dictated by self-interest or by the circumstances of the moment but are founded upon considered general rules of correct behaviour. At times these rules may conflict, but the sign of the man of principles is his moral concern to proceed with care and humility in these circumstances.

Policy

A policy may be taken to mean a formulated programme designed to achieve a specific objective by the use of authority. Thus a policy might take the form: 'On taking office we will relieve the housing shortage by making more public funds available for municipal building'. Simply to have the intention of relieving the housing shortage would not comprise a policy since it conveys nothing in the way of a programme.

A statement of priorities. 'Our policy is to bring the balance of payments back to equilibrium' may be meant to convey the intention to review other programmes in the light of their possible contributions, or otherwise, to this primary purpose.

A policy may be an explicit form of group identification. 'As socialists our policy is such-and-such' is one way in which a group of socialists may identify themselves.

A call for support. 'My policy is such-and-such' may be a way in which a leader or a potential leader attempts to identify himself and to rally a large following.

An explanation and a claim to consistency. 'Throughout, our policy has been . . . .' This kind of usage attempts to establish a clear pattern in the conduct of a line of public affairs that may seem to have been disjointed or that may have taken place behind a veil of secrecy.

Policy may be implicitly claimed to be a rationally selected strategy of authoritative conduct. In the image conveyed by this usage the policy-maker is supposedly confronted by a finite number of fully worked-out alternative lines of possible action for dealing with a clearly perceived problem: superimposing his order of priorities in terms of values and preferred objectives on this 'map' he then selects the 'route' or policy that optimises progress in terms of effort and available resources.

A process whereby social forces, political pressures, the law, and bureaucratic and other rigidities are maintained in some kind of equilibrium. This meaning assumes that large-scale problems do not present themselves in such a way that any simple notion of rationality can be employed in their solution. In practice, the problems of government occur in confused and constantly shifting forms and almost invariably many conflicting interests and arguments are embedded in them. Policy-making is thus a continuous process of authoritative adjustment to the problems of achieving an ordered and, occasionally, a directed form of social existence.

Policy may be seen as an elementary administrative necessity. In large organisations like government departments decisions must be made continually at all levels. If this were not possible, business would come to a standstill because almost everyone would have to wait for explicit instructions from above before doing anything. The practical necessity for daily decision-making throughout an organisation thus requires that policies exist that (a) confer on personnel at all levels an appropriate decision-making capability and (b) make it possible for those in the lower echelons of an organisation to distinguish those matters that must be passed on for higher decision. In the latter sense policy is a necessary negative; it distinguishes novel kinds of difficulties that may require a new decision and new policy.

Policy may contain an assumption of the possibility of progress in the well-being of a society. It assumes the existence of a social entity capable of coherent advance to new goals. It believes that a society can make its own future. It improves itself through the development and application of policy. Policy is thus social self-improvement.

Foreign

Most simply, territories that are foreign are taken to be those that lie beyond the jurisdiction of a particular national government.

Foreign social forms and habits are different from those that are familiar and directly experienced.

Something that is foreign is taken to be unamenable to ordinary understanding. It requires explanation of an unusual and special kind.

Foreign societies are those with which one is likely to feel little sense of affinity and for which one has relatively little sense of responsibility.

People described as foreign are commonly taken to have been born in another country, though outsiders of virtually any sort may also be called foreigners.

Foreigners may also be those whose behaviour is expected to be unpredictable. It may be assumed that their actions are not likely to be influenced by familiar modes of discourse and persuasion. Foreigners cannot therefore be readily associated with a social order that depends on the use and appreciation among its members of a mode of communication that contains the pressures and tensions among them in a peaceful form of political change. Foreigners who do not comprehend this language of political change may have to be influenced by threats of the use of force or by its actual use.

DEFINITIONS OF PRINCIPLES OF FOREIGN POLICY

This lexicographical exercise now enables us to put together a number of plausible definitions of what principles of foreign policy may be taken to be. It seems that all that we have to do is to test each of these against the complexities of foreign policy and to select the definition that seems to address itself to the more important of them. We may then press forward by actually attempting to specify principles in the form required by the preferred definition.

Definition one

The correct procedure for framing / a programme to achieve an objective / in the world beyond the territorial jurisdiction of one's own government.

A number of simple difficulties attach to this formulation. The world beyond domestic jurisdiction is mostly made up of other domestic jurisdictions. A policy towards this world is therefore in large part about what goes on, or may go on, within these domestic jurisdictions. Reciprocally, it follows that other governments must have policies relating to what goes on, or may go on, within one's own government's domestic jurisdiction. Foreign policy as a whole is then substantially about what goes on within the domestic jurisdictions of different governments. It must therefore be the case that foreign policy is not only about conduct directed towards external jurisdictions but is also about conduct within internal jurisdictions, which is part of the material of other foreign policies and which not only affects them but is also affected by them. Much domestic policy is thus logically foreign policy. The present formulation contradicts itself because it contains terms whose effect is to destroy the distinction it intends to make plain.

Moreover, domestic jurisdictions are not the same in themselves or in their relations with one another. Domestic jurisdiction in the Soviet Union, Czechoslovakia, the German Federal Republic and Britain means different things in the sense that the authority of government (its relationship to constitutional law, to federal authorities, to political opposition and to the jurisdiction of the courts) differs greatly inside each of these countries. More importantly

in the present context, Czech domestic jurisdiction in relation to Soviet
Russia is markedly different from Czech domestic jurisdiction in relation to
Holland: in the first case it is relatively permeable, in the second it is relatively
impermeable. Similarly, British domestic jurisdiction in relation to that of
the German Federal Republic or of the Netherlands (which share in the
jurisdictions of the European Community and of other European institutions)
is fundamentally different from British domestic jurisdiction in relation to the
Soviet Union. So domestic jurisdiction itself is a variable, as are the linkages
between different domestic jurisdictions. The notion that what takes place
outside domestic jurisdiction constitutes an environment upon which foreign
policy works does not stand up to examination. In some cases the nature of
differing domestic jurisdictions and their linkages form the material of policy
regardless of whether it be called domestic or foreign. Competition among
Nato partners in armaments developments presupposes the existence of a
defence community among them. Western attitudes to eastern Europe are
directly related to the peculiar nature of domestic jurisdiction in eastern
European countries both internally and in their relations with the Soviet
Union. Nor does domestic jurisdiction denote the capability of governments
to achieve a major class of objectives through specifically domestic action.
Again we come to a variable. What is attempted domestically in many
important problem areas, such as the control of inflation or the improvement
of defence, is often complementary to what is attempted externally. Relative
success or failure is both an internal and an external matter.

Given this to be so, the validity of the rest of the present formulation
collapses. Foreign policy cannot be a programme aimed at the achievement
of an external objective. It contains many programmes of all degrees of
clarity and obscurity, many of whose objectives are both internal and external
at the same time. It likewise follows that there can be no correct procedure for
framing foreign policy as such since foreign policy cannot, it seems, be
reduced to a specific kind of activity. The correct procedure for deploying
naval forces during an international nuclear crisis is unlikely to be the same
as the correct procedure for arranging a fresh line of credit with the IMF or for
obtaining a specific piece of European Community legislation that will have
the direct force of law in several countries.

Definition two

A discovery / leading to the rational selection of lines of conduct / for dealing
with those whose actions are unlikely to be influenced by familiar modes of
discourse and persuasion and who may have to be resisted by force.

The idea of familiar modes of discourse and persuasion is an important if
unclear one. There is a good deal of sense to the view that foreign policy is
centrally concerned with a different kind of dialogue from that practised in
domestic politics and that the difference lies essentially in the danger of

rge-scale violence traditionally associated with many foreign policy opera-
ons. However, far from all foreign policy is linked with the possibility of
ar. Between many governments no such possibility exists; in many issues of
iternational relations violence is an irrelevance regardless of the nature of
ie governments involved; many internationally active governments are far
oo weak to be able to threaten war convincingly except very locally if at all;
ore confusingly, violence or the threat of it may be a close accompaniment
f domestic policies in a number of countries. Yet it is undeniable that
otential for violence on the largest conceivable scale is peculiar to inter-
ational relations of some kinds, just as it is undeniable that differences in
ocial values and habits of authority are usually at their greatest internationally.

In contact across large value-discontinuities the relevance of the notion of
ecision as the rational selection of consistent lines of conduct is more than
rdinarily dubious. If by rationality is meant the logical application of
ommonsense axioms to clearly perceived problems, then a foreign policy
eld in which information of a reliable kind is scanty, authoritative behaviour
npredictable, attempts at communication prone to misperception and
eans of doing physical harm plentiful, would seem to be one in which the
onditions of rational conduct do not exist. In place of abstract ideas about
ationality must be put the traditional diplomatic habit of caution based on
s much strength as can be mustered. The central point about this traditional
osture is that it accepts as axiomatic the existence of large value-differences.
Vhere the premises of government and social relations differ there can be
ttle in the way of a common mode of rational deliberation among authorities.
1 its place must be put a language that is founded on strength and that con-
entrates on precise practical issues where a common interest, if only in the
voidance of inadvertent mutual annihilation, may exist and where there is
ttle opportunity for potentially harmful misperception or deception. Here
ie optimum diplomatic achievement is limited agreement without retreat.

This kind of minimal diplomatic rationality has little in common with, say,
ie rational discourse surrounding the negotiation by a British or Australian
overnment of large credits from the IMF. In the latter case a number of
xioms will be held in common by the negotiating parties. These will not lead
o identical lines of reasoning because of differing interpretations of complex
ata, differing policy priorities, and, more importantly, differing interests.
ut this kind of negotiation is part of a rich tradition of economic discourse
ommon to the parties and in normal circumstances it is likely to come to an
greed conclusion having nothing to do with the application of threats of
orce.

Rationality at the minimal diplomatic level and rationality within a
ommon tradition of discourse are different in nature. At the minimal
iplomatic level only two kinds of discoveries could alter the associated
iode of rational conduct and negotiation. First, there could be a purely
echnical discovery rendering one of the parties safe from the possibility of

large-scale military harm. But in practice conflicting parties of comparabl
strength constantly exert themselves to forestall any breakthrough that coul
worsen their individual power positions. Second, there could be the dis
appearance of the value-gulf that is the premiss of this kind of minima
diplomatic rationality. But such a change could not be the outcome of
discovery. All that could actually occur would be a value-change within on
of the parties. This could be observed but hardly discovered.

On the other hand, an intellectual tradition of free discourse is continuall
subject to readjustment as a result of discoveries and novel hypotheses. I
such a tradition, rational thinking changes its immediate form as the para
meters and categories of discussion and enquiry alter as a consequence o
original theorising and the observation of unexpected events. A rationa
tradition of discourse[12] is thus one that incorporates the possibility o
fundamental change that cannot itself be subject to rational prediction. Wha
seems to be rational economic policy at one period, shortly afterwards ma
appear to be irrational because of fresh economic insights associated, as a rule
with an unexpected turn of economic events.

The static rationality of minimal diplomacy and the dynamic rationality o
common traditions of free discourse are utterly contrasted. No union betwee
them is possible. A deep problem of foreign policy is immediately apparent
The two forms of communication typified in this manner do not exist i
complete isolation from each other in an otherwise empty environment. Eve
a totalitarian state must, if its government wishes it to keep up with worl
technology, allow a degree of open participation in the discourses of th
scientific tradition, to which scepticism is intrinsic. In international society a
a whole, relations at the two levels often intermingle. But in the nature of thei
differences they cannot merge. Discoveries cannot come out of thin air bu
only out of distinct modes of action, observation and reflection. But in inter
national society as a whole, there is no distinct mode but a mixture of modes
No discovery can emerge from this mixture as such.

Definition three

The correct picture of the evolution / of the foreign environment in whic
behaviour is unlikely to be influenced by familiar modes of discourse an
persuasion / making possible a consistent explanation of foreign policy
operations.

As we have seen, the existence of a boundary of 'familiar modes of discours
and persuasion' beyond which potentially violent hostility plays a central rol
in human contact, governmental or otherwise, is basic to the substance o
foreign policy operations. The possession of a correct evolutionary pictur
of this dangerously uncertain setting would contribute much to an under
standing of foreign policy problems. It could not offer a consistent explana
tion of all foreign policy dealings since many are wholly intra-boundary i

orm and content and these, as indicated in the previous chapter, must be xplained from the inside.

However, a correct picture of the whole environment external to'familiar nodes of discourse and persuasion' is not possible, in the first place because his environment is not a coherent entity. It has not evolved as a unit, tribe-ike or otherwise. It is made up of many different kinds of units, each the roduct of different kinds of cirumstances. The authoritarian propensities f Soviet society cannot be explained in the same way as the emergence of a rutal tyranny in an African country. These are different kinds of experiences, hough in terms of human suffering they may encompass some similarities. 3ut the environment as an entity cannot be convincingly explained in volutionary or any other terms because it does not exist as an entity.

The idea of 'correct' evolutionary pictures of particular settings only ecomes relevant inside the boundary of 'familiar discourse'. It is in no way anciful to suggest that a picture of the evolution of western international nonetary relations is possible and that it is necessary to an understanding of, r regulatory involvement with, international monetary problems. Inter-ational monetary relations have four basic elements: monetary operations f a broadly private character taking place in large currency markets; the nonetary performances of governments and official agencies; relations etween governments and official agencies on monetary issues, into which nternational organisations have been drawn; a plastic body of doctrines nd of empirical and theoretical studies of international and national nonetary affairs. An evolutionary understanding of this complex and hifting entity is essential to those wishing to take an active part in it. It ontains no threats of violence yet governments are deeply involved in it. It is vholly within the boundary of 'familiar discourse and persuasion' and this s why an evolutionary picture of it is possible. This picture is a part of this ntity. In much the same way an evolutionary picture of physics is a part of hysics and is shared among physicists. The same sort of picture of the evelopment of, say, Anglo-Soviet relations is not possible: first, because no icture of any subtlety could be even partially shared by the principal parties o this relationship; and, second, because this minimal relationship, though ubject to some change as a result of governmental shifts of emphasis, has ot grown as any kind of lively entity of open ideas and actions and rguments.

Definition four

A process of dealing with the problems of relations with foreigners/towards vhom the domestic sense of responsibility is relatively slight/that is never-heless ethical.

As an implied description of cross-national relations within the habits of vhat has so far been called 'familiar modes of discourse and persuasion', this definition misleads in four ways. First, cross-national issues are various Problems of European agricultural policy, problems of international liquidity and problems of weapons standardisation in Nato are different sort of issues to which different processes attach. The notion that foreign policy is one process is clearly false.

Second, cross-national issues obviously engage people of different nationalities, and negotiation and deliberation in this human setting may call for special patience and insight. But the particular difficulties of operations inside the foreign policy category of 'familiar modes of discourse and persuasion are those not of dealing with foreigners as such but of tackling complex problems that deeply engage diverse authorities that are each subject to different domestic constraints. It is the complex structure of authority in cross-national issues that makes for special problems, not personal differences of eating habits and suchlike.

Third, reference to a want of a sense of responsibility for foreigner similarly misleads. It is impossible for any individual to involve himself in the lives of more than a handful of other people; whether these are foreigners i largely a matter of fortuitous personal circumstances. Responsibility in public matters is entirely different and shows itself in two ways: first, in attachmen to the principles of constitutional rule, which is a means of preventing govern ment from falling into the hands of tyrants, absolutists, oligarchs and specia interests; second, and relatedly, in attachment to self-government in the form of political processes that at once render uses of constitutional authority acceptable to those affected and ensure that these uses of authority are responsive to the interests, needs and wishes of those affected. In all public matters in the circle of constitutional states, responsibility shows itself a respect for these two principles. In part this is a negative matter: cross-national relations are never used as a means of evading constitutional constraints and political processes at home or abroad. It is also a positive matter: responsibility in cross-national affairs shows itself in the establishment of new political processes and new forms of constitutional rule appropriate to this level.

Fourth, given this kind of responsibility, cross-national issues do not create special ethical problems. The ethics (not the content) of the conduct of inter governmental affairs in meetings of western finance ministers are no different from the ethics appropriate to meetings of British cabinets; nor are the ethics of parliamentary conduct in the European Assembly any different from those appropriate to the British House of Commons. This is not to suggest that the ethics in question are simple or without ambiguity or that everyone engaged at all these levels is to be expected to be ethically above suspicion. Far from it But no special ethic is appropriate at one level and inappropriate at another

In the case of foreign policy dealings across the boundary of 'familiar modes of discourse and persuasion', the present definition is not so much misleading as inadequate. Dealings with foreign governments whose domestic structures of authority have not been touched by cross-national issues and linkages o both a practical and a cultural kind may fall into a negative category; that is, they may seem to occur wholly outside 'familiar modes of discourse' since a premiss of such discourse is that communication is based on similar forms of domestic political language. It does not follow that across-the-boundary dealings are of a simple single-process nature. Multilateral negotiations with Soviet Russia and other eastern European governments on issues of arms control in Europe do not occur in a single process alongside bilateral diplomatic crises occasioned by the actions of a tyrannical ruler in an impoverished African country. Nor are issues raised by attempts to regulate the prices of primary products exported by poor unconstitutional countries the same as prospective territorial issues in Europe upon which might turn the use of nuclear weapons. Though the possibility of war figures in some issues that cross the boundaries of constitutional statehood, it does not figure in all of them.

The problem of responsibility in handling relations across the boundary of constitutional statehood is a perplexing one. Inside this boundary it may be assumed that public authorities are responsible to and for their constituents and are constrained by impersonal general rules. Populations within this boundary may therefore be regarded as self-governing. Across the boundary of constitutional statehood so such thing can be assumed. The boundary exists because governments beyond it are tyrannical, absolutist, conspiratorial and otherwise irresponsible. Yet how should responsible constitutional governments treat irresponsible unconstitutional governments? In part this is the traditional problem of observing domestic political norms while making arrangements with external authorities for whom these standards may seem at best meaningless and at worst threats to their internal positions. But the problem goes deeper than this. By definition, responsible authority observes impersonal constitutional and other rules; it could not otherwise be effectively made responsible for its actions or responsive to the demands and criticisms levelled at it. But it follows that a sense of constitutional responsibility cannot be wholly locked within physical boundaries around particular populations. Constitutional authority is responsible because it is limited by rules not because it is limited by contingent national frontiers. The central foreign policy problem now becomes one of behaving responsibly towards people who are not themselves constitutionally governed and are not therefore self-governing. One might argue that constitutional governments should regulate those of their actions that might affect populations governed irresponsibly by tyrants, absolutists, conspirators and the like *as if* they were citizens of constitutional states and able to express their own interests and opinions. This is conceptually attractive but, given the omnipresent form of the independent state, how is this extra quantum of responsibility to be imparted? And what anyways, can be its content or special quality? An *as if* fiction may seem an uncertain basis for authoritative conduct in practical circumstances.

Definition five

The essence / of group identification / in an environment that is not clearly understood.

There is no common essence of issues as diverse as nuclear deterrence and the support prices of western European agricultural products. The present definition sidesteps this fundamental difficulty of getting to grips with the nature of foreign policy. Instead it pronounces that the central principles of foreign policy are to be found in the group. But which group? Manufacturers, bankers, professions, trade unions, diplomats are all active internationally. The state can hardly be a group; it contains groups. A government is not a state, though it may often claim to represent a state; governments may change rapidly, whereas a constitutional state is apt to maintain a constant, though not static, structure. The essence of the state may be imagined to be many things, but in no exact sense can it be a group. It is more plausibly the legal, institutional and political setting in which groups pursue their substantive ends. Yet a setting of this kind is unlikely to be utterly peculiar to one territorial state. The constitutional states are at least comparable in these respects; and similar, and sometimes even identical, groups are active in them. In these circumstances the essence of group identification as a whole defies formulation. Teachers and conservationists identify themselves as such and not as states. Groups are different; what they share is the setting of constitutional statehood. So it may be here, and not in real or imaginary groups, that we should look for the foundations of an understanding of foreign policy.

The present definition's reference to an 'environment that is not clearly understood' strikes a familiar emotional chord. The sense of a threatening external world is common enough in many social units, particularly in rigorously structured ones. Imperfect understanding and the feeling of being threatened are similarly often associated. What is not understood is mysterious and what is mysterious may strike as swiftly and destructively as an avenging angel. In an obvious sense, understanding of universal society must always be imperfect. It is impossible for anyone to be familiar with all the world's cultures, ideas, discoveries, movements, leaders, inventions and policies. But limited knowledge is not the same as superstition and it does not necessarily assume the existence of threats in the unknown.

It is fairly easy to grasp principles of constitutional rule such as adherence to open and known procedures in the passing of legislation, regular free elections, the rule of law, equal access to legal process and the like. The essence of constitutional order is that known rules are a condition of individual practices and enterprises. They do not dictate what shape these should take. In many areas they are positively designed to ensure the possibility of free individual choice. Constitutional order thus assumes the existence of a diverse society that is capable of spontaneous and unpredictable changes. In other words, it assumes that knowledge of society must always be partial. A perfectly known society must be a perfectly controlled society. But this kind of order is

1e opposite of constitutional order, which makes no pretence of perfect
nowledge of human personality. In such an order, law establishes common
onditions that must be observed in all the shifting circumstances of social
ehaviour. But imperfect understanding of social relations in a constitutional
rder does not also imply the existence of mystery and threats within such a
etting.

World society as a whole is not subject to the conditions of constitutional
rder and it certainly contains threats of an horrific magnitude. Yet the
mperfection of ordinary understandings of world society can be exaggerated.
: is quite possible to understand the nature of tyranny without knowing the
ull details about a tyrannically ruled country. In the same way, it is possible
o grasp the nature of modern absolutism without a lifetime's study of, say,
`hinese history and society. Imperfect understanding of the world is not
ecessarily to be equated with an imperfect understanding of the nature of
ule in the world. Some forms of rule are threatening, some are not. This is
ot a mystery. A diverse and imperfectly understood world society is not in
self a threat; it is a fascinating fact of human existence. It is certain ways of
uling in world society that can be threatening, and these may be relatively
ell understood.

CONCLUSIONS

The procedure employed in the present chapter could be continued until
ll the possible combinations among the individual meanings listed at the
utset were exhausted. Enough has been done to show that this procedure
ill not produce a sensible definition of 'principles of foreign policy'. Really
1is is a way of confronting oneself with challenges that bring to mind
ssential points that should not be neglected. Prominent among these essential
oints is the existence of a fundamental discontinuity, or boundary, in inter-
ational relations that marks the outer limits of certain possible kinds of
amiliar' or 'quasi-domestic' processes, issues and structures.

This chapter's procedure could not be expected to yield an acceptable
esult because it assumes that the problem of grasping the nature of foreign
olicy is simply one of selecting the right combination from an existing stock
f possibly appropriate general terms. The existence of foreign policy as a
efinite entity is thus mistakenly taken for granted at the start. As importantly,
1e deep conceptual difficulties created by foreign policy show themselves as
tadequacies in the established use of language in relation to it. Juggling with
1e individual terms of this language continues to reveal its inadequacies.

This procedure has shown the futility of attacking the problems of foreign
olicy as if it were a wholly distinct body of actions and concepts. It is con-
equently clear that foreign policy must be approached from a basis that does
ot contain any such assumptions about its concrete form.

CHAPTER 5

The State:
A Fresh Start from an Old Base

The term 'foreign policy' conveys a false image of the world. It suggests tha
there is a clear distinction between domestic and foreign affairs; it therefor
sets one to looking for this frontier instead of explaining its absence. It declare
that from inside the state the foreign is always an environment; one is therefor
set to explaining the nature of this environment as a whole when one shoul
be looking for fundamental differences within it. Equally erroneously thi
term creates the assumption that an actual or projected plan of action toward
foreign states comprises the fabric of foreign policy; one thus expects states t
produce coherent programmes that can be classified as foreign policy instea
of enquiring into the postulates of different kinds of programmes, some o
which may be neither strictly domestic nor strictly foreign. This term als
insinuates the absurd assumption that in their general form all foreig
policies are the same and that, in their international aspects, all states ar
therefore the same; one is in this way drawn into an *a priori* world of inappro
priate conceptual simplicity when one should turn firmly in the opposit
direction to face the complexities of a world in which states can be deepl
different in all their aspects.

So we must now attempt to approach foreign policy from premisses that ar
not contained in the term itself. We have already been brought to accept tha
foreign policy is not in fact one kind of policy; that states are not the same
that foreign policy ought not to be invariably conceived as a line or as lines o
actual or projected conduct at all; that the external does not consist of a
entity beyond the borders of the civil state; that the distinction between th
internal and the external is a variable; that within international society as
whole there is an important boundary that does not coincide with the frontier
of any one state and that need not be thought of in strictly spatial terms; tha
the position of this boundary must be plotted from the inside. All thes
conditions of this enquiry stress variability except the last, which suggest
that inside a vital international boundary there is a specific form of socia
relations upon which all other variables depend. The traditional method o
setting out the internal foundations of foreign policy is to define the state
We, too, must arrive at a conclusion about the nature of statehood. To thi

88

nd we shall consider specific conceptions of the state from two general
tandpoints: the first sees the state as a tangible actuality, a concrete structure,
erritory or purpose; the second sees the state as the basis of order in a
hanging civil society.

THE STATE AS CONCRETE STRUCTURE AND PURPOSE

s historical actuality

'he state may be taken to be a concrete historical artifact. It was created in
.urope; was rapidly copied elsewhere; and is now the dominant structure of
uman relations throughout world society.

In a sense this must be true. But here again we have an apparently common-
ense view that assumes what needs to be shown: that the state is a simple
oncrete entity that can be readily understood and reproduced. The historical
act of the state in no way substantiates the assumption that it was created
ccording to some clear plan or theory. The territories and populations of the
lder European states were put together during lengthy and erratic processes
f conquest, inheritance, marriage, murder, rebellion, acts of parliament. For
nuch of modern history European states coexisted with territorial entities
nat were not states (independent cities like Hamburg, principalities like
Moldavia or, currently, Monaco). The boundaries of states rarely remained
ettled for long; and the habit of boundary manipulation has remained a
articularly lively one in the twentieth century, during which the European
nap has twice been radically redrawn. The traditional European state was
ot assumed to be a community or some kind of popular movement. Not only
vere rulers often foreigners, but laws, languages and even loyalties within
neir realms were also commonly mixed. No European state was created out
f a single ancient community, and enthusiastic recollections of diverse
lentities (among Scots, Basques, Bretons, Croatians) remain active in many
f them. Statehood did not come into existence as an absolute concept with
n appropriate set of practices, but was penetrated by inter-state entities such
s the church and natural law and, later, by ideas and movements like
ationalism, liberty and various forms of socialism. There never was a settled
neory of the state, only a variety of theories, some of which (marxism most
ifluentially) could hold statehood to be a matter of secondary and not
rimary importance. Copying the European state was no easy matter. In a
vay the American revolutionaries of the eighteenth century created a new
ind of state, which was conceived as a rejection of what they thought to be
ne current European model. In later periods, in the underdeveloped world
nd elsewhere, the European state has been copied as different things: as a
ational movement, a means to achieve large ends like economic moderni-

sation, an opportunity for the exercise of power by a personal leader, as a form of international respectability. But in fact none of these can be held to be the quintessence of the European state.

As the concrete realisation of authority

This view argues that the emergence of the European state was largely the emergence of a new kind of ruler, the monarch. The state defined the authority of this ruler, his status, in two senses: first, in terms of an hierarchical social structure; second, geographically in terms of a specific territory and population.

This apparently clear and consistent notion of statehood also fragments on closer inspection. The authority of monarchs was hemmed in by established laws and customs; by the power and wealth of lords and corporations and by their resistance to taxation; by the claims of religion, if not always by the claims of the Roman church; and by all sorts of practical limitations, from crude physical means of communication and widespread illiteracy to the inefficiency and venality of sparse and badly organised state functionaries. The power of monarchical authority was often a fragile thing, most impressive when on the point of collapse; frequently it was held together by subterfuge, bribery, titular preferment, violence, threats, spurious dynastic and religious doctrines. The actual power of governmental authority was (and largely remains) something strenuously sought after, not a settled structure of human acquiescence generously made available to rulers by the fact of the state. Dissent, rebellion, lawlessness and inertia were the recurrent accompaniments of rule. The decline of monarchy and the institution of fresh concepts of legitimate rule (nationalism, parliamentarianism, republicanism) did relatively little to bring the certainty of power to the uncertain European heritage of state authority. Even in the relatively uncomplicated territory of North America an outstanding republican constitution was challenged in major civil war. Nor did the coming of democracy to France or to Europe generally bring with it settled patterns of government authority. Constitutions began to appear and disappear with a rapidity not dissimilar from the turbulent exits and entrances of earlier monarchs. The nature of the power of rulers and the nature of the authority of state offices seemed to remain as confused as ever.

The state as apparatus

The state from this standpoint is a massive historical aggregation of bureaucratic agencies and hierarchies and networks of official communications; of tax-gatherers, police forces and inspectorates of all sorts; of assemblies, councils, committees, commissions, panels and tribunals; of mechanisms of public subvention to businesses, schools, theatres, universities. Modern

overnments inherit this interminable apparatus of state power, upon which
irge proportions of their populations are apt to be directly dependent for
heir incomes.

Accumulated apparatus is undeniably a tangible daily manifestation of
tatehood. But what it implies about the nature of the state is unclear. Though
irge numbers of interests attach to this apparatus it does not stir the loyalties
f vast populations; the reverse seems sometimes to be the case. It is a tangle
f institutions that itself engages a great amount of governmental energy;
olicy change commonly boils down to apparatus change. It is certainly
xpensive; yet it is much easier to extend than to diminish. Its leading echelons
aonopolise the skills essential to its operations; so their interests and values
ecome significant elements in policy execution and administration. It is not a
ighly manoeuvrable mechanism deploying immense power, if by power is
neant the capability for rapidly obtaining large social and economic results
esired by governments. It consumes wealth but can create very little of it.
t can distribute funds but is less effective at ensuring their productive use.
jeneral aims, such as the control of inflation or the improvement of industrial
fficiency, not only often evade it, its own existence may constitute an impedi-
nent to their achievement. Nor is apparatus peculiarly the manifestation of
ne national state. The most apparent reality of international organisations
ke Nato or the IMF or the European Community are their directorates,
oards, assemblies and committees, many of which merge with little apparent
ffort or stress into equivalent national structures. Nor is this to be wondered
t. If apparatus itself attracts no exact loyalties there is no reason why it
hould not extend itself cross-nationally. If it is simply the instrument of
urposes like defence or economic growth, which are necessarily cross-
ational in many of their aspects, there is a complete case for it doing so.

s the instrument of rule

he state has been used to extend the domains of monarchs and other rulers;[13]
o maintain or to alter particular distributions of property; to maintain or to
lter religious observances; to achieve and maintain full employment; to alter
ne distribution of incomes; to manage particular industrial operations; to
uild houses, roads, drains and factories; to secure public subvention for
ertain associations.

The state as an enterprise is a common modern assumption of political
ction. But again nothing precise is conveyed about the inner nature of
atehood by such a conception. If the state itself is an enterprise or a collection
f enterprises then the state itself is a subject of contention. The fundamental
natter of statehood now resides in arguments about whether a certain project
nould be undertaken, about how it should be undertaken, or about whether
lternative projects should be preferred. The more projects the state takes on,
ne more it must shift and turn. Running specific industrial and commercial

operations; using taxation to achieve a variety of economic and socia
objectives; channelling investment to officially preferred uses: enterprises lik
these often run into unforeseen difficulties leading to contradictory resul
requiring frequent changes in government policies and alterations in comple
bodies of legislation. The greater the extension of the state into diverse enter
prises, the larger the scope for mistakes, for the occurrence of unforeseen an
unfortunate results of government action, and for possible arbitrarine
among state functionaries; consequently ever greater efforts are required t
monitor the state, to frame and re-frame legislation, to supervise functionarie
The state further extends itself to examine and control itself. For all its endle
intricacies the state as a set of projects is a humdrum thing, unlikely t
stimulate the romantic imagination. There is no reason why its enterprise
should not be cross-national in objectives and organisation; and there
every reason why cross-national state projects should be subjected to bot
national and cross-national investigation and judicial and legislative regula
tion. Nor is there any reason why one state should not take the closest interes
in the internal projects of another. The states that have committed themselve
to the GATT have undertaken to liberalise international trade by the reductio
of tariffs. But states have also engaged themselves in a multiplicity of projec
that can constitute non-tariff constraints on trade. It is thus unremarkabl
that governments should scrutinise the details of one another's interna
enterprises and bring pressures to bear accordingly.

An organic form of leadership

The state may seem to be statesmen; and statesmen may seem to be th
spokesmen, leaders and moulders of societies on the grandest scale. The tru
great statesman may thus be one who identifies himself organically with th
state and sweeps all before him to achieve its purposes. The state become
the embodiment of sovereignty in the person of the leader.

An organic concept of the state can authenticate immense personal powe
If the state is the essence of society's purposes, society is a movement embodie
in the state. The effects of leadership conducted in these terms are familiar
the statesman comes to hold himself above legal controls; judicial and othe
offices of state become tokens of discipleship to the leader; the legislature i
bribed and bullied into sanctioning with the form of law all the leader'
arbitrary actions; citizenship comes to mean obedience, not the exercise c
free individual decision in terms of consent to ordered constitutional rule
rebellion becomes a moral imperative.

The constitutional state is a collection of practical devices to protect citizen
from these horrors and abuses. An independent judiciary, regular election
a balance in the powers of the executive and the legislature, the federal diffusio
of law-making functions: these principles and institutions deny the need an
opportunity for the exercise of personal sovereignty by the statesman. If th

ivil state is a structure to prevent the appearance of a personal sovereign,
must also be a structure that can cope with the social problems and stresses
hat might otherwise summon a personal sovereign into existence. It therefore
nakes its authority available for social purposes such as the relief of poverty,
he regulation of conditions of work and the like. Offices of state are open to
eaders concerned with these and other social ends. But the prominent
haracteristic of legitimate authority in the civil state is the formal and
nformal limitations placed upon it. The constitutional offices of the civil state
re defined by the constraints their occupants must endure: by the necessity
o proceed by and through legislation; by the massive weight of existing law,
which cannot be put aside; by the multiplicity of state authorities, which
annot be dominated as a whole; by the need to maintain electoral support;
y perpetual open criticism.

If the state is not personal sovereignty but a device to prevent its appearance,
follows that there can be no argument in principle against its careful
xtension in cross-national structures and other linkages having the same
ffect. The civil state is against sovereignty and lawlessness at home. It should
herefore be against sovereignty and lawlessness abroad, because what is
wicked at home is no less wicked elsewhere, and because foreign sovereigns
nay disturb international society to the detriment, possibly the destruction,
f civil statehood. The civil state should therefore extend itself to regulate the
nternational environment in ways detrimental to prospective sovereigns and
o strengthen the roles of assemblies, judiciaries and elections cross-nationally
nd thus nationally too.

means of obtaining specific external goals

Because the state is the dominant actor in the international arena, it may
eem that international purposes can only be pursued through the medium of
he state. The state is therefore a necessity to any particular foreign objective.

In its most extreme form this view interprets the state itself to be a grandiose
nternational enterprise concerned with the pursuit of ends peculiar to its
nternational nature such as the acquisition of territory and subjects or the
mposition of continental hegemony. There is much historical substance to
he view that the state as a tax-gathering organisation was initially put
ogether to maintain the armies of rulers and to support their foreign
ampaigns.[14] But the state as the expression and vehicle of such enterprises is
learly full of potential for harm. Possessions like territory are in limited
upply so their attempted acquisition must, sooner or later, be the cause of
onflict with other similarly motivated states. And placing external popula-
ons in a vassal condition by denying them the possibility of their own forms
f statehood is likely to cause resentments of an eventually explosive intensity.
o inspire statesmen to such purposes is to encourage them into corruptly
elieving themselves superior to the application of the ordinary moral

criteria of human conduct both abroad and at home. All these effects contra
dict the nature of civil statehood.

At the mundane level of contemporary cross-national relations, it is clea
that the state in no way monopolises the pursuit of external objectives. A
sorts of domestic bodies, commercial and otherwise, are active across stat
frontiers. At the same time, large numbers of domestic interests are affecte
by events abroad. The state may be held a necessity to the protection of thes
interests. Yet even this unheroic role is far from clear-cut. The protection of
sector of the British electrical manufacturing industry from, say, Japanes
competition may seem to require the existence of a state with the traditiona
capability to impose direct limitations on unwanted foreign manufacture
but this commonplace function of statehood is full of complications, of whic
these are a sample:

1.   British consumers have an obvious interest in the ready availability c
     inexpensive electrical goods and this interest will be harmed if such good
     are denied them by act of state. In being of service to one interest the stat
     is of disservice to another.
2.   Relatively few British governments are likely to see the long-term suppo
     of inefficient industries as a proper use of the state's capabilities since th
     represents a wasteful allocation of total economic resources. The prohib
     tion of fair external competition is likely to have this effect. Thus a genera
     long-term concern and a particular immediate demand are in conflict. Th
     field of interests within which the state subsists is not a simple one.
3.   One government may be more sympathetic to the use of the state to serv
     a special interest than another government of the same country. But in th
     case the operative factor in the furtherance of an interest is the views c
     governments, not the nature of the state.
4.   A particular interest (British electrical goods manufacturers or any othe
     is unlikely to be much concerned in the description of an institution that i
     of use to it. If the European Commission can effectively bring pressure t
     bear on a Japanese government to restrict certain Japanese exports, n
     advantaged British group is going to cavil because its interest has bee
     served by something that may not seem to be a state. In these circumstance
     the question of the nature of statehood may seem a wholly metaphysica
     one of no practical relevance to active groups.
5.   As has been indicated (chapter 3), interests exist in distinguishab
     settings. The setting of cross-national economic interests is one to whic
     governments have given much attention. Parts of it have been structure
     under the terms of the GATT in such a way as to place some constraints o
     the unilateral use of the sovereign capabilities of statehood. Thus th
     state's pursuit of the general external goal of an orderly yet open an
     expanding trading system (which necessitates ascribing moderately exac
     meanings to norms like 'fair competition') places limitations on it
     capabilities as an agent of specific internal interests.

The effect of complications like these is not perhaps to destroy the state but is to involve it in networks of general and special interests and issues, and to diffuse its structure among national and cross-national environments and institutions. One might thus say that the state is a vehicle for the pursuit of internal interests externally and of external interests internally. Or it might seem that the state is simply a mechanism for registering some kind of temporary order of priority among goals of all kinds rather than an active principle in determining the pattern of responses to national and international issues and interests.

THE STATE AS THE CONDITIONS OF ORDER IN A DIVERSE SOCIETY

The conceptions of the state that have just been reviewed suffer from three sorts of deficiencies. First, the more historically concrete they attempt to be, the more empirical and conceptual inaccuracies they can be shown to contain. Second, the more practical and matter-of-fact their emphasis, the more natural the state's fusion into cross-national structures and enterprises seems; and the more elusive its fundamental nature becomes. Third, the more heroic the conception, the more obviously is it the antithesis of the actual principles of civil statehood. It does not follow from these weaknesses that there is no grain of truth in each of the above notions of the state. There are many grains in some of them. But they cannot be put together, selectively or as a whole, to make a coherent picture of statehood because of their excesses, contradictions and inaccuracies. The practical thus shows itself to be impracticable; so we must now turn to a view of the state as the conditions of order in a changing society, as a kind of premiss of human relationships, rather than as something analogous to a physical object.

The state as the ground-rules of individuality

The term 'civil state' may be taken to describe a society of individuals whose distinctive quality is not to be found in common practices or enterprises or communal loyalties or languages or religious beliefs; but in an order that depends on the acceptance of certain rules as the necessary condition of the fulfilment of individuality in all its public and private aspects.

This notion of the civil state does not concern itself with sovereignty or specific loyalties or with nationality or power. The state is fundamentally and ideally a set of general rules that do not require the citizen to engage himself in any particular enterprises or practices, or to espouse or to appear to espouse any essential causes or beliefs. If individuality is free development, and if the state is the condition of individuality, then the state cannot determine the forms that individuality should take. But in a society engendering an almost

infinite variety of practices and projects the expression of individuality mus
be constrained in order to preserve the possibilities of individuality from the
effects of intolerant, grandoise, perverse and otherwise obsessive realisation:
of human nature. These constraints must be of the form of general rules. A
its foundations the state is thus an order, nothing more or less. Within this
order, governments, groups and organisations may pursue a variety of public
enterprises. These may make, or fail to make, all sorts of valuable contributions to human welfare. But they do not comprise, individually or collectively
the essential idea of civil statehood. This is an order that is the condition o
these activities; it is not their substance. Authority in the state is available to
social purposes; but authority used in such enterprises is not thereby release
from the operation of constraining principles.

This notion of statehood resolves many of the difficulties attendant upon
views of the state as an activity or a leadership or a collective identity. These
are now to be thought of as enterprises and views and communities within the
order of the state. If this view of the state as the conditions of civil order is
accepted, it follows that efforts to make fundamental distinctions between
one actual state and another may be misplaced. Except in practical ways
two or more states may be part of a common notion of statehood. As ar
example, let it be accepted that the following constitutes a rule that denotes
the existence of civil statehood: that no man may be lawfully held in custody
unless a charge of a particular offence against a known law of general application is publicly made against him. Now a rule like this is actually observed in a
number of states. What then is the fundamental difference between them'
In this respect there need be none, though there may well be practica
differences relating, say, to the period that may elapse between arrest and
arraignment. Another condition of civil order might be this: that no proposa
should become law without the positive and public consent of at least one
body of freely elected representatives drawn from the population likely to be
affected by it. This too may be taken to be a mark of a common statehood
subject to particular variations in legislative procedures and electoral systems
Given this to be so, it follows that the institution of, say, an elected assembly
in the European Community should be interpreted as a manifestation of ar
existing form of statehood rather than as a radical, even outlandish, attempt
to create a new kind of state.

Civil statehood as the form of an international order

An individual civil state is an intrinsic part of an international order. Its
sovereignty is not a weapon for use against this order but a mark and
qualification of membership of it. The international order of civil statehood
is self-governing. The individual civil state is the principal, though not the
exclusive, form that self-government takes. A country that is without civil
statehood cannot be self-governing since its government must be in the hands

of an autocrat, an oligarchy, a conspiracy, an aristocracy, a priesthood or some combination of these; it cannot be a self-governing society of individuals subscribing to general rules as the foundations of order. The international sovereignty of civil states denotes the way in which their governments relate to one another, not the substance of what they relate about. It denotes their tolerance and caution, their propensity to proceed by discussion and agreement, their respect for the practices of self-government. It is also the reserved ability of elements of the international civil order to withdraw from particular arrangements that may be interpreted as impositions born of the superior strength of other elements: the imposition of import quotas by one civil state against the products of another may thus be a legitimate defence of a country in balance of payments deficit against a surplus country taking positive measures to prevent an upward revaluation of its currency. This sort of sovereignty is the practical framework to consent to cross-national forms of rule. It is a defence of civil society rather than the reverse, and it has nothing whatever to do with the threat of war. Internationally it places no prohibitions on novel organisational departures or involvements within international civil society. On the contrary, it stimulates a constant search for new forms of relations, in the matter of exchange rate policy in this example, while ensuring a measure of stability and modesty in any experimentation that may occur. It requires that international order can only be expressed governmentally in a restrained and sensitive manner. It prevents order from becoming, or from being imagined as becoming, orchestrated governmental unity. International governmental enterprises within civil statehood as a whole are always likely to be partial affairs. But this is as it should be. Civil order contains enterprises, it is not itself one massive enterprise; it is a condition of self-government, not of total centralisation.

Complications attach to this conception of an international civil order. States are universal in the sense that they cover almost all of the world's land surface. But relatively few are founded on anything like civil principles. The universal system of states is therefore not a civil order and it certainly contains threats of unimaginable violence. It is nevertheless the case that the form of the state provides such order as exists in the international system as a whole. Its emphasis on territorial boundaries serves to place geographical limits to the cruelties perpetrated by numbers of tyrants. It also conveys some sense of the notion, at least, of self-rule and self-direction to the world's diverse population. The conventions, rules and institutions of inter-state behaviour provide a diplomatic order that permits, given vigilance and some dispersal of military power, radically different governmental habits and ideologies to coexist without the necessity for war. But there is a vital distinction between the world system of states and the international society of civil statehood. How is the civil state to relate itself to the non-civil state and how is the latter to be transformed into the former? Civil society cannot be wholly conservative towards its antithesis.

A necessity of defence

The civil order of constitutional statehood is not in itself an active principle. Only in the widest international setting can this rule be in any sense qualified. Civil order must generate, or in part give way to, an active military concern with defence if its existence is threatened. The maintenance of military preparedness is the only apparently positive activity necessary to civil statehood, given that it exists in a world containing many non-civil states. Projects of other kinds (providing medical services, organising the provision of education, regulating public transport systems) may be very important governmental and administrative activities within the order of the state; yet they do not characterise civil statehood itself because they may be undertaken in all kinds of different official and unofficial ways. Security, on the other hand, is an essential aspect of civil order. However, the maintenance of security is not required by civility itself, but by civility in a dangerous setting. Security is not a practice or enterprise or project; it is a condition of all the shifting enterprises and practices of civil order. The state-as-defence has the appearance of an enterprise activity because it has to create some kind of military organisation; but it is not substantively an enterprise activity and should not be allowed to become one. Defence does not, and should not, yield any substantive products like territory or raw materials or subject peoples. Security cannot be a product. It is the medium of the existence of civil society. The maintenance of security in a world system that is not a civil order requires the concrete military manifestation of the civil state. But in the lives of individuals, security is simply the civil manner of whatever they choose to do, of their practices and public enterprises and causes. Thus state activity whose purpose is the maintenance of security cannot be equated with military projects of other kinds, with foreign domination and the like.

Defence and external security are not the same thing. Defence may be taken to refer to the capability of the individual state to defend its society in a broadly geographical sense. External security refers to a safe condition of affairs in the international environment. Thus in a perfectly secure international environment there is no need for defence; whereas in a completely insecure international environment the need for defence is absolute. An international society entirely composed of civil states would be a perfectly secure one in which there would be no call for defence. On the other hand, an international arena containing many large states unconstrained by civil order and antipathetic to it would elevate the defence function of the civil state to one of almost unconditional importance. But this would create the risk of altering the nature of civil statehood. Forestalling the need for absolute absorption in defence requires that attention be paid to international security. This in turn may require that arrangements of a practical sort (relating, say, to arms control or to limited territorial understandings) be made between civil states and states that confront civil order with incomprehension and hostility.

The civil conception of statehood disengages the military apparatus of the individual state from unique and exclusive attachment to purely national defence. The military arm is now concerned with the control of violence in the international arena to the purpose of preserving civil order, which of course includes the order of individual states. But civil order itself cannot be conceived as a kind of nationalist cause, though it contains numerous manifestations of national feeling. There is thus no conceptual hindrance in terms of national sovereignty to the interlocking of the apparatus of defence forces among civil states or to mutual dependencies in terms of supply and planning. There are plenty of practical difficulties. An alliance of civil states, however structurally advanced it may be, is liable to traditional alliance stresses; to differences of perceptions of external threats, petty jealousies, indecision and the like. But cross-national military arrangements among civil states are highly untraditional in the sense that they are not intrinsically impermanent. The sources of their creation do not lie in purely temporary conjunctions of partial interests. They are not the outcome of a shifting nineteenth-century balance of power system. The concern of a civil alliance is the defence of civil order from the forces deployed by strong anti-political states. This concern is not temporary or partial. When civil order coincides substantially with world order the need for defence will disappear. Until then the mutual defence involvements of civil states are not rendered impermanent by the existing nature of the international environment. On the contrary, if they are impermanent it is because of internal carelessness or decay or corruption of purpose or pettiness.

The priority of civil statehood

The civil notion of statehood contains no contradictions of the modern novelties of foreign policy. It is an entirely general set of conditions of activities, particularly public activities, in civil states. The state as a territory or as an historical structure of rule are not somehow alien to it; but civil statehood prevents these conceptions from becoming fundamental definitions of the state itself. What matters is the manner of rule, not where or in what language it takes place. The structure of rule is a variable. There may be all kinds of federal, quasi-federal and functional relationships among civil authorities. What is vital is the order, the rules, that authorities subscribe to, not their structural peculiarities. State authority is available to all kinds of national and cross-national enterprises. This is as it should be. But the authority of civil statehood is always constrained, wherever it becomes available. It can never be concentrated in one institution. In cross-national affairs it is usually much less concentrated than it is in domestic affairs; but this is a distinction of degree, not of kind.

Civil statehood is not a concrete object like a piece of land or a palace or a parliament building. But it is not abstract either. It is mostly a set of rules that are in no way obscure. It is a principle of civil statehood, for example, that a law must take the form of a general condition on all citizens within a known area of application, whether this be national or cross-national, wherein constitutional means are available to secure its repeal. There is nothing mysterious here. Yet civil statehood is an ideal as well. Its rules are always under pressure from the misguided, the ambitious, the ignorant, the narrow. Movements and leaders are constantly prone to place some other notion of the state (as a nationality or a language or a religion or a race or a welfare ideology or an economic doctrine) in the position of absolute priority that can only be legitimately occupied by civil statehood. The idea of the civil state will always be a source of radical challenges in public affairs because it does not accept the absolute truth and permanence of other ideas or of movements or leaderships. But it is also a stabilising ideal since it should always qualify all that is done or proposed or conceptualised in political affairs. In a sense this is what politics is: an approach to public affairs and the use of authority that, whatever its particular manifestation, is also committed to the maintenance and extension of civil statehood.

THE PEACEFUL INTERNATIONAL SOCIETY OF CIVIL STATES[15]

From the inside, the notion and affairs of civil statehood locate a fundamental boundary in international relations. Within this boundary there is a multiplicity of states, religions, languages, governments, policies, organisations and national and other loyalties; it contains and engenders hosts of private and official, national and cross-national enterprises; it is saturated in arguments, conflicts of interest, movements and ideas of all grades of realism. But where the priority of civil statehood is accepted there cannot be war or the threat of war.

The civil relationship excludes war

The civil relationship subsists among all citizens accepting the rules of political statehood. This is a relationship between individuals via rules. It is not directly personal like friendship or comradeship. It does not express itself in shared practices or enterprises or causes but in the civil quality of practices and enterprises and causes. It is the impersonal conditions of public action and of the language of public action among citizens of civil states. These conditions are general. It follows that those subscribing to them cannot seek to impose themselves on one another by the use of force because the conditions of what they all do are the same. The civil state can only be expressed in terms of violence when it is defending itself. But defence is not a project specifically aimed against anyone. Nor is it the rules of civil statehood in active form. It is state activity on the borders of civil order. If a war were launched inside international civil society, a particular civil state would have to become an organised violent enterprise attacking the conditions of its own existence elsewhere. But this could only be a self-contradiction. The rules of civil society are conditions of the expression of individuality. Their point is best realised in diversity. An attack by one civil state on another civil state would be a violent attempt to abridge variety and would constitute an attack on civil statehood itself. Here are more self-contradictions.

Constitutionalism excludes war

War can only be the outcome of three circumstances: first, a quarrel about ideas; second, a quarrel over governmental control of a particular territory; third, a clash of specific interests. But, first, civil statehood is not an idea, it is the practical conditions of the free evolution and interplay of ideas. Two civil states cannot go to war over an idea relating to their mutual affairs. The civil state is a condition of a variety of ideas in and on the conduct of political relations, it does not itself sponsor any particular idea. Second, territories within international civil society are constitutionally self-governing. An attempted seizure of such a territory would therefore be an attack on the constitutional conditions of self-government, launched by another constitutionally self-governed state. But the only general point of such a state is the maintenance of self-government, not its overthrow. Third, the civil state is the conditions of a diversity of enterprises; so much so that political affairs may, simple-mindedly, be seen as the shifting relations of a mass of interests and nothing else. The governments of civil states invariably operate in a complex field of all sorts of interests in their own and in their mutual affairs. Again, civil statehood is the conditions of these interests, it is not itself an interest. It qualifies the ways in which interests are expressed and related to one another. Two civil states cannot come into head-on violent conflict over an interest in this field of interests. Such an interest is already qualified by the field and by civil statehood. This civil qualification is in no way abridged when interests cross frontiers among civil states. Though interests are often espoused by a government in its relations with another civil country they are not thereby held to be above the law in that country or anywhere else in civil society. But for a government to go to war in these circumstances it would have to make just such a claim.

Civil statehood is the condition of self-government. A state used purely for the promotion of the social or economic dominance of a particular group or religion or idea or race cannot be a civil state because at root a civil state is a relationship between its citizens in respect of wholly general rules. In the absence of this relationship a state may become the instrument of a tyrant or of a clique. But this is not self-government; it is government by a tyrant or a clique. The civil state always places two kinds of limitations on governments: first, the limitations contained in constitutional rules, among which must be the duty to uphold constitutional rules; second, the related limitations of political processes of open debate and free association that, in a constitutional setting, enable differing combinations of interests and causes to exert direct and legitimate influence on the making and unmaking of government projects. Given the necessity of these conditions to the existence of civil government, there can be no fundamentally legitimate cause of war within the society of civil states. One civil state cannot disregard or overturn constitutionalism and its associated political practices in another civil state by the use of force. To do so would be to hold constitutionalism and politics in contempt. But this would be to hold itself in contempt.

Political process excludes war

Political war is a contradition in terms. Political governments are subject to known rules both in the shape of constitutions and the bodies of ordinary law that they each inherit; and they are subject to the familiar but less formal processes required by the need to hold together support for their programmes and their continuance in office. The activities of governments in their cross-national aspects are as much subject to these circumstances as are their more narrowly internal activities. A political government embroiled in questions of trade discrimination or with the terms of credits from the IMF is not thereby somehow released from its involvement in the field of pressures and arguments that is its normal medium of life. Political conditions apply domestically and cross-nationally at the same time. Constant and involved negotiations on numbers of different but often overlapping subjects each located by the interplay of conflicting interests and arguments expressed both nationally and cross-nationally cannot be distinguished as occupying a category distinct from domestic political processes. The domestic and cross-national affairs of civil states merge into one another politically as well as functionally.

In their nature political processes exclude legitimate violence. This is so, first, because they are founded on civil statehood and accept its priority. This condition of public affairs is the same throughout the plurality of civil states and therefore applies cross-nationally in this society just as much as it applies domestically. Second, it is so because the different elements of political processes (arguments, pressures, interests, opposition) overlap and shift and vary in intensity in so many ways as to prevent the relentless and unyielding collision of simple, massive and totally oppposed positions. Political processes are absorbed in innumerable issues, not in a single issue. The non-coincidence of such issues generally ensures that one citizen is commonly aligned with another on some matters and divided from him on others: two individuals united in a campaign against blood sports may be in strong disagreement on questions of housing policy, so that no starkly simple relationship of either complete solidarity or hostility between them results. The same sort of characteristic shows itself in the cross-national dealings of authorities: two political governments cooperatively involved in tackling an international monetary issue may also be at loggerheads on problems of agricultural policy. The issues within the international society of civil states are so diverse that no two authorities are wholly at one or wholly opposed; they are divided on some issues and united on others. Third, issues in political states are never ones of life-and-death intensity. This is as true cross-nationally as it is domestically. Given civil statehood's emphasis on generality in the use of authority and on dispersion in its location, there cannot be a political issue to which there is no remedy but massive violence. An attempt at a violent resolution could only legitimately occur if authority became entirely concentrated and thereby unaccountable and, sooner or later, arbitrary; or if, with or without concentration of authority, generality were abandoned in favour of using the legal apparatus of the state against a particular religious or racial or other group. But in these circumstances civil statehood would have ceased to exist anyway. Within the society of civil states authority is certainly dispersed. Close mutual observation, plus specific agreements, ensure a lively attention to equity and generality in cross-national arrangements. On top of this, a government can often withdraw from any arrangement or project with another government that proves uncongenial to it. The unviolent emphasis of political processes in cross-national issues is even more marked than it is in domestic issues.

Civil statehood as explicit commitment

The priority of the civil relationship qualifies all the other relations of the citizens and authorities of the civil state. The acceptance of this political qualification of public arrangements, arguments, exhortations and actions comprises an ideal framework of social existence. But the political qualification is in no sense a fixed pattern of opinion or behaviour and it does not refer to the achievement of some imagined form of human solidarity. It is an ideal (from which citizens commonly fall) because its effect is the indefinite maintenance of the conditions of individuality, of open public discourse, self-government and an endlessly extending multiplicity of practices. Political society is not a massive joint enterprise of its members whether they be individuals, groups or national or cross-national authorities. In part its quality lies in its endless investigation of the possibilities of political rule in a diverse setting endlessly given to spontaneous change. Many of these possibilities are revealed in the contingent problems of political states. But civil statehood is not itself contingent. Though, say, the state of West Germany is a contingent product of a large number of historical forces and circumstances (many of a strategic kind), it does not follow that the civil statehood of West Germany is contingent. Civil statehood comes into being as a result of clear and authoritative choices to adopt constitutional rule, open legal process and the like. Though international factors such as foreign domination may conspire to prevent their adoption, the structures of political rule are not themselves the product of circumstances but of choices. And these are not mysteriously abstract or inaccessible to ordinary understanding. Similarly, the decision to maintain civil rule is not one that can be taken once and for all. It must be constantly renewed in the daily conduct of political relations in the face of all sorts of corruptions ranging from direct attempts to subvert legality to petty distortions of political langauge in the service of purely personal ambition. A state adopting political rule joins political society. Though states may be contingent, civil statehood is not. The affairs of political society involve a plurality of political states. This is a tautology, not a principle. The principle lies in the obligation of individuals to maintain the civil state and the responsibility of civil states to maintain political society.

CONCLUSIONS

1.   The more exactly social or geographical or purposive a definition of the state attempts to be, the less plausible it becomes.

2.   Civil statehood is exact but it is also general. It qualifies other ideas of the state.

3.   The circle of civil states comprises a political society. This society is clearly demarcated from the rest of the international arena by the civil conditions of its existence.

4.   The conditions of political relations inside the society of civil states exclude the possibility of war. In the sense that the state is a basis of a diverse, changing and peaceful order, international political society is one state containing numerous authoritative forms of statehood among which there are all kinds of connections.

CHAPTER 6

The Political Society of Civil States

There is nothing obscure about civil statehood. A political society of civil states exists and can be described. No grandiose *a priori* inventions need be brought to bear on it. It is an ideal international society in that it excludes war and provides the foundations of widely diverse forms of living and an open future for its members. It is not an ideal society if by that is meant one that is without corruption, folly or bigotry or that conforms to some abstract unhistorical model of rationality in its government. Its actual structures and uses of authority are disjointed. But if they conform to no pattern they are not bound by one either. In this area, as in every other, international political society is productive of endless suggestions for national and cross-national change. Yet the social circumstances that create the need for change themselves always change, so political society is ever in some degree of disequilibrium. Neither nationally nor cross-nationally can it surrender to the total dominance of any particular theory, movement or leader. To do so would be to abandon civil statehood. It does not deal in the irrevocable and can never turn its back on the perpetual problem of balance in social, economic and governmental affairs. International political society always offers the opportunity to learn from mistakes; but it always creates opportunities for making fresh ones.

CHARACTERISTICS OF INTERNATIONAL POLITICAL SOCIETY

A multiplicity of jurisdictions

Political society has nothing in the nature of central law-making or law-adjudicating bodies. Each part of political society (the British, French, Swedish, American parts) has an abundance of law. There are thus many jurisdictions and they are not all confined within the borders of particular civil states. The law in political society contains many variations. The conception of law as general conditions formulated in advance of their application and enforceable only through open judicial process, itself regulated by known rules, is shared. Variations in the details and practices of law constitute a

105

continuous form of experimentation into the place of particular kinds of law in a free society. The multiplicity of jurisdictions also provides individuals with some degree of choice in their legal circumstances, which would be unavailable to them in a society with one body of law and one jurisdiction. Thus a personal taste or want that may be constrained in one jurisdiction may be indulged in another. Pornography legally suppressed in one jurisdiction may be openly available in another. More seriously, a requirement to perform particular kinds of military service in one jurisdiction may not exist elsewhere. The freedom to subject oneself to different laws is far from unqualified, nor can it be indulged without financial and other costs. But it may be exercised without moving out of political society, without accepting exile from the rule of law.

A decentralised economy

National and cross-national public authorities in international political society play a variety of economic roles, some of which bring them into conflict. For this if no other reason the economy of political society cannot be centrally directed. Economic relations concentrated in the United States are a large element in this international economy. The economic actions and inactions of American governments are therefore of signal importance. But American governments do not consequently occupy a position of international economic hegemony. Large quantities of capital have been exported directly and indirectly from the United States. American economic interests are thus diffused through the western economic system. American governmental action persistently harmful to the rest of the economy of political society would be injurious to many interests inside the United States itself. Additionally, there are massive centres of economic strength outside the United States, in the German Federal Republic and elsewhere.

The decentralised nature of the economy of political society does not make it an arena of struggle between governments wielding unconstrained state authority against one another. This is partly because of the qualifying effects of civil statehood; the political relationship is not one of brute contention. It is partly a question of simple necessity. The breakdown of the international economy into withdrawn national entities would be generally impoverishing. Some would suffer more than others but all would be hard hit. There is also the fact that the domestic economic authority of civil governments is often far from secure and apt to confer relatively little strength on them in their external dealings.

Economic conditions throughout political society are not uniform. In one area the problem of inflation may be particularly acute, in another the problem of structural unemployment. But the efforts of an authority to dampen inflation in one place are likely to impede the efforts of another authority to alleviate the problem of structural unemployment elsewhere. For such reasons a single line of authoritative policy is always likely to be inappropriate to the international economy as a whole as well as being impossible to achieve. Numbers of governments cannot have identical policy priorities and their overall use of policy instruments is likely to be disjointed. Given the high measure of relatedness between the national economies of political society it follows that the regulation of the international economy is a matter of constant argument and marginal adjustment. Explicit general constraints on economic policy to which governments from time to time formally subscribe may rarely be uniformly and rigorously applied. But it is seldom that there is any marked neglect of the implicit rules of continuous mutual observation, critical argument, advice and persuasion; of regard for the maintenance of both the institutional and informal conditions of a constantly high level of cross-national communication and mutual support; of the recognition of the peculiar interests and limitations to which each government is subject. Though international economic affairs are not without government, it is government of a particularly complex and partial kind. This is not necessarily deplorable. The relatively free markets of the international economy can be argued to confer on political society a means of rapid and spontaneous adaptation to some large economic shocks. In a way western financial markets were able to absorb large increases in the surpluses of oil-producers in the 1970s far more smoothly than most civil governments were able to deal with attendant policy problems.

A multiplicity of practices

Political society as a whole is constantly diverse and changeful. Differences of habit and attitude towards social class, religion, entertainment, the rearing of children, sex, food and suchlike, are readily communicated among many of its members who are thereby partially released from subjections to rigid social norms and institutions. The forms of artistic and intellectual expression are similarly continually developing. If the cinema is torpid in Britain it comes alive in West Germany or France or Sweden. Repetitive theatre in France may be refreshed by talent from Britain or Italy. New departures in mathematics or genetics are not only rapidly communicated among cross-national communities, they also stimulate fresh spurts of energy in other specialisms. Dull political thinking may be enlivened by impulses from economic theory; philosophy may be driven in fresh directions by mathematics and social science. New intellectual and artistic groupings may quickly attach to discoveries and novel hypotheses. Enthusiasms appear and disappear within and across existing communities. But political society does not of necessity constantly stress novelty. The innovative engineer may be wholly conservative in his religion or in his musical tastes. Innovation can be both furthered and resisted at the same time. Yet inertia in political society is never complete. This is not because civil statehood itself requires innovation: other ideas of the state (as an enterprise to change a society or even to change man) do this. Civil statehood is the essential condition of variety. The effect of variety is change and innovation at social, economic, governmental and intellectual levels. But this is an effect of civil statehood not its intention or purpose. A state built for the purpose of a certain kind of change will in fact produce relatively little that is truly innovative because it establishes the conditions of an absence of variety.

A multiplicity of projects

New products and new productive processes are continually generated in the international economy of political society. Unlimited opportunities for communication ensure rapid diffusion of such novelties. Economic projects are frequently cross-national. Manufactures may be assembled in a trading process among many countries; or they may be produced inside single cross-national corporations. But enterprises in political society are far from being exclusively economic: movements to conserve the countryside, reduce the noise of aircraft, limit the impact of high density accommodation on urban life, promote religious ideas, and so on, are common throughout it and often pay little heed to state boundaries.

Most political governments commit themselves to a wide range of projects. They provide direct services, they organise industrial operations, they subsidise some private enterprises and commission goods and services from many others, they seek to influence the distribution of income and wealth. In some countries official involvement in materially productive projects is common, in others it is not. Socialist government, say in Sweden, does not necessarily lead to large programmes of nationalisation; on the other hand, a substantially private enterprise economy, as in Japan, is not necessarily one that excludes close governmental involvement in many sectors of economic life. In political society as a whole, the nature and scope of governmental projects vary greatly. A civil government in India may be concerned to distribute land among owners of small units whereas a political government in France may be concerned to encourage the concentration of land in large farming units.

A comparing and critical society

A high intensity of official and unofficial communication throughout political society ensures that comparison is intrinsic to all its activities. Projects and practices of all sorts are juxtaposed in constantly shifting ways. Values and standards (of provision for public health, education, housing, of public honesty and official disinterestedness) are subjects of enthusiastic cross-national comparison, as are government measures of all kinds, often on the basis of data provided by cross-national organisations. The extent and variety of political society ensures that critical comment on almost any structure, law, project or practice can point to alternatives about which detailed information is likely to be obtainable. Cross-national comparison forms a major element in most important political arguments.

International political society is a critical, discursive and adjusting one. It is immersed in argument, much of it cross-national. Talk, enquiry, speculation are both a means of obtaining consent to authoritative action and a kind of experimental, trial-and-error method of making decisions. By this method the possible consequences of suggested courses of action can be rehearsed in advance by the decentralised process of verbal proposal, counter-proposal, comparison and criticism. Between governments mutual criticism is usually discreet but is not necessarily any the less effective for that, particularly when foreign comment and suggestion corresponds to views expressed by important sectors of domestic opinion, as it often does. The more intemperate demands made by the government of the United States during an international currency crisis in August 1971 were abated in the following month partly because foreign criticisms were supported by much expert American opinion.[16] The critical communities of political society are not divided by national boundaries. Critical attitudes, and their associated inter-governmental demands and pressures, may also be partly channelled through cross-national organisations. Much of the finance made available to Britain at the beginning of 1977 was conditional on retrenchment in government expenditure. The views of important foreign governments in this matter corresponded with much opinion inside Britain. But the British government's acquiescence was only made explicit in its formal arrangements with the IMF.

Structural variety in government

In the international society of civil statehood there is immense variety in terms of electoral systems, federal and quasi-federal constitutions, party systems, degrees of separation between the organs and functions of rule, among methods of attempting to make governments financially and otherwise accountable, among forms of central and regional administration. Few of the structural reforms that are suggested in a country like Britain (to change methods of voting, to devolve government, to improve the effectiveness of parliamentary scrutiny of the executive, to provide open access to many processes of public administration) cannot be referred to exemplars elsewhere in political society. The possibility of proceeding differently, structurally as well as programmatically, is almost always present because somewhere else things actually are proceeding differently. Given the premiss of civil statehood, no proposal for change can categorically exclude the relevance of data drawn from within political society.

The association of international political society with wide structural variety in government tends to militate against a sense that particular forms of the state are somehow immutable. And a fairly calm approach to the flexibility of the structure of the state in internal terms is apt to induce a similar attitude to cross-national forms of civil statehood. If it seems reasonable, though not necessarily convincing, for constitutional structures in the German Federal Republic (its electoral system, its kind of federalism) to be held to be relevant to proposals for internal adaptations of the British state, it can hardly also seem unreasonable that West Germany and Britain should join in cautious experimentation in the adaptation of their states in cross-national constitutional undertakings. Though it may take fundamental unease out of the prospect of structural novelty, the variety of forms of rule in political society also has the balancing effect of militating against a too easy causal association of programmatic failure or success with particular structures of government. The view, for example, that a two-party system yields more effective national economic performance than a multi-party system no more stands up to comparative examination in the context of international political society than does its converse. In the same way, it does not follow that a new cross-national organisation will of itself guarantee sensible and effective responses to cross-national problems.

A constraint on the abstract

Political society is a constant limitation on theories (about sovereignty, rational economic policy, methods of education) as recommendations. Theories produce counter-theories, and the vast availability of data on the variety of structures and programmes in international political society means that a purely theoretical argument is of itself unlikely to be widely persuasive. Abstract suppositions get drawn into the complexities of political society where particular interests can conjure up data to support almost any case. In this intellectual and practical setting, abstract recommendation tends to become practical persuasion and pressure, and successful policy implementation may be largely a matter of exhaustive bargaining and of luck. The theories of political society are partial affairs, much given to locating their roots in the past; more prone to criticise existing worlds than to design wholly new ones; as often cautiously following in the wake of social change as scudding off in the van.

   The fundamental relationship between individuality and civil statehood is a powerful constraint on governmental dedication to the abstract. A theorised individuality is a contradiction in terms. Individuality that obeys a theory cannot be individuality. It is simply obedience to those who propound the theory in question. In a civil state individuality must be taken to be a fact, not a theory. Political man cannot be designed and is prone to all kinds of waywardness. He guarantees that official projects will have unexpected and unintended results, and is thus prone to instil some measure of humility in governments disposed to the reconstruction of society. He regularly shows the basest ingratitude for the mighty enterprises that governments undertake for his benefit. More deeply, individuality substantiates two opposing public arguments: first, that state authority should be deployed to release individuals from the cramping effects of circumstances; second, that state authority used for this purpose can soon itself become a cramping circumstance from which individuality should be released. The attempt to deploy authority in response to the first argument without fulfilling the prediction of the second is one that preoccupies all civil states. No theory can solve this problem, since such a theory would have to be a theory of individuality. Only practice can hope to establish tolerable working solutions. The existence in political society of a plurality of such attempts, each with its examinable unfortunate results, discourages sensible men from imagining that this problem can be reduced to an equation with a determinate solution.

THE FUNCTIONS OF THE STATE IN POLITICAL SOCIETY

It has been established that there can be no general theory of the geographical state. Each such state is the product of a different mix of historical forces: dynastic, strategic, economic, nationalist, imperialist, revolutionary, religious, linguistic. But there can be, and there is, a general observance of the conditions of civil statehood in and among a multiplicity of geographical states. On this civil basis we have, from the inside, distinguished the existence of an international political society and have listed its principal characteristics. This society generates no imperatives relating to the specific features of its states: whether they should be militarily strong or weak, geographically large or small, whether or not they should be intimately integrated in cross-national structures, whether they should be predominantly rural or industrial, or Asian or African or European, whether they should have federal or presidential or parliamentary constitutions. Given the variety of civil states, important generalisations about their relations must be framed in functional terms. This is now possible because we have distinguished a larger entity, international political society, of which they are the principal components. So the most significant international role of civil states is to be found in the functions they perform in maintaining the inner nature of international political society.

A condition of policy experiment

The state is a necessary condition of authoritative experiment: first, because it provides the institutional apparatus that makes policy departures possible; and, second, because it limits the unfortunate effects of policy departures that turn out to have been mistaken. Thus the existence of the British stat made possible a number of policies whose unintended outcome was a exceptionally high rate of inflation in the mid-1970s. But the more unpleasan effects of this inflation were mostly restricted to Britain itself. Meanwhile th less inflationary activities of other political governments provided salutar examples of alternative modes of response to not uncommon economi problems. Given that political society cannot be described in terms of a collective linear progress through history, then it is also given that th possibilities of political society are partly investigated by actions that turi out to be unfortunate. Political society engenders all kinds of communication and pressures that tend to moderate the extent of authoritative experiment This capability nevertheless remains and it is largely provided by states Yet the state also limits the effects of ill-considered experiment.

The state provides a necessary condition of the variety of policies an policy objectives in political society. At any one time the combination o policies to obtain full employment in civil states must be expected to differ Not only this, there are also likely to be variations in the priority given to ful employment in relation to other objectives. Even definitions of what con stitutes full employment are to be expected to differ. In these circumstance close mutual observation and comment among its members constitute a system in which the consequences of the dissimilar application of a variety of policy instruments may be studied and in which different criteria of policy effectiveness may be compared. Each individual political state is able t experiment simply by closely observing the travails of other political states

Political society's regulator

The plurality of civil states locates and contains the problems of politica society. The sharp rise in world oil prices in 1973 and thereafter had a majo impact on the economic life of political society as a whole, but it did no reduce it to collapse. The effects of this crisis were not identical among th political states, which could respond to it in different internal and inter national ways. Political society as a whole provided an important servic in the absorption of the immediate balance of payments shock of this crisi in that the cross-national capital market proved a convenient means o attracting and recycling the suddenly swollen currency reserves of the oil exporting countries. But international political society as a whole did no have to, and did not, respond to the problem by attempting to act in massiv unison.

The system of political states provides a kind of grid that locates differen aspects of, and different insights into, the vast bulk of a problem like this The diffusion of governmental responsibility tends to constrain any inclina tion to excess in the response of the society taken as a whole. All kinds o different policies towards specific oil-exporting countries emerged. Th

pread of governmental stresses among the large number of states in political
ociety also goes some way to ensuring their absorption without the
estructive measure of mutual tension that a centralised system would
xperience. At the same time the existence of cross-national interdependencies,
epresented by the capital market in the present example, provides a direct
timulus to political states to assist one another over particular difficulties
nd to take account of a variety of attitudes in their individual policies
owards the rest of the world.

A condition of cross-national structural change

tates are a practical and necessary condition of departures in the forms of
ross-national association in political society. First, they are a condition
f longstanding obligations to new institutions. The creation by one set of
overnments of the European Court of Human Rights binds their successor
overnments to acquiesce in the Court's jurisdiction whatever embarrassment
his may cause. Second, states are an essential component of the structure of
ovel international organisations. The detailed work of the Commission of
he European Community and its apparatus is made possible by its close
inkages with the bureaucracies of the Community states. Moreover, the actual
xecution of Community rules is the operational responsibility of states. The
olding of direct Community elections would be inconceivable without
xisting state electoral mechanisms and experience. Similarly, the masses of
ata assembled and analysed by international organisations such as the OECD
re largely provided by the information gathering facilities of states. Third,
tates ensure the existence of consent to novel forms of cross-national
rganisation. The undoubted capability provided by the state to disrupt
nternational organisation is an essential condition of organisational
nnovation. The participation of governments and legislatures in novel
ransnational structures is in part forthcoming because the existence of the
tate ensures that if novelty turns out to be oppressive it can be substantially
eutralised. The state provides the initial confidence that is the condition of
eparture. Fourth, the state constitutes an essential contact with social
ealities in cross-national organisations. The existence of the state ensures
hat all the pressures and constraints on governments operating in free
ocieties can be emphatically transmitted to international structures where
he limits of political rule may thus be fully appreciated. Furthermore, the
ivil state provides some kind of assurance that interests (like those of
he very poor or of the unemployed) that are unlikely to be directly expressed
nternationally by strong enterprise associations, may nevertheless receive
ue attention in international bodies, which, through the medium of the state,
eel the full force of popular opinion on the electoral fortunes of governments.
The civil state can represent internationally groups and causes which are
therwise unrepresented.

The state as a stabiliser

The state moderates change. First, the forms of the state can act as a token of identity in communities undergoing the general perplexities and tedium associated with urbanisation, secularisation, standardised eating and entertainment, computerisation, nuclear family life. It is thus not uncommon that a demand for some version of regional statehood rises as regional identity in terms of language, customs, religion and the like declines. Second, the idea of the state is highly elastic and it is able to provide a sense of continuity when in fact there may be very little of it. In the forty years between 1937 and 1977 both the internal and the external nature of the British state, and perhaps of British society as well, underwent fundamental change, yet the sense of the presence of the same state remained throughout. Third, the state moderates change in more practical ways, sometimes by blocking entirely legitimate international agreements. In western Europe in the postwar period, particularly in the 1960s, a general movement of labour from the land took place in response to large market forces. During this period legally valid American pressures in the GATT to free trade in agricultural products, which would have intensified this movement and its concomitant social stresses, were firmly resisted both by European states and by the European Community at some cost in American antipathy. Fourth, the plurality of states is a guarantee against the central direction of change in political society. The large-scale social and economic changes that come to political society are largely the result of impersonal shifts in technology, efficiency, tastes, incomes, enterprise and the like, which governments are usually involved in but hardly ever direct. No state commands change in political society as a whole; the plurality of states grapple with it and attempt to adapt it to local circumstances. Fifth, the state may confer confidence to face change through its capability to regulate it. Multinational companies are powerful transmitters of technology and organisation and in any given region they may be substantial employers. As such these companies are commonly welcome in their host countries. Governments, both local and national, often vie with one another across national boundaries in offering inducements to this kind of immigration. But it is largely because of the existence of the state that these structures are usually congenial presences, since the state ensures that they are constrained by municipal law and are responsive to local interests. The state is not so much a hindrance of cross-national enterprise as a fundamental condition of its existence.

A defence against collective aberration

The plurality of civil states is some assurance that the role of open debate, criticism and dissent in public affairs throughout political society will not be easily diminished. Contagions of ideological mania do not easily cross state boundaries. Paranoid reactions to social and international problems may occasionally reach something approaching authoritative status in individual countries. One thinks here of the example of McCarthyism in postwar America. But this phenomenon was by its nature exclusive to the United States. The idea of the state can hold a contagion of this sort within a particular territory while internal forces muster the strength to overcome it. Additionally, foreign civil states may provide refuge for those needing respite from personal attack and may also constitute sources of deprecative observation and comment. Civil states are always as a whole immune from outbursts of a single collective passion. This is perhaps the greatest merit of international political society. Intense romantic sensations cannot attach specifically to it.

Civil states at large constitute a curb on crusading national foreign policies. In this enquiry politics has been identified as a civil quality of action, opinion and structure rather than as specific kinds of action, opinion and structure. It is essentially because politics has this qualitative sense that it is possible to conceive of an international political society that is not to be subsumed under the terms of any particular treaty or organisation. From time to time it may happen that a particular political government launches itself into a foreign policy that by violent means aims to propagate values said to be shared among civil states. Yet such a policy is unlikely to muster anything like the united support of political governments and peoples. Domestic dissent may thus be sustained by the sceptism of much of political society and perhaps by the explicit criticisms of some of its governments. It is not a quality of political values that they should take the form of official doctrines, subject to authoritative interpretation only by single governments. Any individual authority claiming singly to act for the 'free world' is likely to encounter free condemnation in it.

The nature of political society and the plurality of states within it is similarly something of an antidote to grandiose pretensions to national and international power on the part of any one of its governments. The distribution of strength and influence among civil states is clearly uneven, but it is never wholly centralised. An attempt by one government to impose a single policy or structure on a group of civil states, let alone upon the generality of civil states, is highly unlikely to be an unqualified success because of the diversities of views and interests expressed in the context of separate and equal statehoods. In this setting, large general changes must invariably be negotiated over the long term. As well, the mass of detailed connections that bind the larger states of political society together has the inherent effect of drawing any new and ebullient national government into a variety of crossnational concerns that do not all progress at the same pace or fit together in any simple pattern. Under this weight of disjointed detail, heroic images of national foreign policy usually wilt. Yet the traditional sovereign is master of itself externally as well as internally. A government that cannot act masterfully in its cross-dealings is likely to be moved to a certain modesty of self-conception in its more purely domestic affairs.

The plurality of civil states may constitute a structural support of minorities. The existence of an external political audience may have a moderating effect on repressive modes of expression of domestic orthodoxies and prejudices. A minority may gain some sense of strength from its ability to make cross-national connections. And among civil states there are likely to be many examples of authoritative accommodation to minority needs that presage reforms in those states where no similar accommodations have yet been made: the experience of legislative action against racial discrimination in the United States contributed something to later British enactment in the same field.

The variety of political society is in part conferred on it by the diversity of its states. These contribute to the richness of debate within any particular state. Movements aiming to change a national pattern of taxation or to extend individual rights against an executive or to decrease poverty by some specific means can almost invariably point to exemplars within political society. A characteristic of political debate on public affairs is its high empirical content and this is in part a contribution of the plurality of civil states.

A constraint on power

A civil state locates its authority but does not concentrate it. Invariably distinctions are made between different state authorities that are thereby constrained by one another as well as by constitutional rules and by accumulated bodies of ordinary law. In locating authority the state does not confer power of a positive kind. The constitutional existence of an executive conveys nothing about its control or want of control over a legislature; this is essentially a product of the configuration and discipline of party groupings. The constitutional existence of a legislature conveys nothing about the effectiveness or quantity of its legislation; this is an effect of a mass of social and party circumstances, not of constitutional arrangements. The social power of a judiciary is dependent on the cases that come before it and on the conflicts and uncertainties contained in the body of law that it must adjudicate.

Once it is grasped that internally the state allocates authority, not power, and that this authority is largely set against power, the way is clear to seeing the state as an allocater of authority and a constrainer of power at cross-national levels as well. Within political society there are numbers of non-national authorities: the European Assembly, the European Court of Human Rights, the Nato military command structure and so on. National authorities also comprise cross-national authorities by virtue of their cross-national linkages: thus, for example, finance ministers associate formally and informally to influence the course of international monetary affairs and in this sense constitute a formidable international authority.

Civil states legitimate international authorities in two broad ways. First, they create national authorities of a limited kind that interlink to form authorities in relation to cross-national affairs. Second, they legitimate the constitutions and procedures of formal cross-national bodies. In keeping with their domestic character political states locate authority internationally in such a way as to constrain power. This effect is in part achieved by the decentralised nature of the collectivity of political states and by the limited nature of authority within each of them. As well, formal cross-national bodies are constrained by the terms of their constitutions, by their close linkages with states and by the disjointed nature of the distribution of authority among them.

CONCLUSIONS

1. The characteristics of international political society can be distinguished without reference to what lies outside it.

2. This society contains a plurality of states that are all founded on the conditions of civil statehood. These states maintain the diverse, structurally plastic and experimental nature of political society.

3. This society is an ideal one in the sense that it provides the basis of an open and peaceful future for its members. It cannot spare them the difficulties of self-rule.

CHAPTER 7

Inside Political Society:
Civil Perspectives on Issues of
Foreign Policy

The third chapter of this enquiry attempted to get to the core of foreign policy by analysing a selection of foreign policy issues. The results were inconclusive. Foreign policy itself emerged as a variable, and the different doctrines comprising most of the fabric of the issues examined were not in themselves suggestive of any coherent principles. The important result of these analyses, and of the verbal excursions of the fourth chapter, was that principles of foreign policy could not be expected to be directly produced by foreign policy itself. A secure position would have to be established independently of foreign policy. This position would have to be founded on a conception of statehood that would not be bound by the contingent pecularities of particular states. It would also be required to establish, from the inner nature of statehood, the boundaries of an international order distinct from the world arena as a whole. Given that foreign policy denoted forms of linkages between the national and the non-national, only in this way would it be possible to explain the variability of foreign policy and to bring order to its apparent incoherence. This requirement has now been met. On the basis of the notion and practice of civil statehood we have distinguished a peaceful international political society whose interior character is not determined by what lies beyond its boundary. We may now briefly review the third chapter's foreign policy problems as issues occurring entirely within this political society.

THE PROBLEM OF EXECUTIVE DOMINATION

Treaty-making powers

Three sets of harmful possibilities were previously delineated under this heading: first, the acquisition by the executive of obligations on behalf of the state leading to potentially catastrophic war; second, the acceptance by the

ecutive of external commitments whose fulfilment might so stress the state's
apabilities as to hazard the internal political order whose preservation is a
stification of the executive's existence; third, the accumulation of exag-
erated power by the executive as a result of the duties and status conferred
n it by international agreements.

This chapter is entirely concerned with relations and arrangements within
ternational political society that are conceived as having no bearing on,
relationship with, what lies outside. It therefore follows that for the
resent we may exclude from consideration relations containing the threat
war because, as established in chapter 5, relations among civil states
annot incorporate this possibility. The civil state exists as a qualification of
oncrete political circumstances. It cannot be a territorially bound concept.
shows itself as a constraint on power and as the legal conditions of
atheorised individuality. War between civil states would be analogous to
vil war. It would occur within one kind of statehood. A war inside a civil
ociety is only possible if authorities or groups therein cease to modify their
ctions and purposes to the requirements of the preservation of the civil
lationship. Such a civil war is the result of the collapse of political conditions.
war inside international political society would thus have to be preceded
the demise of civil statehood in some part of it.

A civil executive cannot enter into an arrangement that could lead it into
ar inside political society; nor could the commitments made by a civil
ecutive inside political society be the direct cause of a breakdown of its
ternal order. A disruptive consequence of this order could only result from
aplacable external pressure to fulfil ruinous cross-national commitments.
ut political governments have no interest in imposing structural breakdown
one another because this would diminish the extent of political society
ad increase the dangers of the international arena. Nor could they exert
ayielding pressure on one another to such hazardous effect. Political
lations, which exclude the possibility of war and depend on consent, can
aly include pressures that may be peaceably resisted. From an internal
andpoint a civil executive cannot drive its own polity to collapse in fulfil-
ent of an external commitment because, most obviously, in this dire
tremity it would lose domestic support and thus be deprived of the
apability to act. However, international political society is not a dreamer's
yll untroubled by practical difficulties. A civil executive must attend to
umerous domestic and cross-national stresses. In doing so it may expect
me assistance from other civil executives and may enter into exact commit-
ents in return. The civil relationship is never a paternal one and no political
overnment or combination of governments is under an obligation to provide
definite open-handed material support for another political government.
merit of political society is self-rule; so no element in political society can
endlessly protected from the consequences of its own follies nor can its
wn authority be removed into other hands. External political commitment

cannot in itself be a cause of the collapse of domestic civil order. But it mus
be true that the deterioration of an internal civil order (in panic or dissensio
or the pursuit of grandiose and inconsistent government programmes) ma
lead to the external assumption of obligations that cannot be met.

The status of a civil executive in international political society cannot ad
massively to its domestic power. It cannot in this context be a foreig
conqueror able to intimidate its own citizens by its international might. I
practical terms, the intergovernmental agreements of political society mor
often limit the scope of executive action than otherwise. Typically thes
agreements require an abandonment or reduction of particular tariffs o
taxes or borrowings. Among some affected citizens these constraints may b
felt as impositions, but they cannot be argued to be large increases i
executive power. The authority of such agreements derives from the politica
nature of their negotiation, in which reciprocal consent plays a central role
This kind of authority is not itself an accretion of executive power, thoug
it may add appreciably to the administrative complexity of executiv
responsibilities. However, a special situation may seem to be created b
cross-national organisations in political society. Many of the decisions of th
Council of Ministers of the European Community have the direct impact o
law in Community countries, and the members of the Council are member
of national governments, which may therefore be argued to have acquired
direct legislative authority otherwise constitutionally denied them. But th
Council of the European Community is not the instrument of any on
executive. Its actions are the product of laborious inter-executive negotiation
(sometimes involving parliamentary committees at the national level) i
which formal provisions for majority voting are substantially ignored i
favour of decision by unanimity. It may with some substance be argued tha
this process has effects that limit national legislatures because it produce
laws they cannot overturn. But this is not necessarily to be equated with a
increase in executive power, since an executive may have more difficulty i
moving the Council in a preferred direction than it is accustomed to in it
dealings with its own legislature. In a sense what has happened here is tha
a novel kind of cross-national legislative process has been superimposed o
more traditional national legislative process. The result is an unfamilia
structure of law-making. In any political setting the constraints on civi
authority are not static because civil statehood does not dictate any particula
national or cross-national structure of authority. The constraints on th
authority of the Council of the European Community (which are anywa
almost crippling) may thus be legitimately complemented by nationa
legislative involvement in executive negotiations in the Council or by mor
novel involvements on the part of the European Parliament. No arrangemen
peculiar to the affairs of political society can be such as to undermine the lin
between authority and constitutional limitations. But this is not a principl
that rules out constitutional novelty at any level.

Secrecy

It was previously suggested (chapter 3) that the executive's disposition to secrecy in international dealings might have the unfortunate effects of surreptiously extending the range of executive discretion, of tempting the executive to proceed unscrupulously, of limiting the information available to opposition groups and thereby encouraging executive folly, and of concealing foreign commitments of a potentially onerous nature.

In their usual domestic travails civil governments are apt to cultivate a measure of secrecy for familiar reasons: to conceal negotiating positions from domestic groups with whom they must deal; to give themselves some freedom to alter their positions without embarrassment to their supporters; to allow arguments to be conducted freely inside the executive; to confer on civil servants discretion to proffer alternative forms of advice without being drawn into public debate. A measure of secrecy for purposes like these may seem reasonable. If it may be reasonable to be secret domestically, then it may also be reasonable to be secret in dealings across traditional national boundaries inside international political society. There are no criteria of reasonableness that are particular to either category, since this distinction is a contingent not a substantive one. It obviously does not follow that executive attempts to maintain secrecy in political relations should be conceded. If it may be reasonable for an executive to conceal its positions from opposing parties in a set of negotiations, it may also be reasonable for these parties to try to find out what is being concealed. Secrecy that encourages argument inside an executive may also cripple equally legitimate argument outside an executive. The case against secrecy is in no way lost simply because there may be a case for secrecy. In all political circumstances an executive's own standards of secrecy are widely unacceptable. There will be an almost constant struggle between governments and groups and persons and institutions outside government over what reasonable secrecy may be taken to be. Actual executive secrecy is practised amid a constant argument over its validity. No new and compelling case for the reasonableness of secrecy enters into this interminable argument simply because more than one civil executive may be involved. If different national conventions of secrecy are awkwardly conjoined in cross-national political relations, so much the better. If otherwise secret information about the policies of one's own executive becomes available elsewhere in international political society, then one of the virtures of that society is thereby revealed. Similarly, domestic pressure on the boundaries of executive secrecy loses none of its legitimacy simply because the issues in question are of a cross-national character. Within political society there is no special foreign policy case for secrecy. If secrecy in the apparatus of the European Community cannot be readily penetrated by national legislatures, there is every reason to strengthen the European Parliament so that it may take up this cause. In general terms, uses of authority anywhere in political society are legitimated by the legal and structural limitations placed on them and by the political process from which they emerge. The attempted abridgement of this process by the excessive cultivation of secrecy by an executive or by a combination of executives strikes at the legitimating principle of open argument and enquiry. In any national or cross-national situation the case against secrecy is thus *prima facie* to be preferred.

Legislative involvement

Chapter 3 discussed the view that an executive's place in foreign relations should be controlled by the constant attentions of a legislature's specialist foreign affairs committee and by strict legislative priority in the ratification of treaties.

Treaties within political society come in two broad shapes: first, they may change the nature of government procedures; second, they may either require specific authoritative performances or, more commonly, they may place constraints on possible authoritative performances. In relation to the first of these categories, a political community always approaches anything in the nature of constitutional change with particular attention. In part this is a statement of fact. Given that civil authority is always constrained by known rules, it follows that widespread disregard of change in constitutional rules is a characteristic of a community that is not political. But there is also a powerful argument for particular care in constitutional matters. Political government is a product both of general rules and of consent. Rules could be thoroughly unpleasant: as an extreme example, there could be a rule of obedience to a particular ruler. Consent to the practical actions of civil governments in most concrete circumstances requires that numbers of citizens put up with some authoritative decisions that they find uncongenial. Over a medium period the total of such people is likely to comprise a large majority, because virtually all citizens consent to some government policies that they find personally disagreeable. The social conditions of this consent are complex, but its fundamental manifestation must be large-scale support for a particular constitutional order. What is done is accepted because of the way it is done and the way in which it may be undone. It is therefore a common feature of political communities that constitutional change requires special legislative (and sometimes other) procedures. Wherever cross-national authority in political society is exercised, or is going to be exercised, in a regularly allocative manner there is good reason why it should be constrained in a constitutional way by a treaty. But bringing about this state of affairs is likely to have some effects on the existing constitutions of the countries involved. Treaties having this consequence should be (and for the most part are) regarded as at least equal in importance to internal constitutional amendments and should therefore be subject to a process of ratification similar to, or the same as, that required for constitutional change. But their special status lies in their being new constitutional law not in their being treaties.

Similarly, the category of treaties requiring specific governmental performances, or forbearance from future possible performances, should be treated legislatively in much the same way as these performances, or constraints on future possible performances, would be were no treaties involved. In neither matter is it plausible to argue that cross-national political agreements should have anything less than the legislative attention usually accorded such issues in a purely domestic setting. There is no persuasive exception to this rule. Where the actions of some kind of cross-national executive are constitutionally removed, wholly or partially from the attentions of national legislatures then what has been lost at this level should be replaced by an equivalent competence on the part of an assembly at a cross-national level.

The same kind of principle applies in relation to legislative committee involvement in executive policy-making. Cross-national affairs conducted entirely within international political society are always substantive; no general questions of defence and security arise. So these affairs resolve themselves into matters of a constitutional or other kind. In this context there is no general category of foreign affairs policy-making, so a legislative foreign affairs committee has nothing to contribute as such. But legislative specialist committees in all other areas (in agriculture, finance, the arts, industry or whatever) have everything to contribute. The activities of such committees should in no way be bound by purely territorial considerations when the specific matters requiring their attention are of a cross-national character. And, again, any cross-national constitutional curtailment of the competence of national specialist committees in cross-national matters should be replaced by an equivalent competence on the part of the specialist committees of a cross-national assembly.

If a special foreign policy category is inappropriate to cross-national issues in political society, it must equally be the case that the executive has no legitimate claim to a structural monopoly of external–internal official linkages. The view that the state must be coherently represented internationally by a single authority collapses in the context of international political society. Here the individual state is not a contained territorial entity but a concentrated set of political relations penetrated by all kinds of cross-national connections. It does not struggle for life in a hostile setting from which fundamental threats to its existence proceed. Neither its citizens nor their parliamentarians have to subscribe to the myth that the state connects with other states only along a single, government controlled frontier. The involvement of legislative committees in investigations and discussions abroad; the participation of parliamentarians in cross-national assemblies; the direct election of representatives at cross-national levels: practices such as these are inherent to the nature of civil statehood. Civil executives are executives, not masters of states.

INTERNATIONAL ORGANISATION

Political society contains and engenders a host of official and unofficial enterprises. But it cannot itself be defined as an enterprise. It is a plurality of states. But the concept of civil statehood is not a territorial one. Inside a civil state authority does not concentrate power but attempts to limit it. Political power (that is, power qualified by civil statehood) is always decentralised in the sense that governments are constrained and diverted by law and custom, by the diversity of state authorities, by argument and competition for office, by the need to maintain popular support, by the social diversity in which large official decisions are invariably met by unforeseen consequences.

Many of the forces and interests with which a political government contends, and many of its own purposes, are of a cross-national character. Numerous organisations have been created that embody cross-national aspects of political rule. These organisational departures cannot be subsumed under some imagined grand design whose purpose is the creation of a territorial state to conform with the boundaries of the whole of political society. They do not fit into any clear pattern, actual or imagined. Such a pattern would anyway be entirely contrary to the nature of political society. To attempt to create a coherent territorial state coterminous with this society would be to attempt to reduce the notion of civil statehood to the level of a geographical space defined by an official boundary. To the moral and intellectual failings of such a conception must be added its practical deficiencies. The realisation of this immense figment would be the grossest imaginable cross-national official project, generating levels of opposition that could probably only be overcome by violence. This would be an enterprise to destroy international political society.

So cross-national organisation in political society is not, and cannot ever be conceived to be, a stage in the creation of one immense territorial state. Organisation is thus not an indeterminate and unstable admixture of two kinds of statehood, one a plurality and the other a unity. Political society exists in civil states. Cross-national organisation among them is an empirical investigation of the unterritorial aspects of this kind of statehood. All sorts of frictions and inconsistencies occur within and between these organisations. This is to be expected. The point is that no special kind of theory has to be manufactured to account for, or to prescribe for, cross-national political organisation. The plurality of diversely placed states is a structural fact of political society. Cross-national organisational departures are not replacements of this plurality but investigations of forms of the political state that arise from it. Existing states provide a firm base from which these advances may be made. And they ensure that consent is as fundamental to cross-national as to more familiar forms of political rule. But civil statehood itself is not the monopoly of territorial states; being general, it can just as legitimately be expressed in cross-national organisations and processes.

Traditional diplomacy

Diplomacy is an important institution of international political society because it exists; because the relations between civil governments can no more be held strictly within organisational frameworks than can be, or should be, the relations between civil governments and all the domestic groups and authorities with which they have dealings; because the flexibility of diplomacy provides an authoritative means of responding quickly to unusual alarms; because delicacy in arguments between governments is generally more necessary than in arguments at other levels, so that, for example, the traditional discretion of diplomacy may provide a necessary lubricant for the smooth working of more novel cross-national arrangements; because diversity, inconsistency and partial membership among cross-national organisations create the need for this authoritative traditional institution that can facilitate the conduct of public affairs throughout political society regardless of its piecemeal formal structure.

But diplomacy is as much subject to limitation as any other political institution. It is one means, among many others, of communication between authorities. It cannot claim to represent civil states in their entirety. It does not hold a monopoly of knowledge of the affairs of international political society. It has no right to undermine cross-national political structures or relations or to claim general priority among them.

The status of cross-national organisations in political society

Cross-nationally organised projects among governments do not exist on a different political plane from other kinds of governmental enterprises. They take cross-national shape because any other would be insufficient to the purposes governments have in mind. This is sensible but it does not confer a special status on them. Cross-national folly, incompetence or blind orthodoxy are no less reprehensible than their more usual domestic manifestations. The insulation of government projects from criticism is no part of the functions of any cross-national political organisation. A state that is conceived purely as an enterprise can never be a civil state because no legitimate defence against any kind of official rule within it is possible. Civil government is always bound by rules and by constitutional political process. This principle is as applicable at the cross-national level as at any other. Where cross-national projects begin to evade domestic constitutional rules and processes there is every reason to ensure the institution of similar constraints cross-nationally.

Citizens of international political society may relate to one another through numberless practices and enterprises. None of these relations is more than partial. As a whole, the citizens of political society are to be identified not in terms of their active relations but in their impersonal legal standing as individual citizens within the boundaries of civil statehood. Among the political aspects of this standing is that the conditions of the enterprises of governments (or any other kinds of enterprises) should be set out by known laws subject to open legislative repeal. Cross-national enterprises are no exception. If the relevant legislation is itself of a cross-national character, adjudicated by cross-national courts, so much the better for the experience of political society.

In a civil state rules set out the conditions of enterprises and are subject to known and open processes of repeal. The rules that establish the status of individual citizenship are not subject to repeal during the existence of the civil state. This status is in no sense an enterprise or mission or belief or practice. It is the requisite of practices and projects, whether they be national or cross-national. The preservation of this status is fundamental to the nature of civil statehood. The case for constitutional bills of rights is a strong one both nationally and cross-nationally. The specific structure of a civil state is secondary to the maintenance of civil statehood. The subjection of civil governments to cross-national judicial processes in international political society does not raise novel problems about the nature of civil statehood. This is a form of civil statehood.

The actions of civil governments are responses to perceptions of human needs and interests in the invariable circumstance of conflicting political demands for particular uses or non-uses of the authority of the state. A constitutional structure that cannot match authority with contending interests and with the practical problems to which they attach in such a way as to contribute to the long-term social equilibrium of political society is at best irrelevant and at worst damaging. This applies locally, nationally and cross-nationally. It is not a principle that substantiates any vast rational plan of government. And it is far from being an invariable recommendation to size. There is no point in grandiose schemes to create directly allocative organisations to deal with matters that do not require scale in their treatment or that would bring into intimate contact mutually abrasive interests best expressed locally and related to one another through diplomatic contact among separate authorities. Mutual adjustment among all levels of civil government is not necessarily a prelude to tight organisation.

International political society does not itself summon into existence organisations concerned with the deployment of large-scale instruments of violence because its interior relations do not include the possibility of war. Within political society, therefore, no traditional state-like stereotype fixes the possibilities of structural innovation. Cross-national organisation in political society is not subject to some imagined internal logic that establishes the structural concentration of all the known functions of rule, including defence, as the ultimate structural achievement of statehood. Civil statehood is a qualification of structures. It is not itself a structure. Civility is not an *a priori* design but the essential conditions of variety, experiment, criticism and enquiry. This is what civil rationality means.

The Pursuit of National Interest

The relevant passages in chapter 3 distinguished four senses of national interest. It is a simple matter to review these from a civil standpoint.

As geography

Once the relationship between geography and the civil state is recognised to o be a contingent one, the link between interests and geographical circumstances in international political society becomes wholly unremarkable. Governing is a practical activity and every government, local or otherwise, operates in a geographical setting. A government of a highly urbanised population is subject to pressures distinct from those that a government of a predominantly rural population is likely to experience; so in their relations, at whatever level, two such governments are likely to press different viewpoints on each other. A government whose constituents endure an intemperate climate is likely to have different kinds of practical concerns from those of a government of a population that is not so afflicted, simply because different climates tend to evoke different agricultural, industrial and social responses. In a diverse civil state, which is not dominated by one industry or by one pattern of social life, the pressures on government will not mysteriously fuse into a single interest superior to all its constituent parts. It is likely that some unsteady kind of balance will be struck among interests by a particular national government at a particular time and the outcome will be particular kinds of governmental responses to cross-national problems. The place of geography in this process is obvious but not fundamental. Nor is it invariable.

As defence

War, actual or possible, has no role in political relations as such. Situation, in a strategic sense, only touches importantly on political relations when a state like Finland is barred from full involvement in political society because of its close contact with an anti-political state or with anti-political forces. Strategic situation thus only becomes vital at the margins (which need not be spatial in nature) of international political society, where it may force on some governments constrained modes of conducting their cross-national affairs. But it follows that where strategic situation overrides other considerations it is because of pressures from outside political society, and actions so determined cannot be political in nature.

As the pursuit of wealth

Most civil governments, at whatever level, are often concerned about the material prosperity, or lack of it, of their constituents. This is what their constituents most generally become agitated about. Also the scale of particular government performances is related to overall levels of national income; in the long term, what a government spends cannot also be spent on private consumption. This is true, but nothing whatever follows in terms of an understanding of national interest conceived as the dominating economic force of specific government policies. It will always be the case that much argument will turn on what government actions are most likely to increase national wealth; or, just as significant, whether any positive acts of government ment can have this effect. National wealth is not a single object that can be acted upon by clear and direct measures. It comprises large numbers of wealth creating activities, many linked together in cross-national enterprises or chains of production and exchange. A government action that brings benefits to one part of this complex system may very well impede another part. Levels of wealth and levels of trade are closely linked; but increasing international trade can never, by definition, be an exclusively national interest. Official efforts to increase international trade most often take the form of mutually agreed reductions in government interference in the cross national movement of goods and resources; so here a national interest is really an international interest that limits the use of instruments of national government. Where a country is in balance of payments difficulties its government may be urged by some interest to ignore international obligations and impose direct controls on imports; but the more efficient sections of the economy will recommend that this pressure be resisted. When there is severe inflation its abatement will seem widely desirable; but complete national consensus on the implementation of specific programmes to this end is highly unlikely. The notion of national interest is an empty one unless it conveys something determinate about actual policies. It does no such thing.

Engagement with cross-nationally related economic problems is common among the governments of international political society and it is the source of many intricate arguments among official and quasi-official authorities. What governments actually do, individually or jointly, is an aspect of this cross-national dialogue. It is also an effect of what they each conceive to be possible in their individual circumstances. It is never the revealed outcome of mystic communion with an entity publicly described as the national interest.

As core values

In the civil state the core values on which individual men and women build their lives differ. This is the merit of the civil state. The central place of individual citizenship in the civil state is a condition of values; however active some citizens may be in public affairs, citizenship itself is not a value in the sense of something that dictates positive lines of authoritative action. It is a space that the individual fills with his own values and these may have no bearing on official performances. Its relationship to specific kinds of non performances is likely to be more precise. In civil states there will from time to time be movements of opinion (about the merits of different forms of education for example). These are movements of opinion, not core values, and it often happens that such tides turn quickly. Within international political society the standing of individuality is generally recognised. No fundamental challenge to it can come from this source. It follows that in the relations of political society this common status of individuality, which is in no way national, dictates nothing in terms of exact government action.

The national interest as a symbol

In each of the above categories it quickly emerges that national interest is empty of specific substance. In international political society it remains a term much used by governments and by those pressing particular schemes on governments. One is thus driven to conclude that in this context it is a symbol. It is futile to attempt to ascribe a determinate meaning to a symbol because if it had a determinate meaning it would cease to be symbolic. One can only enquire into its functions. National interest frequently appears in arguments to denote that a suggested course of action will bring rewards to many besides its immediate proponents and principal beneficiaries; while critics of government policies may use it to suggest that the interests to which authority is responding are narrow and selfish. On the other hand, it may be used to call upon those severely treated by authority to bear their discomforts quietly for the greater good. In referring to their international dealings governments can use it to signify their belief in the merits of multilateral as well as of unilateral undertakings. In another common usage it simply signals that a balance of interests has been struck and a decision made, whether in domestic or in cross-national affairs. And so on. It is a term that derives what meaning it has from the circumstances in which it is used. Occasionally it may refer to a wide consensus; more often it signifies that attempts are being made to create a consensus. Its general function in political affairs is to mark and encourage a concern with the large scale and the long term. It is a harmless expression when qualified by civil statehood.

STRENGTH

The application or threatened application of military force has no legitimate place in political society. But international political relations are not conducted by etiolated contemplatives. The unevenly distributed strength of governments must be a substantive part of their contacts with one another. Different national authorities are acutely aware of the facts of their differing capabilities.

Effects of strength

A particular internal use of authority may be widely felt abroad. A change of levels of personal taxation in the United States tends to have a wide overseas impact through its balance of payments effects; a similar change in Denmark has relatively little external significance. The authority of a government in a large and strong national economy generally ensures that its actions will have a substantial effect in the cross-national economy of political society. The effectiveness of traditional instruments of foreign policy is likewise related to strength. A threat by the United States to raise its tariffs to obtain a change in Japanese exchange rate policy is far more powerful than a similar threat issued by, say, a Canadian government. Similarly, the consequences for prospective joint governmental enterprises of the withdrawal of a possible partner usually varies according to its strength. The refusal of a French government to participate in a new international monetary arrangement is unlikely to be crippling if the remaining partners include the United States and the German Federal Republic.

Strength not an analogue of military power

Strength plays an obvious, though highly variable, role in the official relations of political society. But it is in no sense to be equated with, nor is it an analogue of, military power.

Cross-national influence in political society almost invariably seems to boil down to uses or possible uses of authority to influence economic events. But authority used in the economy rarely obtains the specific ends that governments wish for, regardless of whether these ends are internal or external or both. They are not the same as military objectives, which can, by definition, be achieved given superior force and generalship. And the difficulties of life in the cross-national economy of political society are not somehow thrust on states in some quasi-military way. A government may use the instruments of state to stop trade; to confiscate foreign capital; to suspend markets in its currency. A siege economy can be created by such measures. But a state used by a civil government in this way would also create relative poverty among its citizens. Remaining a part of the cross-national economy may entail exposure to the effects of foreign uses of authority, but it is exposure in terms of material advantage. This is in no way analogous to being on the weaker side in a war.

Authoritative action bearing on the cross-national economy is generally constrained by continuous negotiation in the context of formal and informal rules (among which is the rule of continuous negotiation). These rules, often indistinct, are seldom to the clear disadvantage of strong governments. This is unremarkable. But in the cross-national economy it is open to any relatively weak state, in the last resort, to opt out of foreign influence if it is prepared to bear the economic cost. Military force is in no way similar to political authority because it positively requires the compliance of the weaker with the will of the stronger, regardless of general rules, and surrender is the only way out of a war that is going badly. Decentralised authority in the cross-national economy is wholly in keeping with the nature of political order. But decentralised authorities are to be expected to bring pressures to bear on one another. This is a merit of decentralised authority. Centralised authority is a dangerous condition of political rule because (*inter alia*) of the inattention to balance among a wide variety of interests that it is prone to encourage. This is why economic dominance on the part of one state (whether it be the United States or any other) in political society is open to legitimate suspicion. But there is nothing intrinsic to the nature of the cross-national economy of political society that requires that the multiplicity of its states should also constitute a multiplicity of relatively weak authorities. It is a peculiarity of this society that states can join to create a potentially strong economic authority such as the European Community that has no standing as a military force.

There are genuine differences in the interests of political governments, which are not to be ascribed to ill-will or to a drive to hegemony. If all political governments had the same concerns, political society would not be the diverse entity that it is. Policy disjunctions among governments are normal. Governments do not expect to have intimate control over the policies of other governments. This is one of the reasons why military force has no place in political relations. If uniformity is not expected or required in the first place, there can be no motivation to enforce it.

MORALITY AND FOREIGN POLICY

No moral problems specific to international political society

International political society is not a moral unity in the sense that moral feelings always attach to the same things in the same way. The death penalty may be widely felt to be a moral outrage in one jurisdiction whereas in another it may be felt to be both a necessary and a just form of punishment. It is essentially the notion and practice of legality that is the mark of political society: no penalty is just that is also arbitrary; rulers are subject to all the laws that they make; law is a condition of individual life not its pattern; and so on. In relations between rulers and ruled, civil statehood categorically requires common regard for legality. The constitutional and political constraints on civil governments can make their relations with one another in international political society extremely complicated. But there are no moral problems specific to these relations. The subversion of legality anywhere in political society cannot be their outcome. This does not mean that the civil statesman does not face moral problems. He does, just as all individuals do. But the moral problems the statesman faces in international political society are no different in kind from the moral problems he faces at home. All these problems occur within the conditions of civil statehood.

International political society is not a system of sharply distinguished states whose individual strength can only be controlled by a balance of power process among their national propensities to inflict violent harm on one another. In his dealings in international political society the civil statesman is not required to adhere to amoral rules generated by a system founded on the military capabilities of competing sovereigns. He is forced into no moral quandary by the existence of a sharp distinction between a legally ordered domestic environment and a lawless international environment whose order is founded on force. All the states of international political society are legally ordered. Together they must therefore comprise a lawful society. The impulses that motivate the statesman in his cross-national associations are likely to be practical and to arise from problems that are neither wholly national nor wholly international. The governments with which he associates will all be subject to the same conception of legality. They may agree or disagree, their enterprises may prosper or founder, but they cannot draw one another into relations unconditioned by civil statehood. The rules engendered by cross-national relations in international political society cannot contradict legality.

In political society some of the actions of a particular government may affect citizens who are not also its constituents. This does not create a relationship whereby the moral assumptions of authorities are imposed on foreigners for whom they are alien. The otherwise domestic economic policies of a government of the German Federal Republic that are deemed to hinder economic recovery in Britain are not in some way foreign impositions on Britain. First, no legitimate interest in political society goes unrepresented. British governments can and do argue the case for particular policies with governments of the GFR. Second, no self-governing part of political society is without choice. In the present example, Britain may have become particularly exposed to the impact of West German economic policies through its own industrial inefficiency, excessive inflation and the like. These are not foreign impositions on Britain but the consequences of large numbers of domestic choices. Third, no part of political society has a legitimate interest in the misgovernment of another part. Governments are under a reciprocal obligation to consider the interests of all those affected by their actions. But this does not include an obligation to behave foolishly at the behest of foreign authorities. Stupid behaviour by a West German government is not rendered less stupid because a British government may have urged it. Fourth, no domestic action of a foreign civil government can force a neglect of legality inside Britain. The internal impact of authoritative behaviour conditioned by constitutional limitations, by the principles of

:gality and by an effective political process cannot be such as would compel
1e neglect of these considerations abroad.

Relations wholly within the boundaries of international political society
annot draw a government into the moral inconsistencies of foreign crusades
:quiring immoral actions to be undertaken for supposedly moral ends.
here is nothing to crusade about. If all states in political society are civil
:ates there can be no moral end that they could wish to impose on one
nother. Civil statehood is the condition of self-rule; it cannot also be used to
ndermine self-rule.

Nationally and cross-nationally, political statesmen are constantly trading
ff possible benefits in one direction against actual benefits in another. The
rguments that infuse this process will often be charged with strong feeling.
ut this does not mean that the statesman is confronted by choices between
·hat is moral and what is immoral. What is practicable in the context of
1stained legality and of limited representative government cannot also be
eeply immoral. Again, these are conditions of moral choice; that is, between
ifferent conceptions of what is moral.

INTERVENTION

Io intervention in practices

1side international political society there can be no government intervention
1 violent conflict abroad, whether it be of an internal or a cross-national
ature. Political conflict occurs within the terms of political relations and
1ese cannot include violence. Nor can there be government intervention of
ny kind in the determination of the substantive nature of practices (art,
hilosophy, religion, chess and such), since a virtue of the civil state is its
eparation of official projects from the conduct of practices.[17] In the latter
ense political society is one state and there can be no such thing as legitimate
itervention anywhere in it. Laws may set some conditions of practices (the
iinimum age of marriage for example), and in this respect there may be
ainor differences among jurisdictions; but in no political jurisdiction can
1e substance of a practice be a matter of authoritative direction (artists
annot be required to paint certain kinds of pictures, white people cannot
·e directed to marry only other white people). It follows that cross-national
ules on human rights, supported by appropriate cross-national judicial
·rocedures, are not interventions in political society but a part of the sub-
tance of civil statehood.

itervention and enterprises

Jon-official projects (making, selling, buying, lending, borrowing, building)
egularly cross traditional national boundaries in political society. It is not

the function of the civil state to hold projects within particular territories, but to provide the conditions of law within which projects may be undertaken. The national origin of a project is a matter of no consequence. The central requirement of civil statehood is simply that all projects be equally subject to the law of the jurisdiction within which they operate. If certain enterprises prosper in one jurisdiction more than in another, so much the better for the overall experience of political society. A problem of intervention may seem to arise when projects are subject to domestic laws (relating, say, to taxation) in respect of their foreign operations. In this sort of case it may appear that one jurisdiction is intervening in another. In reality this is a complication, not an intervention. Those engaged in an enterprise in more than one jurisdiction may adjust their arrangements accordingly. One jurisdiction is not subverting another if enterprises are advantaged or disadvantaged by this sort of overlapping. It is open to authorities in overlapping jurisdictions to coordinate their rules or even to create a single jurisdiction appropriate to the class of activities in question.

Enterprises of governments may sometimes seem to be constrained by the actions of foreign governments or by cross-national authorities. The exchange rate policy of a government may be subject to disturbance resulting from the actions of other governments; it may be directly impeded by prior international agreement in the context of an international organisation; and then there are always the rapid movements of cross-national currency markets to contend with. This may be a difficult setting but it is one in which intervention has no distinctive meaning. The civil state cannot be claimed to create circumstances of complete freedom for official projects. Governments must expect to be limited by bodies of law, by other authorities and by the practical nature of a diverse society in which official projects may go as badly awry as any other. Whether a government is limited by a diverse domestic society or by an even more diverse cross-national society, by domestic rules and authorities or cross-national rules and authorities, is largely contingent on the nature of the projects it may choose to undertake.

Intervention as pathology

Intervention originating within political society, if it is to be anything other than a tautological reference to the distinguishing characteristics of this society, must denote cross-national action having the potential to disorder the civil state; that is, intervention has to refer to effects destructive of law, civil authority, social variety, or of self-government. Now it may happen from time to time that a government agency may act cross-nationally in a way that might reasonably be called interventionary. But when this happens an aberration occurs that is not only stupid but almost certainly illegal as well. In other words, intervention is not politically possible. It can only take place because of a loss of commitment to civil statehood.

ECONOMIC PROBLEMS

International political society is an asset to its members. It is a support of political life in that it is a source of much of the variety that gives the notion of the political its meaning. While often perplexing and constraining to governments, it also provides the peaceful external circumstances of domestic political self-rule. It is full of movement and stress, but it is also a condition of civilised life. Its cross-national economy is likewise a stressful asset to its members. It provides large markets in which economies of scale may be obtained and assets and expertise rapidly transmitted. It has a multiplicity of currencies (including a cross-national one supplied by the IMF). It is not centrally directed and is capable of a variety of spontaneous adaptations to the problems it engenders and encounters. As a whole it deeply penetrates the economies of its member countries, whose governments are constantly absorbed in problems of economic policy with many cross-national aspects. Three broad kinds of interdependence are created by this economy. First, there is the interdependence of wealth-creation through trade and cross-national forms of production. Second, there is the responsiveness of economic events in one country to those in another (to changes in tastes or incomes or to technical breakthroughs). Third, there is interdependence in terms of the high impact that actions of governments are apt to have on one another. Interdependence is clearly not to be taken to mean identity of specific interests. A government practising some form of discrimination against imports is likely to obtain an advantage for its national economy from countries whose governments are less discriminatory. Governments of countries in balance of payments surplus are often able to resist external pressure from deficit countries to allow the upward revaluation of their currencies. Governments enduring high rates of inflation are likely to view the policy priorities of governments of low inflation countries in a different order than they do themselves. And so on. Yet such is the interlocking nature of the economy of political society that its well-being as a whole is intimately related to the well-being of its parts. Uses of governmental authority that secure national advantage at direct cost to other countries are likely to provoke retaliations. And rounds of retaliation must quickly enfeeble all the national parts of the whole. Governments are thus placed in the familiar political predicament of operating in an environment productive of large numbers of arguments and policy conflicts while at the same time having to care for the well-being of this environment as an entity. The difficulties of this situation can be exaggerated.

Political society creates its economy

Its economy does not create international political society, political society creates its economy. This is true in a logical sense. Mutual suspicions of the possibility of military attack could not coexist with industrial interlocking among national economies. Similarly, the pursuit of national autonomy by governments given to the untrammelled and arbitrary use of economic sovereignty would prevent the evolution of large cross-national markets in capital and expertise. The uneven distribution of authority among governments in an intimately integrated cross-national economy would prove widely unacceptable were not strong government assumed to be committed to the conduct of their economic affairs in open conditions of critical observation from all quarters and to be amenable to rational argument at cross-national levels. The creation of potentially authoritative international economic organisations would also be impossible were they seen to be available for the subversion of the principles of self-government and the rule of law. Similarly, the provision of assistance to countries in balance of payments deficit could not be a routine feature of the cross-national economy were it to be equated with submission to irrational alien domination. Direct investment would be unlikely to flow massively across traditional national frontiers were these to represent fundamental distinctions between the existence of the rule of law and its non-existence. All the conditions of the growth of the cross-national economy are primarily political in nature. No economy could *ab initio* call these conditions into being. They depend on the prior evolution of the notion of civil statehood and of its wide acceptance. The political is the necessary condition of the existence of the economic; not the reverse.

It is also historically true that political society creates its economy. The notion of the civil state clearly has distant origins. Here our concern is with a cross-national economy that is novel in its combination of qualities: in its unexampled size; in the number of large currencies in which its business is conducted; in the scale of the cross-national markets in these currencies and the magnitude of the borrowings facilitated therein; in the numbers of economic structures, official and non-official, crossing national boundaries; in the complexity of the official and unofficial observations, arguments, contacts and understandings running through it; in the number and variety of governments engaged in the affairs of this economy and the freedom of the relations between them. The combined features of the economy of international political society mark it as an entity emerging from the second world war. Four conditions facilitated its birth and early growth. First, economic strength was almost entirely located in the United States, a constitutional country with decentralised institutions of government and an economy unamenable to close governmental direction. Second, the construction of large cross-national economic organisations was begun during the war principally by the United States and Britain, two intimately related political countries that conducted their economic arguments in a cultural and strategic setting that precluded anything in the nature of military hostility between them. Third, those territories of the principal enemy states falling to western occupation rapidly resumed self-government along constitutional lines and were major beneficiaries of the cross-national economy. Fourth, the substantial international aid provided to many countries by the United States in the immediate postwar period, though not unaccompanied by policy pressures, was not conditional upon specific internal governmental performances among recipients. These conditions grew from the existence of a link between a political form of domestic rule and an open pattern of relations among states. In this setting an economy could develop unhindered by, and unproductive of, war-like hostility between governments.

In a fundamental sense the priority of the political simplifies the problems of the cross-national economy. The maintenance of political forms of rule is the primary condition of its existence and of its capacity to develop and adapt, organisationally and otherwise. Traditional concerns with the maintenance of individual liberty thus retain their primacy.

Obligation and the economy

That governments should have economic interests and that these should periodically conflict is no novelty. But an interest cannot be separated from the setting that gives rise to it and in which it is expressed. The environment of interests, so far as the present chapter is concerned, is international political society. This is a kind of common civil statehood that provides the external conditions of peaceful self-government for citizens within it. An obligation to maintain political society is therefore shared among its member governments. The fulfilment of this obligation does not guarantee that the economy of political society will be free of disturbance or that it will always grow. But political society is not itself a joint enterprise to get richer. It is a way of conducting affairs that is open to new ideas and to the creation of new structures, yet that is also inherently resistant to the imposition of gradiose schemes on governments or on individuals. Governmental regulation of the cross-national economy is always likely to be partial, much given to policy disjunctions of all sorts. But it is flexible and spontaneous as well, and these qualities could not be contained in massively coherent plans. Given the common obligation to the maintenance of political society it follows that governments, particularly strong governments, should be attentive to the foreign effects of their policies. Similarly, economic support between governments derives its proper motivation not from identity of policies or from mutual admiration or from the desire to exert influence abroad but from the obligation to maintain the political manner of conducting affairs whether these be national or cross-national.

The language of economic relations

The political denotes a qualification; it does not describe some overarching rational principle or edifice. A large variety of rational discourses exist, and can only exist, on the foundations of civil statehood. It can thus be accepted in political society that economic rationality is not to be subsumed under some other kind of rationality. But economic rationality is not one abstract formula, since human behaviour is an intrinsic part of it; nor is it a totally distinct language, or category of relations, upon which extraneous conditions and purposes can have no bearing. It is an arena of open action and discourse to whose problems there is no coherent *a priori* non-economic solution. It is because the political outlook exists that economic rationality can continuously develop. Political governments are to be expected to be variously active in attempting to regulate economic affairs and in organising particular economic enterprises: this is so because, among many other factors, the economy generates structural problems (technological unemployment) and distributional problems (regional poverty) to which representative authorities must be sensitive; and because many governments may believe official organisation to be best suited to overseeing and, perhaps, supporting some specific economic projects for social or other reasons. The plurality of states in political society ensures that government enterprises take place on a variety of scales in almost all the different sectors of economic activity. The open discourse of the rational tradition of economic thinking ensures that the actions and arguments of governments are always subject to comparative criticism in an international language. The view of, say, a French government on agricultural policy is subject to sceptical examination in a community of economists stretching far beyond the frontiers of France. And the existence of a massive cross-national economy ensures that individual governments are subject to many economic criteria of a practical kind that they cannot manipulate. A nationalised motor company that ignores purely economic criteria of efficiency will either have to contract because of declining cross-national demand for its relatively expensive products, or it will have to pay its employees less than foreign wage-rates in order to keep its prices down, or it will be obliged to make constant inroads into public funds; but it will not be possible for its government to manipulate cross-national markets or the cross-national community of expert critics and enquirers so as to obviate or conceal the nature of these choices. Neither the language of economic relations nor many practical economic constraints are subject to the apparent regulation of one government. They must in this sense be objective. At the same time (though it clearly cannot infallibly yield acceptable answers to economic problems) the discursive language of economic rationality constitutes the indispensable medium of cross-national communication and authoritative decision among the self-governing components of political society's statehood. The innumerable forms of official cross-national coordination, agreement and organisation, which are a distinguishing mark of the economy of political society, would be impossible were they not all immersed in a language that can never be available to serve the exclusive purposes of a single government or movement.

The state not an exclusive enterprise

The historic emergence of much of the economic apparatus of the state (as chief tax-gatherer, as monopoly supplier of legal tender) can be convincingly explained in terms of the requirements of rulers to finance their costly military enterprises against one another.[18] The state came to be the dominant form of rule largely because it was better at providing for such activities than were its alternatives. But military conflict has no place inside international political society. So in this society the argument that the traditional state should always be available to provide each government with monopoly economic powers is a weak one. In terms of political society there is no compelling reason why properly accountable cross-national organisations should not acquire tax-gathering capabilities; or why new cross-national currencies should not be created; or why two or more currencies should not become legal tender within any one state.[19] In the economic language of political society there may be arguments against arrangements of these kinds. But there can be no compelling non-economic case based on the imperative requirements of the competitive military enterprises of rulers in political society. The propensities of governments to create and operate domestic monopolies are in small part offset by the inherent tendency of the cross-national economy to resist designs of a governmentally monopolistic kind. The structural penetration of this economy into national economies raises no fundamental questions about the nature of civil statehood. It does tend to call into question received assumptions about the use of the state as an exclusive enterprise of national government. But this is not a challenge to statehood because it is wholly intrinsic to civil society that the directing role of governments should be open to perpetual inquiry and dissent.

CONCLUSIONS

1. The third chapter's issues of foreign policy have now been reviewed wholly within the terms of the international society of civil states. In this context these issues are emptied of peculiarity. They are not foreign. No principles are applicable to them, or occur in them, that do not also occur inside individual civil states.

2. The plurality of states in political society establishes no categorical constraints on cross-national enterprises and organisations that are not also categorical constraints resulting from the acceptance of the priority of civil statehood. The plurality of states creates problems but not problems of principle.

3. Political society is an ideal society. This means that it will always abound in arguments and in difficulties without single determinate solutions.

CHAPTER 8

Outside Political Society: The Anti-political State[20]

This enquiry now addresses itself to the environment of the society of civil states. It does so from inside civil society. There can be no question of its shaking off, or pretending to shake off, its origin in civil conditions. It is concerned with a civil appreciation of foreign policy, not with inventing an abstract formula. Civility's international setting must comprise states from which civil statehood is absent. This is a negative categorisation. It contains no supposition of any element of coherence in the category as a whole. Of the many special cases in this category the most clear from the civil viewpoint must be those wherein the civil relationship is positively, explicity and effectively rejected. These can be called anti-political states.

ANTI-POLITICAL PROPENSITIES

From within the civil relationship it must be possible to distinguish propensities to reject the conditions of civil statehood. It may well be that in some degree these propensities from time to time figure in the individual lives of almost all citizens. In an anti-political state they are integrated into a massive structure of doctrine and power. However formidable such a state becomes, its character as a state can be distinguished not in its own preferred terms but in terms of the civil relationship of whose explicit denial it is a product. This method of approaching part of the environment of civil statehood avoids exclusive concentration on purely geographical demarcations between states. If the boundary of civil statehood is conceived as a distinction of propensities, then it is one that may feature in human relations within any given civil state as well as in the relations between civil states and states that reject the conditions of civil rule.

The domination of abstraction

Politics, the word, has no place in this enquiry because it does not refer to any specific action, theory or structure. Instead, the qualifying term 'political'

s used and it is taken to distinguish those public projects, proposals,
rguments, institutions, groups and organisations that subject themselves to
ivil conditions. These conditions maintain the priority of the impersonal
elationship between citizens in terms of rules over their more intimate
elationships in projects, quarrels, practices, organisations and associations.
Civil statehood is not abstract though it is general. Knowledge of the
onditions of civil rule is easily come by. It does not confer the gift of
rophecy. It is not a guide-book to the ramifications of civil society nor is it a
ictionary of its language. The maintenance of the civil relationship requires
he political qualification of the doctrines that citizens espouse as well as of
heir actions. The priority of civil conditions is in effect a standing denial of
laims to certainty in public matters. In political society all abstractions are
artial and no abstraction (reason, welfare, nationality, the public good,
rder, duty, national interest) can claim immunity from argument over its
ature or its supposed interpretation in action. Civil statehood is not a
efinition of a society. It is the necessary and sufficient condition of open,
iverse and changing social relations.

The propensity to arrange abstractions in coherent systems (as in species
f marxism and national socialism) claiming to be totally explanatory of
uman relations and individual consciousness is one that will neither under-
tand nor readily endure political qualification. Clashes between adherents
f different abstract worlds are likely to be deeply resistant to processes of
onstant mutual adjustment in the context of common impersonal conditions.
And disagreements among those otherwise conceiving themselves to be
ined in unqualified habitation of one abstract world must become mutual
uspicions of heresy. The consequence of heresy is likely to be total separation,
chism, or, where possible, the imposition of orthodoxy by the use of power.
n a state without statehood the latter course may well be available because
edication to an ordered system of social abstractions itself encourages and
ustifies absolute rule. Abstract cohesion establishes the norm of practical
ohesion, and practical cohesion justifies power in pronouncing the orthodox
nterpretation of events and situations that might otherwise be a source of
ncoherence. The supposed imperative of solidarity made its inevitable
ontribution to the absolutisms of Stalin and Hitler and others. And a state
uled in a language deriving all its general terms (duty, order, justice) from a
otal system of abstract categories (relations of production, dialectic,
istorical consciousness, racial consciousness) must be anti-political. Such a
tate cannot create authority constraining to power because there can be no
uthority independent of ideology and ideology is at the service of power.
ower justified wholly in terms of abstractions acquires the metaphysical
tanding of unchallengeable rectitude. This does not mean that an anti-
olitical leadership obtaining possession of a state is thereby spared the need
o exercise cunning to secure its position. But nothing independent of power
an actively limit the anti-political ruler. Statehood as autonomous constraint

disappears, partly because a source of its validity in practical affairs is
acceptance of the fact of human fallibility and partiality, and the purely
abstract can be neither fallible nor partial.

A widespread propensity to accept a completely explanatory system of
abstractions puts a highly adaptable legitimating device into the hands of
leaders. An officially supervised abstract frame of social reference cuts off
the possibility of open and legitimate independent criticism which is uncongenial to power. Arguments drawing on exterior sources of inspiration
whether practical or theoretical, must by abstract definition be irrational
and therefore inadmissible. The absence of independent bases of criticism
means that official language, exercising a monopoly of public discourse, is
completely freed from exterior moral or other criteria and can be bent to
explain and justify virtually any use of power. No previous contract, duty or
traditional value need be allowed to contradict correctly interpreted historical
purposes. An absolute duty to support one use of anti-political power in a
possessed state can be quickly transmuted into an equally absolute duty to
support its reversal. Abstraction of this order places only one limitation on
leaders: they are committed to conflict. If order is perceived as social and
ideological coherence, then that which does not cohere must be ideologically
hostile. Order itself cannot be seen to be variety maintained by tolerance,
argument, adjustment, open legislative and judicial process.

Citizenship equated with identity

Civil statehood does not require unity. The civil relationship is not one of
community of belief or enterprise or practice or habit. A civil society contains
communities; it is not itself a community. Citizens subscribing by way of
political qualification of their pursuits to the maintenance of civil statehood
do not have to be of the same colour, speak the same language, share the
same social customs, subscribe to the same religion, be active in public affairs,
identify with a particular nation, clan, class or profession. Political citizens
are disposed to be polite to one another because, though the civil relationship
is entirely impersonal, it is inspired by a regard for individuality. Citizens are
under no obligation to support public or private enterprises of any kind.
If the mechanisms of a particular state are used to the benefit of the individual
citizen he is in no way obliged to be humbly grateful or to support any group
or government claiming to be the legislative initiator of this beneficence.
A citizen who receives a state education or is kept alive by a state hospital is
under no obligation to subscribe to doctrines stressing the desirability of state
education or state medicine.

The equation of citizenship with identity is anti-political. A movement or
doctrine that would require all citizens of a state to be of one nationality or
one colour or one class or one religion or one anything makes a fundamental
definition of citizenship out of what in a political society is itself simply

ualified by citizenship. The fulfilment of anti-political criteria of citizenship
aay require the impossible (a change of ancestry) or the immoral (a change of
elief) or it may justify the use of violence (the forcible transformation of the
ndividual into a member of the proletariat). In all circumstances anti-
olitical criteria transform what is irrelevant to citizenship in a civil society
nto the defining characteristic of membership of the anti-political state. The
ubject of such a state cannot subscribe to the maintenance of general
onditions of individuality but must conform to official criteria that pattern it.
n these circumstances equality means common identity within an officially
efined class, race or belief. To exclude oneself, or to be excluded, from this
lentity is to become an enemy of the state.

he state as project

he civil state may be conceived to comprise two components: first, the
onditions of enterprises and practices; second, the apparatus and processes
hereby official projects are undertaken. The civil state as a project (to obtain
ull employment, provide medical care, alleviate poverty, run postal services)
an never escape the civil state as general conditions. These conditions are
ot static but they always have priority. All the projects of the state are open
o continual debate about their structure and their particular operations and
bout whether they should be undertaken at all. The way in which a given
vil state organises provision for, say, medical care is subject to constant
isputes, among which comparisons with other civil states will figure
rominently. Whether the state as a medical provider should dominate other
inds of health provision will also be argued about. But what is not arguable
a a civil state is that the state as an active project in the matter of medical
are (or anything else) may therefore exclude itself from the general conditions
f the civil relationship. The mentally disturbed are to be as legally protected
om abuse in state hospitals as in private hospitals. In undertaking a project,
owever desirable it may be, the state and its agents do not escape the civil
rder of statehood.

The civil state undertakes projects; but it is also the prior general conditions
f projects. If a state is treated purely as an instrumental mechanism, the
teans to achieve some wholly imperative social purpose, then it becomes
self the antithesis of the political qualification. Where some abstract entity
class, a race or a nation) is officially held to be the central reality of social
elations, then the state must become that entity's instrument. The state, in
is conception, is simply a superstructure that is given meaning only by the
urposes to which it is put. It becomes a massive social project. It cannot
nbody in itself any constraints on the programmes required by the 'real'
1aracter of society. A movement with an unqualified propensity to claim to
nbody this character which seizes the state must attempt to transform it into
s instrument. Such a movement cannot also subject itself to the state

conceived as prior general conditions. The state treated in this way is simp
a mechanism given its meaning by its purpose, which is that of the moveme
to which it falls victim. Such a state can know no prior impediments. Leg
and constitutional processes must become no less instrumental than burea
cracies and railways. The law thus becomes 'class' law or 'race' law ar
law-making becomes the pursuit of the programmes specified by anti-politic
leaders. Rules are subsumed under the project. The agents of the state are r
more subject to prior conditions to their enterprises than is the moveme
from which they claim to draw their inspiration. The less autonomous tl
state the more arrogant it becomes.

ANTI-POLITICAL STATES

The propensities to refer policies to large coagulations of doctrine or
inflate a sense of social identity into a central principle of statehood or
become so absorbed in grand programmes of state action as to be dismissi
of prior constraints are all too familiar. In excess they must destroy the ci
relationship. No civil state is free of them but normally they are held in chec
The ubiquitous critical dialogues of political society are conducive to
general mood of scepticism towards doctrinaire assertiveness and tl
pervasiveness of this mood is apt to induce acceptance of the political quali
cation in all but the most fanatical. The civil state invariably sets authori
against power, so those given to anti-political excess who attain office a
eventually baulked by the state itself. The civil relationship, being entire
impersonal, is the bedrock of a society comprising an endless variety
communities, projects and practices, and in this diverse society the proce
of gaining widespread support for policies and personalities is one th
emphasises the habit of moderation and compromise. The laws of the civ
state are really sets of general conditions that, within any given jurisdictio
admit no exceptions; so defence of legality is a standing denial of all clair
to exceptional extra-legal status based on the supposed inferiority of civ
statehood to ideological, racial, religious or other principles of soci
dynamics.

The anti-political state has no existence of its own. It does not set itse
against power but serves it. It is wholly the victim of orchestrated anti-politic
propensities. It is totally incapable of providing the conditions of fre
individuality, so the habits of tolerance, compromise and modesty in gover
ment are alien to its affairs. The anti-political state is the instrument
orthodoxy; it thus transforms the open scepticism of citizens into the possib
treachery of subjects. Its laws conform to the tactical requirements of leade
who justify themselves by way of abstract figments of almost infinite pliabilit
It has no authority to exert over them.

Sovereignty

Inside political society there is no sovereign. Civil statehood is the antithesis of concentrated and legally unconstrained power. As an individual the citizen is under an obligation to defend the civil state because it is the necessary condition of his individuality. The act of defence may of necessity exclude itself from political qualification. Whoever, or whatever, performs such an act may be said at that moment to take on the role of a sovereign. Sovereignty is response to challenge. But civil statehood can only be attacked by that which is external to it. Sovereignty therefore denotes no more than the possibility that it may at some time be necessary to 'step out of' civil statehood into some exterior domain in order to counter the endeavours of enemies of the civil relationship. Sovereignty can thus never be the creation of the civil state or of the society of civil states.

Beyond the boundary of this society lie anti-political states that are by definition disdainful of the notion of civility and of prior constraints of a general nature. In these, sovereignty cannot be the possibility of acting without political qualification. The mover of the anti-political state (the party, the race, the leader) successfully claims superiority to legality and to statehood. The anti-political state is thus in itself the concrete manifestation of sovereignty, which is not something summoned up by alien forces but is the constant interior principle to which this kind of state subjects itself. Sovereign rule cannot be equated with the civil state; it can exist only in the absence of civility.

The anti-political sovereign is not necessarily incautious, though the Nazi sovereign certainly became so. Sovereignty and power in the anti-political state reinforce each other but they are not identical. Power is a capability to act, and this is regulated by circumstances. Sovereignty is government in total command of the state. The affairs of such a state may be conducted with sagacity. This is never to be confused with civility. The cautious sovereign is sensitive to limitations imposed by the existence of external power over which he has no control and to the difficulties of pursuing a number of goals among which scarce power resources must be carefully allocated. The sovereign may be accommodative towards other kinds of rulers. But the sovereign is a sovereign because it does not, and does not have to, accept the priority of the civil relationship. The accommodative sovereign cannot be a politically qualified sovereign. Modesty in the sovereign is an uncertain virtue. It is the product of a cautious temper and, possibly, of inertia. Neither is reliable. In the sovereign, caution is predominantly a human not an institutional quality and is subject to the vagaries of mortality and character. Inertia (supplied by the sheer accumulation of the apparatus of the state in the case of the Soviet Union) may at any time be overcome by the dynamic potential of an official doctrine of rule so comprehensive in its interpretation of human affairs as to be almost entirely wanting in any interior qualities that might fill its adherents with a sense of modesty. There can be no such thing as a ideology of scepticism.

No society of anti-political states

The international society of civil statehood is not a specific association organisation, bloc, alliance, practice or enterprise. Its essential characte resides in the civil relationship, and fundamental to the maintenance of thi is rule subject to prior general conditions. The anti-political state is not th prior general conditions of acts and forms of government. It is withou qualification the instrument of a sovereign. Such an absolute instrumen cannot provide the basis of an open society. Having no autonomous existenc of its own, it is incapable of being the shared premiss of essentially disparat projects and practices. This is just as true internationally as it is domestically Being only an instrument, the Soviet Russian state cannot create the condition of a freely diverse society inside Soviet Russia. Nor can it be possible for th Russian and Chinese states between them to create the conditions of a freel diverse cross-national society. Whether they are officially in internationa accord or disaccord, such states separate their subjects. When their govern ments come to diplomatic understandings, these states have nothing more i common than these understandings. The supposed content of officia ideologies cannot qualify the impossibility of society among anti-politica states, since it cannot affect the absence of common statehood among then other than by accentuating it. Being the perfect master of the state, ideolog must be the perfect negation of a statehood that can be shared. The anti political state concentrates power partly because it cannot qualify ideology It is this absence of any capacity for resistance in the state that is important not the supposed content of the ideology to which the concept of the state i surrendered. The national destruction of statehood places power at the centr of the national and international affairs of anti-political states. The Chines and Soviet Russian sovereigns cannot be jointly constrained by a supposedl common ideology if they are not individually constrained. But an intrinsi part of their sovereignties is their regulation of doctrinal orthodoxies. I these circumstances ideology is subsumed under the calculus of power. Th relations between sovereigns are power relations because the anti-politica state is in itself entirely arbitrary. Anything approaching an equal relation ship between these sovereigns depends on some kind of a balance of powe and interests in which mutual suspicion plays a central role.

Civil statehood is a condition of the undesigned individuality of citizens So civil statehood must also be essential to the existence of self-government if by this is meant government within a society of individuals whose con ceptions of self are independent of authority. Contrastingly, the anti-politica state can only provide government in terms of officially authorised pattern of human personality. This is government at the cost of individuality and i annot for that reason be self-government. It is the domination of a sovereign ver subjects, whether they be willing or unwilling. Because of the relative ecurity of individuality within the boundaries of political society, a civil overnment is always liable to be assailed by novel criticisms. There are no xed or officially orthodox forms of public argument in the society of civil tatehood. The only constant is civil qualification. And an effect of this ualification is that public discourse is always held open to fresh shifts and novements. Civil statehood means self-rule, so no civil government can onsistently deny self-government to another civil state however inferior its ower capabilities may chance to be. Whatever the depths reached in a uarrel between a Canadian and an American government, the latter cannot, vhile itself claiming civil authority, forcibly deny the civil authority of the ormer nor can it justly require Canadians to subscribe to some doctrine ronounced orthodox by itself. And if such an American government emains within political society it cannot act to destroy the joint practices of itizens who happen to be Canadians and citizens who happen to be Americans. These may continue to read one another's books and newspapers, orrespond with one another, conduct love affairs, listen to one another's roadcasts, talk by telephone, arrange parties, sports fixtures, even business eals. While the civil relationship lasts, the individual citizen is in no way bliged to participate in the affairs of civil governments. Here power is an relevance.

The anti-political state is a denial of self-rule since it contains none of the onditions of individuality. Its affairs are the affairs of its subjects. It main-ains a unity of government, doctrine and society. Those who attempt to gnore this unity, publicly or privately, strike at the state itself. A rupture in ne relations of two anti-political governments must thus be a clash between wo deeply distinct entities. Such matters are not to be ignored in the private onduct of subjects. The Russian subject who would join in a life of practices vith Chinese subjects in the face of the mutual hostility of their respective overnments would (apart from attempting the impossible) expose himself to ne fate of a traitor. And where a 'community' of apparently closely related nti-political states is maintained, as in eastern Europe, the effects of the bsence of general conditions of government are likewise compelling. In ffect such a community is a domain of power. The anti-political state exists o maintain the sovereignty of power. Wherever the full power of the overeign runs, the existence of lesser sovereignties cannot be conceded. The ssence of sovereignty is its absence of self-qualification. The sovereign can nly be constrained externally by other sovereigns. In a territory in which it xercises large-scale direct strength through substantial military garrisons it annot recognise the regulatory power of another sovereign because this ould be to accept major qualification of its control of itself. The sovereign 1ust be master of its own power. Within the domain of this power, the anti-olitical state may indulge the whims of vassal rulers, be indifferent to their

personal conduct and even understanding of their governmental difficultie
and aspirations. But it cannot concede them sovereignty. An anti-politica
community cannot contain a plurality of sovereigns, each capable of acting i
an unqualified and unpredictable way towards the others: this would resul
in the strict demarcation of the domain of each sovereign and hence th
destruction of the community; or it might develop into a direct struggl
between sovereigns from which the strongest would emerge victorious as th
only true sovereign in the community. Because the sovereign is itself withou
general qualification it must treat all lesser states within the scope of it
direct control as being unprotected from its power. To do otherwise woul
be to accept qualification. Thus the only conditions that can exist throughou
an anti-political community are those created by a dominant sovereign
A community of this sort has to be defined as a project or a movement (i
cannot be subsumed under any substantive general notion of statehood) an
only the sovereign can formulate this definition. Vassal governments, what
ever the space for manoeuvre allowed them, cannot presume to formulat
alternatives to the sovereign's orthodox conception of itself. This woul
constitute an attack on sovereignty. The sovereign controls its own purposes
A movement and a government in Czechoslovakia in 1968 seemed set o
producing a relatively novel meaning of socialist rule. This would also hav
been a novel meaning of socialist rule within the anti-political community o
which Czechoslovakia formed a part. Had it been successful this enterpris
would have established new conditions for the exercise of sovereignty by th
Soviet Union. To act thus towards a sovereign must itself seem to be th
action of a sovereign. Two sovereigns cannot exist inside one community
so the dominant sovereign crushed the incipient sovereign. Within the sam
community the government of Romania can act with some show of inde
pendence. While it makes no claim to redefine the nature of the socialist stat
(or, consequently, to establish its own notion of general conditions in th
community of which it forms a part) it can be indulged. Acting with som
independence is not the same as attempting to subject the sovereign to a
definition not chosen by itself. The anti-political state is wholly an instrumen
because there can be no such thing as anti-political statehood. The anti
political state is thus incapable of creating the general conditions of a cross
national society. The relations between anti-political states are powe
relations and they fall into simple practical categories: those of mutuall
suspicious and potentially belligerent sovereigns; those of a sovereign an
its dominated vassals; those of a sovereign and its clients (these being mino
anti-political states of an aligned disposition that geographical or othe
circumstances place beyond the reach of direct domination); and those o
the major sovereign and minor anti-political states that it seeks to make it
clients. The crudity of the sovereign's conception of the world cannot b
deeply qualified and complicated by anything analogous to statehood.

ae state against spontaneity

irtually any group, person or institution that accepts the conditions of civil atehood may be active cross-nationally within the boundaries of political ociety. Parliamentarians, jurists, journalists, scientists, trade unionists, ankers and businessmen of all descriptions move freely abroad, make eeches to foreign audiences, enquire, observe, argue, gossip and enter into numerable formal and informal cross-national associations. Within the rms of civil statehood there is no determinate sovereign and the relations tween civil authorities can never summon one into existence. The individual tizen is under no obligation or necessity to support, to represent or to obey e executive pronouncements and exhortations of his government, either at ome or abroad. He must simply maintain the civil relationship and act ithin the conditions of the jurisdictions that comprise the environment of hatever operations he chooses to undertake. Though swept by fashions om time to time, political society cannot be distinguished by reference to ay special doctrine, belief, group, association, practice or organisation. he term 'political society' has been settled on in the present enquiry because ternatives that are not outlandish tend to carry connotations of structural eterminacy. The intention in the use of this term is to convey not the istence of a definite structure but the possibility of endlessly proliferating nd changing social connections and communications. This possibility is eated by the conditions of civil statehood, which provide the fundamental isis of social order without propounding any general theory about mankind • its future. Constant conditions of order among citizens (the civil relation-ip) and an open social future are two aspects of political society that are atirely interdependent. Governmental, social and intellectual change can ecome an almost unremarked constituent of individual experience in the vil state. This normalisation of what is not normal requires a sufficiency of curity in authority and in individuality to enable governments and citizens handle change without fear or resort to politically unqualified power. either governments nor citizens are faced by cataclysmic choices between omplete order and complete change inside political society. It is open to em to be committed to order and to change at the same time. The bank ficial who is a model of professional rectitude at work may have an experi-ental attitude towards his private life. The innovative artist or scientist may there to traditional religious beliefs. The campaigner for female emancipa-on may lead an unremarkable family existence. A conservative respect for e traditional substance of education does not preclude a radical attitude to e organisation of education. The citizen is under no public or private cessity to adopt a single-minded approach to change as a whole or to der as a whole. He is able to participate in the initiation of some changes aile putting up a steady resistance to others as a matter of relatively calm dividual choice, provided he is secure in his legal status as a citizen. Like-se, a civil government may suggest large reforms of the IMF while holding

to conservative economic policies at home. It may remain within the jurisdic
tion of the European Court of Human Rights while resenting judgment
made against it there. It may be conservative towards the institutions of th
European Community but radical towards its own constitutional arrange
ments or vice versa. Provided civil governments know that other civi
governments habitually exercise authority and not power, they can propos
or resist or dissociate themselves from cross-national departures withou
recourse to the mobilisation of citizenry or the closure of frontiers or an
other threat or posture markedly at variance with the ordinary delays
confusions and makeshifts of domestic affairs.

There can be no anti-political distinction between statehood and govern
ment. The anti-political society is entirely master of itself. Its leaders ar
therefore placed in sovereign control of the state in all its ramifications
Doctrinally the sovereign is society. Consequently the sovereign must be a
determinate social order, complete self-possession being a central charac
teristic of sovereignty. The leadership that actually exercises sovereignty ma
initiate change but it cannot be seen to have change thrust upon it by move
ments and demands it does not control. If the sovereign within its ow
domain is utterly in possession of itself, change that it does not will must seen
to be a threat to sovereignty itself. Spontaneity in such a society is thu
equated with disorder. The official language that the state places unreservedl
at the disposal of the sovereign makes no distinction between what is publi
and what is private since a secure area of private life could be a site o
spontaneity. The sovereign's fear of spontaneity in part determines it
attitude to the foreign societies in which it has no power. The borders of th
anti-political state are thus taken to mark not a jurisdiction but the extent of a
sovereign social order. What happens beyond these borders is likely to seen
threatening because change there cannot be controlled and its effects coul
shake the social domain of the sovereign. Foreign influences must thus b
tightly regulated along highly fortified frontiers. Visiting foreigners must b
kept under close scrutiny and their contacts with the sovereign's subject
officially supervised. Sovereignty is likely to be asserted at every point o
junction of the anti-political social order with influences that lie beyon
official regulation. Because there can be no such thing as anti-politica
individuality, and therefore no such thing as anti-political citizenship, th
subject is never entirely free of the sovereign. A Soviet Russian subjec
travelling abroad who permits himself to criticise his government is guilty o
treachery. A Chinese sportsman playing in a foreign capital is as much th
agent of his government, and as much subject to its instructions, as is th
resident Chinese ambassador. Whatever the shape of their cross-nationa
involvements, the sovereign as a determinate social order must resist th
open claim to individuality of its subjects. This is a matter of the firs
importance to the sovereign. The international connections of the communis
party of the Soviet Union do not mean that it opens itself to spontaneou

ifts of doctrine and conduct within a multifarious transnational setting.
pparent changes in the attitudes of some western European communists,
ιo have recently hinted at the possibility of their acceptance of political
alification of their conduct and doctrines, have drawn forth the ire and
ndemnation of Russian communist leaders. To question the orthodoxy
the sovereign is as dangerous as to attack it physically, perhaps more so.
it seems that the sovereign's attitudes may be freely questioned cross-
tionally, then it may also seem that they are questionable internally. The
·viet sovereign's boundaries are therefore apt to be brought down within
ε international communist movement wherever its claim to regulate doctrine
εms under attack.

In the humane practices—art, philosophy, literature and such—the
vereign can generally seem to impose its own preferred forms within its
main through its control over means of publication and communication,
rough its penetration of all professional and artistic associations and
rough its regulation of most points of contact with the outside world.
·hind the dull facade thus erected there may be more lively expressions of
dividual creativity but those who involve themselves in these manifestations
spontaneity risk the full weight of the sovereign's power. The regulation of
ientific practices is by no means so straightforward. If the sovereign
trudes itself directly into the substance of, say, the practice of biology,
ree results are likely to follow: the profession given to this study will be
detracked and confused by charlatans prepared to produce results congenial
the sovereign; the ridicule of the cross-national community of biologists
ll be invoked; and this effort to deny the autonomy of the tradition of a
ientific practice will cripple its capacity to yield advances useful to the
vereign's programmes. The public projects of the sovereign can make
mands of scientific practices but the sovereign cannot itself regulate them
thout harm to itself. Here the spontaneous must be allowed some degree
scope within transnational associations that are inherently liable to ignore
vereignty altogether.

ιe rejection of self-interest

ιe economic relations of the international society of civil states cannot be
nply described. Local, national and international markets, businesses and
thorities intermingle with such complexity and changefulness as to out-
ιch the scope of any comprehensive empirical description. Economic
ncepts, and arrangements of these concepts in theories, are absorbed into
εse structures and processes, where they are acted upon, reacted to, debated
d, as commonly as not, rapidly superseded. The theoretical does not deter-
ne more than a part of the actual. Individually and jointly, governments
ν to regulate overall levels of economic activity; they directly undertake
·ge numbers of economic enterprises; and they are almost invariably active

in devising rules and institutions to curb monopolies (other than their own
and to discourage speculation, tax avoidance and a variety of other perenni
economic sins. All civil governments also attempt to achieve economic an
social ends (the relief of poverty, the equalisation of educational oppor
unities, full employment, the encouragement of efficiency, enterprise an
sometimes thrift) by way of taxes, grants, loans, subsidies, tariffs, publi
works and services. These well-intentioned activities are invariably accom
panied by loudly critical debates about welfare and the material nature of th
public interest and about how different versions of both may best be secured
For all this official concern and all this talk about the general good, it i
generally accepted that individual citizens are in part economically self
regarding and are to be expected to pursue their own interests with som
vigour. Though this common propensity may be subjected to different kind
of legal conditions, there can be no serious thought of destroying it becaus
this would entail a revision of the civil notion of individuality. So pressures
appeals and demands for higher incomes for civil servants, miners, old ag
pensioners, company executives, legislators, ministers of religion, farmers
investors, automobile workers and every other interest capable of expressio
occasion no more surprise than the regular movements of the heavenl
bodies. Individual citizens are likewise expected to be vocally resistant t
high levels of compulsory expenditure in the form of taxation. And wha
income they succeed in obtaining they may be assumed to spend in way
suggested by their own needs and tastes and not in ways that might serv
patriotic or other public causes. The acceptance of self-regard as a fact c
economic life is balanced by all sorts of private and governmental preoccupa
tions with welfare and the general good, but in political terms there can neve
be any question of public altruism obliterating private selfishness. Each i
necessary to the other. Economic relations cannot be removed from civ
conditions. In political society individuality and an openly critical attitude t
all official actions cannot be separated. Because self-interest as such doe
not have to be justified, criticism of official policies cannot be required t
keep within approved criteria. And conceptions of general goals preferred b
authorities cannot be imposed as unquestionable public orthodoxies. Th
civil condition means that supposedly public interests have to be kep
responsive to the public. Given the existence of economic aspects c
individuality, the economy of political society is to be expected to be con
tinuously swayed by an almost infinite number of self-regarding decisions b
groups, corporations and consumers as well as by the often uncoordinate
decisions and allocations of a plurality of authorities.

In the anti-political state the will of the sovereign has absolute priority ove
individuality because the sovereign is the governmental manifestation o
fundamental economic or other forces that are held to determine huma
consciousness in its entirety. The anti-political language of official project
and goals must therefore exclude the language of individual self-interes

om the sovereign's domain. As well, there can be no recognised place for he unexpected and spontaneous in the economic life of the anti-political state ecause the sovereign is supposed to represent a society in full knowledge nd command of itself. For the individual subject of the anti-political state he route to personal economic betterment will lie through hazardous private perations of a corrupt or quasi-corrupt nature or through advancement in he service and the favours of the sovereign. The state is unlikely to ignore elf-regarding motivations entirely and in order to promote its goals it will robably find it useful to reward some classes of workers considerably more han others, both to encourage their efforts and to bind them to itself. But y the same token it may also threaten and punish workers whose per- ormances are displeasing to it. The sovereign cannot be seen to be subject to rces it cannot control; it therefore makes detailed allocations of productive ctors to specific uses with a view to the achievement of stated economic rgets. Labour, like any other resource, has to respond to these commands. disposing of his energies the individual subject is thus unlikely to have uch in the way of personal choice. Full employment can easily be achieved the anti-political state because all jobs are made available by the sovereign's ommand. This does not mean that labour is deployed efficiently. Since the vereign is sole employer, sole paymaster and sole planner there can be little the shape of independent criteria by which the relative value of alternative ses of resources may be measured. More importantly, it is open to the vereign to use unemployment as a form of punishment. A subject who ses his job because he displeases his government cannot cast about for nother employer. Since there is no legitimate language of self-interest, the fficials of trade unions will be as much concerned to serve the sovereign's ill as any of its other agents. Though the sovereign may effectively achieve rge goals (the rapid expansion of heavy industry or the development of assive pieces of military equipment) it is singularly ill-equipped to respond numbers of shifting individual demands (for vacuum cleaners, pre-set zor blades, zip fasteners, convenience foods and the like) because in the sence of the stimulus of personal gain there is little to promote agility in e production and distribution of new consumer goods. The sovereign's bsession with self-control through planning also makes for all kinds of onomic mistakes and contradictions because of the sheer load of linked mmands that have to be issued to maintain complex lines of production in fective operation. For the same reason the anti-political economy will be gid in its responses to unavoidable disturbances and frustrations, to the ilure of harvests or to hold-ups in the development of new technologies. he apparatus of the state will be suspicious of innovative enterprise, which nyway cannot have access to risk capital. To compensate for its obvious onomic deficiencies the sovereign may allow partially free markets in some ctors and ignore 'black' markets in others. In the interests of promoting dividual improvisations, which in fact keep much of the economy going,

it may also tolerate a good deal in the way of corruption. But such equivoca-
tions and hypocrisies do not comprise an acceptance of the autonomy of
individual economic decision and the legitimacy of self-interest. Theory
does not openly relax its grip on practice. The sovereign simply acknowledges
its need to ease its own administrative problems. This is not a fundamental
qualification of the sovereign's status.

Anti-political powers cannot enter into the economic language of international political society. Soviet officials may operate as buyers and sellers
in western markets for grain or precious metals but they cannot allow market
forces or cross-national civil institutions and authorities to be directly active
within the boundaries of their sovereign's domain. Anti-political sovereignty
is totally immodest and modesty is the essential condition of the economic
interdependence of civil states. Each civil government is aware of numerous
limitations: of those created by contending national and cross-national
interests; of market forces generated by changing demands, new products
and new technologies, by commodity scarcities and altering relative levels of
efficiency and productivity among national economies; of constitutional and
electoral constraints on its power; of the inadequacy of its knowledge of
complex relations that engender large numbers of transitory economic
notions and prophecies; of the high likelihood of unintended consequences
following from any important authoritative economic action; of the
exposure of its domestic economic environment to the consequences of
policies adopted by foreign governments; of the probability of retaliations
against national efforts to achieve economic advantage through highly
subsidised exports, tariff and non-tariff barriers to imports, long-term
governmental efforts to resist upward pressure on the exchange rate of its
currency; and so on. The international economic language of political
society is not a product of power but of limitations on power. In just the
same way, the ability of civil states to create all sorts of cross-national
arrangements and authorities and to facilitate cross-national official communications at a multiplicity of levels is a product of civil perceptions.
Because the anti-political state contains no civil qualifications, the anti-
political sovereign perceives the economy of its domain solely as an aspect
of its power. This power is not without its limitations, but these are physical
not doctrinal or political or constitutional in nature. Among anti-political
states economic relations thus tend to fall into four broad patterns whose
shapes are determined by power: where a strong sovereign controls vassal
states it is in a position to force inequitable economic exchanges determined
essentially by its own will and unrelated to any objective values created by
open markets; where something approaching an equal power relationship
between sovereigns exists, economic exchanges are really officially regulated
forms of barter; where a sovereign wishes to cosset a client state or a possible
client state it may confer bounties on it, usually in return for fairly specific
government services; and where sovereigns quarrel, trade ends. No

utonomous cross-national economy, limiting to the power of sovereigns, an flourish among anti-political states. Similarly, no cross-national economic inguage beyond the direct control of powerful governments can be expected ɔ be allowed to penetrate their domains. Though sovereigns may seek the ‣roducts of the economy of political society, they cannot open themselves to it.

CIVIL STATEHOOD AND ANTI-POLITICAL STATES

'he international environment outside the society of civil states includes a umber of anti-political states. These have been defined here from within the oundary of civil statehood. From this standpoint the anti-political state is ɔnceived to be the negation of statehood. It is the state entirely at the ‣rvice of anti-political dispositions. Lacking prior resources of its own it is ιcapable of setting authority to constrain power. Instead it maintains and ιstifies power's sovereignty. An obvious problem for this enquiry follows ʻom such an appreciation. For the civil state, it may seem, there is no basis ›r any relationship other than one of unrelieved hostility with its apparently ›tal negation in the shape of the anti-political sovereign. Several empirical ɔnsiderations modify this conclusion, though they cannot completely ιvalidate it.

(1) Just as do most other states, anti-political states denote the existence of ɔvernments in concrete social, geographical and historical circumstances. hough the anti-political state as such does not impede sovereignty (except by s sheer bulk), anti-political governments may be qualified by many other ιctors. The absence of any wide-ranging imperialist traditions in Chinese ιstory suggests that Chinese governments, whatever their claims to internal ɔwer, are unlikely to be flamboyantly irresponsible in their behaviour in ιe international arena. The 'insularity' of much of Russian historical ‹perience is to be expected to engender suspicious and defensive attitudes › the external world but not incautious ones.

(2) The impossibility of an international society of anti-political statehood .eans that individual anti-political states are never likely to be able to draw ›gether, or to want to draw together, to attack civil states simply because ιey are civil states. The sovereign fears other sovereigns. For a particular ιti-political government, relations with civil governments may well be less aught with hostility and danger than relations with other anti-political states.

Chinese government may thus be warmer in its attitude to Japan than to oviet Russia. The limited and open nature of civil governments can render ιem more congenial to sovereigns than other sovereigns.

(3) Civil statehood is not an active principle. It is the conditions of a ιverse society and, therefore, of limited government. Civil statehood as ιch can never be a violent crusade and it cannot be militarily imposed on

any community because this would itself constitute an infringement of civil conditions. There are no grounds here for conflicts between citizens of civil states and subjects of anti-political states. Though civil statehood cannot be forced on subjects, it can certainly be denied them, but only by their own sovereigns not by civil states.

(4) This enquiry has several times drawn a distinction between civil government, which is capable of varieties of action, and civil statehood, which is not a principle of action but of conditions of action. Civil government. occupy a world in which action is possible just as anti-political government do. The existence of practical problems affecting both kinds of government may be a sufficient basis for understandings between them. The dangers of inadvertent military instability, for example, create a common environmen of practical problems in which some kinds of arms control agreements are possible. The recognition of areas of practical action, which need have little bearing on fundamentals, may thus be a basis of more complex relation than can be suggested by the extreme dissimilarity of civility and sovereignty

So the contrasting natures of civil statehood and anti-political states de not mean that civil and anti-political governments must always be separated by unrelieved conflict. But though there may be grounds for a number of cross-boundary contacts, the civil perception of international relation cannot be the same as that of anti-political sovereigns. The political qualifica tion is fundamental to the maintenance of civil statehood. It cannot be abandoned whenever a citizen or authority has dealings in, or thinks about the environment of civil society.

The diplomatic circle

The totality of states may be conceived to be a decentralised structure whose merit lies solely in its capacity to maintain some measure of order in a world society that is without any common values or any consensus on the proper nature of government. States encapsulate diverse and potentially explosiv human materials. Without states, the world would be immeasurably anarchic but to attempt to subjugate so much variety under a single universal stat would be an immeasurably destructive enterprise. States as a whole are to be expected to be permanently suspended between these poles, at neither of which would anything other than misery and death be the common human lot. The world system of states is not a civilisation but the only possibl condition of some measure of civilisation. In their unavoidable historica relations the multiplicity of states have engendered certain diplomatic mode of conduct on the part of their representatives. These are the product not of common attitudes or values but of the juxtoposition of dissimilar attitude and values in a hazardous context that suggests that order is generall preferable to disorder. The stability of this system, such as it is, is an effect of accumulated diplomatic mores, of the armed and counter-balancing watch fulness of governments, of the coincidence of the interests of most authorities in the maintenance of an ordered international setting and of the wide recognition of the state as the fundamental legitimate constituent unit of a regulated world society.

Much may be said for this attempt to see and to typify states as a totality. But it conforms neither to the civil conception of statehood nor to the doctrines of world social forces espoused by anti-political sovereigns. The plurality of civil states is the condition of a diverse cross-national society that is not potentially explosive. The different circumstances of civil governments and the multifarious jurisdictions within which they act do not comprise a diplomatic arena made up of concentrations of power. In the political society of civil statehood governments do not arm themselves against one another. Nor is this political order suspended between poles of disorder and tyranny. It is already immeasurably diverse; and there can be no desire among any of its citizens to subjugate one another. From the civil viewpoint the conditions established by the state are a protection from subjugation. And at a deep level civil states are all the same, because civil statehood establishes three entirely general principles: the state's authority is distributed to constrain power; all authoritative action is subject to prior general conditions; and the impersonal relationship between all citizens via explicit rules is given precedence over more intimate projects and practices and is maintained regardless of any special claims to status or office. Actions, policies and arguments that are politically qualified by acceptance of an obligation to protect civil statehood can never incorporate mutual violence. From the civil viewpoint there can be nothing to be feared in the diversity of world society or in its multiplicity of states as such. The hazardous character of international affairs is an effect of the insubstantial fabric of many of the world's states, not of their numbers or the customs of their inhabitants. For the citizen of the civil state the ideal world would be one in which all states were strengthened by strong infusions of civil statehood. The strong state, not the weak state, creates peace.

The anti-political sovereign regards its state as a possession, no more than its internal and external instrument. Inside its own domain the sovereign recognises no prior general conditions. Outside its domain it recognises only the existence of practical limitations to its power. From the sovereign's viewpoint power can only be limited by power. What the sovereign cannot dominate it thus regards with suspicion. It follows that its formal attitude to the external world is contradictory. To transform all states into instruments of sovereigns maintaining the same doctrine of absolute rule would either (a) subject its own sovereignty to the legitimate intrusion of other sovereigns, all with the internally untrammeled capability to take idiosyncratic doctrinal positions, or (b) make the external environment even more threatening by increasing the number of absolute sovereigns in it. Given that the sovereign invariably retains control over its own means of justifying itself to its subjects, the prospect of sovereigns peacefully discoursing over variable doctrines of rule would seem a remote one. The sovereign puts power at the core of internal and therefore of international relations. In its eyes the state is simply a component of power. In regarding the variety of the external world as intrinsically threatening, the anti-political sovereign is inevitably drawn to wish to substitute a uniform world in its own image. But in fact this would be infinitely more dangerous. The sovereign is inherently disposed to hold statehood in contempt, but without statehood its own situation becomes perilous. If the United States of America had been a communist anti-political state in the years after the second world war, the Soviet sovereign could hardly have survived.

Arrangements

Except for the imperative conditions of civil statehood, there are no necessary (as opposed to contingent) constraints to the cross-national arrangements that civil states may make with one another. Cross-national habits (close and mutually supporting contacts among central banks), projects (high energy research and development in Europe) and authorities (the European Court of Human Rights) can thus come to be a normal aspect of civil affairs. All the governmental and non-governmental arrangements of the society of civil states are subject to constant enquiry and argument and in many cases their procedures and competence are bound by explicit agreements of a constitutional nature. Many of the arrangements initiated by civil authorities (the IMF and the GATT) have concerns and memberships that extend far beyond the boundaries of international civil society. The cross-national dimension of civil society is thus one into which external governments can enter. In this environment the existence of different interests and attitudes is in itself unexceptional, as is a propensity to criticise civil authorities and to make demands on their resources at the same time. Civil relations can thus tolerate without strain the public presence inside political society of all kinds of official and unofficial elements from the non-political world, even though these may be much given to openly condemning the policies and conduct of civil governments. Non-political governments and other bodies that become active in civil society must of course pay a political price: no view or demand propounded in this context will be accorded any particular respect by the citizens of civil states and no protestations of domestic or international virtue will be widely accepted at face value. External interests may likewise be active at the non-governmental level in capital and other markets in civil society, but they will not necessarily be granted any authority to regulate them and efforts to operate secretly are unlikely to be indefinitely successful.

Inside its own domain the anti-political sovereign accepts no general conditions to its behaviour and consequently the affairs of the anti-political state are without exception the affairs of its sovereign. Its international contacts are carefully regulated so as not to compromise the sovereign. Within the sovereign's domain there is no scope for cross-national rules, adjudications or markets; or for unregulated associations with foreign journalists, economists, academics, industrialists. In the absence of the possibility of political qualification, the sovereign can use the state to control both the activities of its subjects and the contents of public discussion of its own doings. No authorities of state (a legislature or a judiciary) can undermine the power of the sovereign, so there can be no cross-national authorities (an elected assembly or a court of human rights) with that potential either. Criticisms and enquiries by its subjects cannot affect the sovereign because officially its subjects are uncritical of its power and the captive state denies them the possibility of free enquiry. The domestic conditions that the sovereign requires are thus far removed from those that governments at large are prepared to accept in their international debates and arrangements. There is a fundamental discontinuity at the borders of the area dominated by the sovereign. In these circumstances foreign policy can be accurately depicted as officially controlled contact between the sovereign and its environment. Anti-political rulers would be threatened by the open existence in their domains of international institutions in which foreigners of all descriptions could legitimately discuss their conduct in a sceptical and disrespectful style. The anti-political state cannot lend itself to cross-national organisational departures that could subject its sovereign to new forms of authority because it has no authority to contribute to such innovations. Nor can the sovereign allow foreign governments and other authorities to carry on in its domain in ways far removed from those it permits in the behaviour of its subjects. For the sovereign, international relations in an open institutional setting are in themselves radical. As it presently conducts itself, the United Nations would hardly be welcome in Moscow or Peking were it to be inclined to remove itself from New York. And the extension of the jurisdiction of the European Court of Human Rights into the Soviet Union would require a fundamental change in both the internal and the external character of the Soviet sovereign.

Practices and penetration

The practices in which individuality expresses itself most creatively—art. literature, mathematics, philosophy, theatre—have traditions of their own that are not bound by any national community, state, doctrine, language or religion. There is Italian opera, but opera is not Italian; there is Christian art, but art is not Christian; there are Jewish composers, but music is not Jewish; there are socialist dramatists, but drama is not socialist; there is British philosophy, but philosophy (even in Britain) is not British. The autonomous tradition of a practice that can incorporate contributions from numerous national and other sources is strengthened by them not weakened. Because civil statehood is completely unspecific, requiring only political qualification from those within its boundaries, an unlimited number of practices are open to development inside its borders, given the sufficient availability of individual talent. Through subventions particular states may encourage art in Paris, theatre in London, opera in Milan; but no civil state can hold itself to be the arbiter of a practice. Most practices are not in any way territorial and they are clearly open to stimulus from sources outside political society. Soviet mathematicians obviously make important contributions to mathematics. But because of the autonomous nature of the traditions in which they occur, outstanding advances in most practices take place more often than not in civil conditions. Artists and historians in political society are seldom much impressed by the work of Russian or Chinese artists and historians, whose efforts are directed by the need to secure the approval of their sovereigns. Where open and wide-ranging challenge and argument are vital to the renewal and veracity of traditions (in literary criticism, history, economic theory, sociology) the relationship between practices and civility is a necessary one.

The anti-political sovereign, drawing its conception of rule from some grand identity with supposedly fundamental social forces, cannot set itself against all practices. Being officially in the van of history and always eager to increase its power, it must cultivate modern science and technology. Being the authentic bringer of an ideal form of human existence, it must also portray its subjects as happy participants in healthy and elevating pursuits. The anti-political state is thus disposed to make much of the more uncritical or abstract practices (sport, dancing, circuses, chess, mathematics) and to regulate, often with minute care, those whose vigour most depends on critical individuality (cinema, literature, history, art). Whatever expedients the sovereign employs, the autonomy of practices is denied. Even science is approved because the sovereign claims to be scientific. A great novelist will be denigrated because he is bourgeois or Jewish; a mediocre novelist will be praised because he confirms official doctrine. The criteria of practices are thus rendered secondary to the sovereign's criteria. Here again there is a deep discontinuity at the borders of the anti-political state. Civil statehood is a condition of the world of practices; the anti-political sovereign sets itself to be master of this world.

CONCLUSIONS

1.   There is a human propensity to reject the political qualification. Extreme forms of this propensity are to be found in the wholly abstract justification of rule; in the equation of citizenship with positive identity; and in the disposition to treat the state as nothing more than the apparatus of a project.

2.   Civil statehood can have no existence where these dispositions are dominant. The anti-political state is without reserve the instrument of the sovereign.

3.   Whatever the stated doctrines of its sovereign, the anti-political state is in all respects a particular and not a universal. There can be no such thing as anti-political statehood since the sovereign accepts no prior conditions. So there can be no such thing as an international society of anti-political statehood either.

4.   There are deep discontinuities between the particular anti-political state and the external world. The actual variety of the world cannot itself be accommodated by the anti-political identity. In abstract terms such an accommodation can only be achieved by a fundamental revision of world society; but the transformation of all actual states into anti-political states would in fact destroy the possibility of a world society of statehood.

5.   The institutional arrangements made among states at large cannot be incorporated into the sovereign's domain. The foreign policy of the anti-political state is the officially regulated contacts of the sovereign with an external world.

6.   The anti-political state attempts to control practices so as to render them useful or congenial to its sovereign. Without autonomous statehood there can be no autonomous world of practices.

CHAPTER 9

Civil Statehood, Anti-political States and Issues of Foreign Policy

This enquiry has distinguished anti-political states by way of certain human propensities and not by way of any positive theory of the anti-political state as such. The effects of the rejection of the political qualification are not restricted to foreign anti-political states but regularly show themselves within the domestic affairs and debates of virtually all civil states. Responding to anti-political pressures is therefore a familiar requirement of everyday civil living. So in crossing the boundary of civil statehood this enquiry is not advancing into totally strange territory. It may begin to consider the relations between civil states and anti-political states by first addressing itself to internal civil experience.

CIVILITY AND ANTI-POLITICAL PROPENSITIES

The defensive response

Civil statehood requires that authority constrain power. The use of authority to apply force within the civil state is consonant with this principle if it prevents citizens from being ruled by power. A band of anti-political brigands is, within its own ranks, governed by power not authority. In preventing this power from invading the lives of citizens, civil authority may be obliged to use force. But it legitimately does so only as a response to the attempted use of power.

The institutions of the civil state formulate and are bound by explicit general rules. In dealing with anti-political manifestations, the individual state's inherited law may seem deficient. In this event new general rules may be adopted; but the civil state does not proceed by ignoring rules.

The rejection of the political qualification shows itself in argument and in the ways in which the anti-political organise themselves as well as in specific actions. Civility is the basis of an enquiring and discursive society. Citizens do not allow their own arguments to be distorted by the intrusion of anti-

162

political dogmatism. And in answering this they maintain the civil tone of voice while persistently uncovering and challenging anti-political premisses. Just as they enquire into their own doings, so do they enquire into the organisational schemes and arrangements of the anti-political. Both these methods of defending civil statehood are intrinsic to civil conduct and require no special justification.

The generative response

Being diverse and changing, civil society is incessantly productive of social and economic problems—unemployment, inflation, disadvantaged minorities and such. In itself civil statehood contains no programme for dealing with the several problems of civil society. Anti-political manifestations that draw the attention of citizens to situations requiring thought and action do civility no necessary disservice. Civil institutions can respond to anti-political propensities by generating responses to civil society's difficulties that yield nothing to the anti-political inclination to force citizenship to conform to a single identity.

In the civil state the politically inclined and the anti-politically inclined occupy the same material environment and this can create issues affecting both in much the same way. In a practical manner they may be equally active in generating acceptable solutions to such problems. The inhabitants of an urban locality are all likely to be assailed by the same traffic problems. In this context particular lines of authoritative action may be agreed by numbers of individuals regardless of the depth of their regard for civil statehood. Acquiring a new set of traffic lights (and obeying them) may be a matter of little ideological impact. Such advances are not necessarily insignificant. Staying alive on the streets has a high priority for most people.

The approximative response

Civil statehood, being inactive, cannot deny itself to anyone. A civil state assumes that those within its jurisdiction who may be subject to anti-political dispositions or influence nevertheless approximate to citizenship and are to be treated accordingly. A person is not denied a fair hearing in court, or in any other civil institution, because his opinions are without political qualification. The approximative attitude has several merits. The political qualification is not a badge or uniform whose absence can easily be observed. Opinions and actions that are simply unexpected or shocking are unlikely to contain any basic contradiction of civil statehood. Civility does not express itself in prejudice. So a civil approach to what may seem to be anti-political is desirable because it may turn out not to be anti-political. And where this is not the case there is the possibility that experience of civil conduct may have the effect of attenuating anti-political obsessions in those possessed by them.

If it fails in this, approximation may at least expose to general view the dangerous and doctrinaire nature of anti-political rejections of the priority of the civil relationship.

Civility is a condition of the expression of individuality in an endless variety of practices. A characteristic of anti-political propensities is their denial of autonomy to practices—to the writing of history or the cultivation of friendships. Yet it happens that the anti-political feel the pull of practices (of chess, gambling, pure mathematics, poetry) in which citizens enjoy and develop autonomous traditions. Approximative associations between those who accept and those who reject the priority of civil statehood in practices may be relatively untroubled. And by patiently maintaining the autonomy of the values of their practices citizens may in some small degree succeed in promoting an understanding of civility among those who participate in them on other terms.

These responses at the inter-state level

This classification of civil responses to the existence of anti-political propensities inside civil society does not constitute a prescriptive theory or a coherent plan of action. It denotes what is possible. It is simply a categorisation that can also be applied in the case of civil responses to anti-political states. Most obviously, the defensive response manifests itself in preparedness for war in order to counter possibly violent use of anti-political strength; the development of special rules relating to the control of potentially unstable armaments and to the management of both spatial and functional contacts with anti-political powers; and in persistent enquiries into the internal and external doings of anti-political sovereigns and the rigorous analysis and criticism of their attempts to justify themselves. The generative response shows itself in the flexibility and effectiveness with which national and cross-national civil authorities deal with the interior problems of the international society of civil states; and in their ability to cooperate watchfully with foreign sovereigns in practical arrangements to contain specific mutual problems. Approximation occurs in innumerable social, organisational and diplomatic situations in which civil patience and humour is extended to the subjects and representatives of anti-political sovereigns and in those practices in which citizens and the sovereign's subjects are able to join in the life of autonomous traditions.

The realist objection denied

Yet the existence of totally different conceptions of the state in the international arena may seem to create a unique environment that ought not to be confused with what is interior to civil statehood. Civil responses to anti-political manifestations inside civil jurisdictions are supported by authority and their effect is to maintain a form of statehood that already exists. But, taken as a whole, relations between civil and anti-political states cannot possibly occur in a similar or even analogous setting. In the international setting in which they actually do occur, anything more complicated than a straightforwardly diplomatic approach, backed by military strength, is frippery at best. Internationally, it may be argued, civil governments should simply accept necessity while guarding themselves against its dangers. In these circumstances the state as such is the fundamental structure of foreign policy; citizens, subjects, practices or general notions about the potential universality of the civil relationship are irrelevant.

Four major considerations weigh decisively against this position.

(1) States are facts. To describe them as necessities assumes that the concept of the state is given and immutable, which it is not. There can be no general theory of states as facts. The concrete existence of the states of Norway and New Zealand can only be explained historically; and the appropriate historical explanations must be fundamentally different because the countries themselves are different. But the broad common acceptance of the priority of civil statehood in both Norway and New Zealand is another matter. Historical factors undoubtedly contribute to this shared priority, but they cannot wholly explain it because it has the form of a large number of decisions that are daily renewed. A non-historical explanation of these decisions is common to both cases: without the priority of civil statehood there is little to prevent the historical state from falling into the exclusive possession of a particular group or of a conspiracy of some kind.

The state of Russia is an historical fact not a necessity, since it could have taken a different shape or failed to have survived altogether. It is the present government of Russia that claims to be a necessity. But though this government possesses the Russian state it is in no way a necessity for its subjects. To concede truth to this claim would be to concede the argument for sovereignty and for the sovereign's right to abolish alternatives to its own rule. But civil statehood is the negation of any such claim, which is both conceptually and empirically fallacious. From the civil viewpoint, the Soviet government claims a necessary status for itself that cannot be accepted except by those who are themselves in the grip of anti-political propensities. Treating the Soviet sovereign as a powerful government is different from accepting the necessity of its sovereignty.

(2) Civil statehood, being entirely impersonal, can never be the exclusive property of any particular state or group of states. If civil authorities attempt to contain all aspects of civility within national boundaries, then either they in effect treat civil statehood as an instrument that they control, or they allow civility to be defined by external power. But, first, civil statehood is never an instrument; it is always conditions. And, second, it constrains, or attempts to constrain, power; it is not constrained by it.

(3) Civil states cannot themselves deny civil statehood to the subjects of an

anti-political sovereign. This does not mean that civil statehood provides a justification for, or a means of, forcible intrusion into domains external to it. It does neither. Questions of practicability apart, a civil authority forcing civil conditions on an unwilling population by violent means would be contradicting its own acceptance of civil conditions; thus it could not in that respect be a civil authority. The acceptance of civil statehood must be a matter of choice. So before a territory or state can become a civil state it must have or obtain or be granted self-determination. Though self-determination may result in forms of rule other than civil self-rule, it remains a necessary condition of the establishment of the priority of civil statehood. Even if self-determination results in anti-political rule, it is still a necessary condition of the adoption of civil self-rule.

Civility shows itself as a qualification of the particular experience of a state. There can therefore be no law about how or when a population accepts its priority: the circumstances of the adoption of civil statehood in Sweden need have nothing in common with the circumstances of its adoption in Spain. If civility were the product of a determinate universal law, civil statehood could never have priority over arrangements and projects. The law controlling civility would have priority over it and therefore over everything else. A civil relationship produced by such a law could not be a condition of individuality because individuality itself would be subject to the same law, and determined individuality is a contradiction in terms. It follows that, from the civil viewpoint, the denial of an anti-political sovereign's claims to absolute rule is not the same as a denial of self-determination to the state that it treats as its instrument. Nor can it be categorically denied that acceptance of the political qualification can never begin to occur in conditions of anti-political rule. It is unlikely, but it cannot be impossible because no law determines its occurrence or its non-occurrence.

Since the civil view includes a commitment to self-determination and excludes a belief in a determinate path to the acceptance of civility, political responses to the anti-political state take many different shapes that do not in total comprise a strategy or a theory. The acceptance of the state as an historical fact, the rejection of the necessity of anti-political sovereignty and the recognition of self-determination as a necessary condition of the emancipation of a population into civil self-rule are fundamental to the citizen's attitude to the external environment of civil society. But they in no way place political responses to the anti-political in an *a priori* straitjacket.

(4) The anti-political sovereign, recognising no prior legal conditions to its rule, is able to justify its denial of self-determination to the states (including its own) that it dominates. The Soviet sovereign has blatantly denied self-determination to states such as Czechoslovakia in eastern Europe. Now if it is urged that the citizens and authorities of civil states should accept external reality, an obvious problem arises: which reality—the reality, in this case, of the Soviet sovereign's denial of self-determination to the state of Czecho-

slovakia, or the reality of the preference of large numbers of Czechs for self-determination?

The civil viewpoint can of course accommodate realities of different kinds. It is quite consistent to perceive the fact of the power of the Soviet sovereign to deny self-determination to states that it dominates while at the same time refuting, as a matter of equally valid reality, any reason or justification offered in support of this denial. However, responding to power is not quite the same thing as responding to sovereignty. The sovereign's claim to superiority over the state is clearly an important aspect of external reality; but it is not real in the sense of being true. Civil responses to a reality that is not true cannot be expected to fit into a crudely simple model of the international system based on a concept of the state divorced from statehood.

FOREIGN POLICY ISSUES

This enquiry may now review, from the civil standpoint, issues of foreign policy as problems that occur in the relations between anti-political states and civil states. In these issues, it has been established, it deals only with the nature of civil responses. Civil statehood is not the substance of a grand strategy.

EXECUTIVE DOMINATION

The anti-political sovereign regulates its relations with the external world by means of the state it possesses. Such a state must tend to summon up analogues in political society. Dealing with the sovereign on something like equal terms may seem to require civil authority to emulate its status, not simply its strength. An emphasis on the executive may therefore seem intrinsic to civil relations with powerful sovereigns like the rulers of Soviet Russia. Yet civil statehood is the contradiction of claims by any person or authority to a status free from its general conditions. In civil society sovereignty refers not to particular institutions or persons but to arbitrary actions that may become necessary to protect civil statehood from anti-political power (and this is their only justification). Even sovereignty in this sense is not in any way congenial to civility. Though sovereign action must be possible (since otherwise citizens could find themselves defenceless from those who reject civil constraints), it is essentially barbarous and therefore to be avoided. So in the life of political society three kinds of concerns are evoked by the international existence of anti-political sovereigns: (1) the concern to guard against structural tendencies in a civil executive to move towards a status analogous to that of a sovereign; (2) the concern to proceed in relations with anti-political sovereigns in such a way as to forestall the necessity for authorities or citizens to have to undertake sovereign actions; and (3) the concern to moderate, as far as possible, the more extreme activities of sovereigns outside civil society.

(1) A civil executive's contacts with an anti-political sovereign must by their nature extend beyond the boundaries of civil statehood and must, in this exact sense, be foreign. In relation to the cross-national affairs of the international society of civil states, no national legislature or assembly need lay much stress on a special structure like a foreign affairs committee to make its authority felt, since all the members of such an assembly and virtually all its committees may be active cross-nationally. But the anti-political sovereign closely controls its state's external contacts in their entirety, so civil connections with such a sovereign must in this sense be specialised. Given the sovereign's inherent tendency to emphasize the role of the executive, it follows that there is good cause for an assembly to make structural provision, in the shape of foreign relations and military affairs committees or their like, to maintain an authoritative presence in this area of the executive's conduct. The argument that this divides responsibility in foreign policy is a weak one; civil statehood divides authorities in order to make them, as a whole, responsible. There is no sound reason why foreign sovereigns, unconstrained by domestic authorities themselves, should not be made aware of diverse, critical and enquiring authorities inside civil states. Likewise, the argument that there is a special case for executive secrecy in dealing with anti-political sovereigns does not withstand civil examination. The sovereign normally proceeds secretly. But the civil state, being the antithesis of all aspects of sovereignty, should therefore proceed as openly as possible in matters relating to sovereigns. The case that ordinary prudence requires the civil executive to conceal its negotiating positions from those with whom it is negotiating is always a respectable one. But it is not inherently superior to the case for denying the executive a status analogous to that of a sovereign. These two cases conflict, but so they should. Since civil authority as a whole protects civility there may be occasions on which representatives of an assembly can and should enter into executive secrecy. Given the anti-political sovereign's addiction to power, military strength must enter into the civil state's relations with it. Here again there is a limited case for executive secrecy in the sense that it is folly to hand an advantage to a potential attacker by making every military disposition public. But there is no case for being secret about strength as such or about broad strategies of resistance to attack; indeed it is important that ill-disposed sovereigns should be reasonably well informed about these matters. A civil executive may feel it more vital to conceal weakness from possible enemies. But if civil statehood is weakly defended, civil assemblies should know it, even if they must participate to some degree in executive secrecy in acquiring this knowledge.

(2) To inflict harm without due process of law is either criminal or sovereign behaviour. War (particularly modern war) requires harm to be done

on a large scale without legal process; it is thus, in the civil perspective, sovereign action and this, in itself, is contrary to the general conditions of civil statehood. An anti-political sovereign may have a preference for peace in any given circumstances but, holding itself to be above legality, the use of arbitrary violence cannot be wholly alien to its nature since it is accustomed to acting arbitrarily in the internal uses to which it puts its state. So military strength has a necessary role in the relations of civil authorities with sovereigns. The civil executive makes military preparations in order to deter possible attack. But it also enters into arrangements with sovereigns to reduce the likelihood of either technical developments or territorial confusions precipitating a war that might not otherwise occur. In none of these functions need the civil executive assume a sovereign-like status. Defence strategies can without danger be conveyed to assemblies (including cross-national assemblies) whose members are anyway likely to have to face the expenditure problems raised by the pursuit of defence effectiveness. Similarly, proposed arrangements to regulate arms can stand examination without thereby yielding some great advantage to foreign powers. In the case of anything in the nature of a territorial arrangement, such as the recognition of the territorial *status quo* in Europe, enquiry and discussion are particularly necessary because the interests of populations subjected to domination by a sovereign may be affected and these need somehow to be expressed in political society since legitimate domestic expression is denied them.

(3) If civil statehood is the antithesis of sovereign tendencies among political institutions it must also, being general, be the antithesis of the sovereignty of anti-political governments in the areas they effectively dominate. A number of policy implications follow. The civil standpoint requires that sovereigns be exposed to whatever kind of political influences are possible. Unhindered by open debate and enquiry in their own domains, their doings are constantly observed and criticised in political society. No civil executive cooperates with a sovereign to conceal its affairs from whatever degree of examination is possible by citizens or their representatives. No civil executive attempts to use its authority to support the sovereign's official view of itself. If only by public protest in political society, legitimate non-official pressures are as appropriate to foreign sovereigns as to any other governmental structures. Nor do civil executives connive at the sovereign's denial of self-determination to the states and subjects it dominates. As nearly as possible, civil authorities of all kinds treat such states as if they were self-governing and their subjects as if they were citizens.

INTERNATIONAL ORGANISATION

The denial of civil statehood grossly limits the kinds of international connections that the sovereign can contemplate without alarm. Its belief in the necessity and the rectitude of its claim to sole and total possession of its state constitutes a fundamental barrier to the merging of the bureaucratic, military and industrial instruments of its purposes into cross-national structures that it does not wholly dominate. Where the priority of civility is established, authorities are released from such deep-seated fears and are able to respond to their problems, which include the international existence of anti-political sovereigns, in a variety of organisational ways.

The defensive response

From the civil standpoint war is not the act of a sovereign but a sovereign act. Preparation for military defence at both national and cross-national levels is therefore preparation to perform sovereign acts, that is, acts that cannot themselves be carried through on the basis of the civil relationship because they entail violence without legal process. Cross-national arrangements for joint planning, command, training and weapons procurement are manifestations of the possible necessity of this behaviour. Sovereignty is thus never an *a priori* constraint on civil entry into cross-national defence structures. It is not an existing entity of any kind but a projected course of action, which, because it is never political, can only be necessitated by events outside political society. Plenty of practical and dispositional constraints of course apply to organisation in this field as in any other.

The international society of civil states is not itself a defence structure and civil states are not necessarily military allies. Civil preparations to undertake sovereign action, because it is always directed to possibilities external to civil society, can take a variety of national forms without thereby alarming other civil states. The presence in western Europe of a large and independent Swiss military capability is entirely tolerable, whereas a similarly independent capability in the middle of eastern Europe would be intolerable to the Soviet sovereign. Equally, it is an important aspect of the liberal genius in international affairs that a defence obligation and interest can exist without formal military ties of any kind; thus an attack on Sweden would concern and involve many other civil states because of general obligations contained in the UN Charter and in other declarations and agreements as well as because of many structural and associational links between Sweden and political society.

Military arrangements are in no way central to civil relations as such. Being specialised matters, there can be many kinds of defence commitments. Simply because France is a civil state it does not follow that its governments need maintain the same depth of defence involvement with the United States as do British governments. Variety in the depth of organised defence can become an important matter of civil choice. Preparing for defence is always an activity stimulated by matters external to civil society, so it may seem necessary for a civil state to move outwards and form an alliance with a state whose government rejects the priority of civility. This is a specialised involvement in the external environment of civil statehood. A commitment to the civil relationship includes a commitment to self-determination as an indispensable condition of the achievement of civil self-rule. But self-rule is not the inevitable consequence of self-determination, which may in fact result in governments that conceive of rule as uses of power and not of authority. Civil statehood cannot be imposed, so such unfortunate consequences of self-determination must be accepted. Yet they need not be supported. Thus an alliance with a Greek state subjected to the control of a junta can only be justified (a) by clear external necessity and (b) by the desirability of preserving self-determination in Greece. But the latter justification contains an obligation, since self-determination is desirable as a means to civility not as an end in itself. So this is an alliance that should not take the form of deep organisation having the effect of supporting the control of a junta and thus transforming a necessary means (self-determination) into an undesirable and unnecessary end (rule by power).

The generative response

In their own responses to problems within international political society, regardless of whether these result from the external existence of sovereigns, no necessary constraints limit the scope of organisations that civil authorities may create. But there are numbers of practical problems that are, or appear to be, mutual to both anti-political and civil states. The common existence of these states on a planet of determinate size and physical character means that organised cooperation between them in matters such as weather-forecasting is likely to be a simple requirement of individual effectiveness. But activities like weather-forecasting yield little in the way of positive solutions to specifically cross-national problems, being merely concerned with the provision of information that may be difficult to come by but is far from secret. More truly generative organisations would deal with weather-modification, supervision of the exploitation of the resources of international seas, tight control of world supplies of nuclear fuels, the regulation of international markets in foodstuffs such as wheat that sovereigns purchase but whose supply (and therefore price) is prone to sharp oscillations from season to season. In organisations in fields like these there would be no reason to expect different civil interests to be easily reconciled. The involvement of a sovereign in such organisations would thus entail its participation in cross-national processes of enquiry, argument, mutual criticism, compromise and, possibly, action and there are no certain grounds for believing it to be much disposed to proceed along these lines. By its nature the sovereign places its interests in an imperative category; it also resists processes and arrangements that might qualify its position inside its own domain. However, these are also good reasons for persisting in attempts to incorporate sovereigns in generative organisations since the qualification of sovereignty is wholly in keeping with civil statehood. But, as such, they in no way carry the implication that civil authorities should constantly wait on the accession of sovereigns in making whatever arrangements they deem to be necessary or desirable, any more than they should passively adjust to the membership of sovereigns that devote themselves to obstruction. There is no sound case for allowing a sovereign, in its capacity as a party to a cross-national generative arrangement, to impose itself on civil states in ways that would not otherwise be available to it.

The approximate response

Inside its boundaries, international political society cannot generate threats of war; and its combination of states with statehood provides the conditions of self-rule. The approximative response suggests that sovereigns be incorporated into international organisations on terms that approach these, even though structural sovereignty is the antithesis of self-rule in its own domain and most accurately expresses its own understanding of international relations by the fundamental importance it ascribes to the capability to use force. Two civil approaches to this intractable approximative problem are possible. First, civil authorities may in general deal with sovereigns, whether inside organisations or outside them, from positions of military strength, so that the operational effect on political society of the power of sovereigns is as nearly as possible nullified. Second, values that approach those of political society may be infused into the whole diplomatic collectivity of states, where they may become an element of the conditions in which sovereigns proceed with their foreign affairs. The liberal genius has exerted itself to the latter end. Two obligations of membership of the UN are, first, the avoidance of violence in the national furtherance of international disputes and, second, respect for the self-determination of states. Now these are not civil conditions: avoidance of war is not an absence of military threats; and self-determination is not civil self-rule. But they do not contradict civil conditions. So if a sovereign participates in the diplomatic circle on anything like these terms, then in some small degree it is turned towards the civil form of order.

In the political society of civil statehood cross-national organisation is by no means an exclusively official matter. Innumerable associative organisations absorb themselves in cross-national practices—bridge, mathematics, folk-dancing, sociology, religion. When its subjects participate in such organisations the anti-political sovereign does not surrender its domination over them. But (depending on what kinds of practices are being undertaken) it may be disinclined to intrude itself too obviously. Subjects approximate to the status of citizens if they are able to participate in cross-national associations on terms in keeping with the autonomous traditions of the practices on which they are based. But from time to time citizens who are active in such organisations may feel the effects of the pressures of sovereigns through their subjects. The approximative response requires citizens to exert themselves to maintain the autonomy of their practices in these circumstances; if they fail to do so, approximation cannot occur.

NATIONAL INTEREST

For groups and authorities in civil states the national interest is a term they can freely use as a means of claiming unusual importance and dis-interestedness for their proposals, decisions and procedures. For the anti-political sovereign the national interest is its specific purposes portrayed as the exclusive expression of supposedly fundamental social and historical forces.

The defensive response

Confronted by the sovereign's conception of its interest the defensive response may require civil authorities to take a matching stand on their own interests. Thus an American government took an imperative view of its national interest when confronted by the emplacement of Soviet missiles in Cuba. But this sort of national interest is evoked among civil states solely by anti-political sovereigns; it is not the creation of political society and has no direct part in the play of interests within it. The national interest imperatively expressed by an American government during the Cuban missiles crisis thus has nothing in common with the national interest that that or any other such government may claim to be defending in negotiations over issues raised by the agricultural policy of the European Community.

It may be necessary for a relatively weak civil state, historically and geographically exposed in its relations with an anti-political state, to bend to a sovereign's interest. Thus Finnish authorities have avoided formal attachments with other civil states that might incur the displeasure of the Soviet sovereign. In proceeding thus Finnish authorities may be said to be pursuing their own national interest. But, again, this kind of national interest is created by the demands and threats of a sovereign; it is not a concrete entity with an existence of its own outside the relationship with a powerful anti-political state. Because international political society is not an alliance it is thus possible for Finnish economic and other interests to be actively linked with the congeries of interests that inhabit civil society as a whole.

The generative response

An interest, even a supposedly national interest, exists in a setting of other interests. The interest of the Soviet sovereign is not its metaphysic but its metaphysic freely interpreted by the sovereign in a complex but mundane context. This practical emphasis of interests provides some scope for generative arrangements between sovereigns and civil authorities. For the Soviet Union to become engaged in lengthy arms control negotiations with civil states does not require its denial of its metaphysic but the practical perception of its interest in military stability. In such matters a common language of interests can be generated when there can be no common language of metaphysics.

The approximative response

A modern, or modernising, state cannot in fact mould itself to a single interest. Acute conflict occurs between different interests and persuasions inside both the Soviet Union and China. Externally, the active interests of both these sovereigns in some western markets and their relatively large imports of western capital goods do not fit easily into their theoretical dedication to the downfall of civil statehood. Also the practical interests of states such as Poland or Hungary that are dominated by a sovereign do not in fact exactly conform to the sovereign's designs. The approximative response treats particular interests that cannot be shown to be manifestations of a single dominating anti-political national interest as if they existed on a similar (though clearly not identical) plane to that on which political interests interact. This does not transform sovereigns into limited governments or anti-political states into pluralist societies. It does not hinder such remote developments. But, more importantly, it contributes to the involvement of sovereigns in a complex variety of practical concerns with the conceivable effect of slowly diversifying and possibly softening the otherwise brutal simplicity of anti-political perceptions of national interest.

WAR

The sovereign governs through power not authority. The possibility of the existence of order and security without domination is alien to its perception of the nature of rule, so it must be suspicious of what it does not dominate, the external world of civil states. Also, as the sovereign rejects submission to prior general conditions, it is able to assert its will in its domain by otherwise arbitrary uses of force. The sovereign, then, is to be expected to place military strength at the centre of its approach to international relations. In contrast, a civil authority never has arbitrary power at its disposal within the conditions of civil statehood; and it does not suspect other civil authorities, over which it may have very little direct influence, of preparing to mount an attack on it. There is nothing in the civil experience of rule that can lead civil authorities to approach international political society as an arena in which to exert military power. In the civil perspective the use of military force is always a sovereign act external to the conditions of civil statehood. Acts of war always occur outside the civil relationship because arbitrary violence cannot possibly occur within it. Such behaviour can be justified by an attack on the established priority of the civil relationship but it is no part of the civil relationship.

The defensive response

Civil statehood is a condition of self-rule, it is not an alliance; but within the political society of civil states deep and complex alliances are possible. The civil relationship cannot be imposed by arbitrary force and even when it must be physically defended the necessary sovereign acts of violence take place outside the boundaries of civility. The plasticity of cross-national structures based on civility combines with its fundamental passivity to comprise a formidable kind of strength. Different anti-political sovereigns may be hostile to civil statehood but its own character cannot push them into strong military combinations to attack it. Civility itself contains no propensities to aggressive military action: only the combined and insane folly of civil authorities, not civil statehood, could throw the Chinese and Soviet sovereigns together in an alliance determined to destroy the society of civil states. Because civil statehood is a condition of self-rule, the defence arrangements of civil states are various. This faces prospective attackers with a daunting range of possible military contingencies. And civil alliances have intrinsic advantages over the military apparatus of sovereigns. Nato contrasts with its counterpart in eastern Europe in a number of ways: it can readily coexist with substantial independent military capabilities such as those of Switzerland and Sweden; it can associate with aligned but unintegrated military forces such as those of France; it can function at different levels in different countries, more deeply in the German Federal Republic than in Norway; because of its emphasis on the defence of self-rule its members do not feel threatened by one another; though the multiplicity of weapons that Nato members develop is a possible source of confusion, it also effectively presents the Soviet sovereign with a wider range of changing military techniques than it can readily outreach. And so on: active defence within the context of the civil relationship has many possible strengths.

But the essential requirement of defence effectiveness is the will to resist. Without this, defence strengths grounded in civility turn into weaknesses. If military attack is to be deterred, the will to resist must manifest itself in military strength and in a sufficient measure of defence association among prominent civil states to convey a high probability of mutual support in resisting anti-political military incursions. If deterrence fails and attack comes, then (military and humane considerations apart) the civil distaste for sovereign acts of arbitrary violence requires that resistance be restricted to what is necessary for defence. Even so, necessary defence could entail the use of nuclear weapons. Certainly, if preparation to use such weapons is not made then a sovereign with a nuclear capability may be tempted to exert pressure by threatening its use. Nuclear weapons clearly tend to exaggerate war's propensity to kill otherwise uninvolved civilians; additionally large-scale nuclear exchanges could have catastrophic consequences for civil states intending to defend themselves. These two possibilities must be faced. By planning to use only such force as may be necessary for defence, civil authorities do all they can to minimise possible casualties among non-combatants. Sovereign acts are justified if they defend civility; if resort to war is made in reply to attack then the initial decision in the matter of civilian casualties is in anti-political and not political hands. The risk of the thermonuclear devastation of civil society must be borne if anti-political threats based on thermonuclear capabilities are to be excluded from the affairs of political society. Though this does not mean that civil states must recklessly deploy unnecessarily large numbers of massive weapons, it does demand the standing civil rebuttal of the argument that, in the last resort, civil surrender is preferable to large-scale war because the preservation of ordered living is a superior end to any that results in holocaust. If this argument is accepted widely in civil society then, of course, anti-political attack cannot be deterred. It is, however, fallacious. It assumes that a world surrendered to the domination of sovereigns would be ordered and peaceful. But such a world would be fundamentally unstable because it would be without any constraints but the danger of war, which would thus be increased and not diminished by civil surrender.

The generative response

The anti-political sovereign reduces the state as a whole to an instrument. The military arm is not distinct from any other part of the anti-political state except in practical ways. Such a state thus contains no inherent constraints on the use of military strength, provided (like the rest of the state) it serves the sovereign's will. Contingent constraints do, however, weigh on the sovereign: the more instrumental the state as a whole is taken to be, the more ponderous and even conservative it in fact becomes; the wider the sovereign's domain is extended, the weaker its control (and its sense of its control) in periphal parts of it is likely to be; and, above all, the sovereign is well placed to appreciate the dangers to its own safety of international military instability. In these contingent constraints on the sovereign can be found the possibility of a generative response to war as a mutual, though differently perceived, problem. From the civil standpoint war is a sovereign act, not the act of a civil sovereign since there can be no such creature. Because civil authorities are able to see war as something extraneous to the state it is relatively easy for them to propose all kinds of international arrangements, utilising and penetrating the state, in order to control it; and, as a matter of fact, most arms control initiatives have come from civil sources. The sovereign is prone to respond to these initiatives for contingent and not fundamental reasons. Even when they are relatively successful, it is therefore mistaken to look to arms control agreements between civil and anti-political states as steps towards the abolition by states of the threat of war, since the distinction on which this perception is based is unknown to the sovereign. What arms control negotiations can do is to reduce the likelihood of war by opening military capabilities to a constant process of detailed international investigation and discussion in what amount to permanent institutions devoted to this purpose. Negotiations on strategic arms control between the first-rank states and on regional arms control in Europe among a wider range of states have developed something of an institutionalised character. In the long run

is institutionalisation is more generative than individual agreements
ecause these must refer to given technologies and to specific military and
ther interests that inevitably change and throw up novel problems to which
existing agreements are likely to be irrelevant.

he approximative response

this institutional setting of arms control negotiations can be detected
me hint of the possibility of approximative change. As the use of military
olence by civil authorities is always a sovereign act and not the act of a
vereign, no necessary (as distinct from circumstantial) consideration
revents the intermingling of their different national forces in terms of their
gistics, training and even command inside civil society. Habits of cross-
ational activity in military matters are in fact commonplace in this environ-
ent. But arms control is also a species of cross-national intrusion into
ilitary organisation and preparedness and it is conceivable that something
pproaching civil habits in military matters could be approximated in it.
might be possible, for example, for arms control as an institution to include
ose inspection of the deployment, and even close involvement in the
mmand structures, of some military forces in limited areas of both eastern
nd western Europe.

MORALITY

is impossible to argue that all the acts of anti-political sovereigns are
ecessarily wrong; some of the changes wrought by the Chinese sovereign
ithin its own domain may not unreasonably be held to have been morally
esirable. It is equally impossible to argue that all the acts of civil authorities
e necessarily right; large numbers of the decisions taken by presidents,
ime ministers, cabinets, magistrates, commissioners, parliamentarians,
vil servants and such are manifestly shaped by self-interest, prejudice,
istaken information, stupidity and exigency and not by moral consid-
rations at all. But this is beside the point. Civility is not morality in either
ublic or private affairs. It is the necessary condition of moral judgement
nd argument. The moral difference between anti-political sovereigns and
olitical authorities is not that the former are always immoral while the
tter are always moral. The distinction between them is more crucial than
is. The sovereign claims possession of amorality, but no civil authority can
aim to be superior to morality or to regulate moral criteria. All civil
uthority is therefore open to moral criticism. The subject's moral character
an be defined by his sovereign. The citizen cannot be required to acquire or
pretend to acquire a public pattern of moral sentiments. Authority can
nly require the citizen to act out his life in known legal conditions but no
ivil authority can require a citizen to be moral. The civil relationship is not
moral one. It is the only condition that allows the individual to adopt.

reject or ignore moral criteria as he wishes. Civility itself does not contain anything that (an earlier example) could be taken as a prohibition of legal punishment by hanging; but it does provide the conditions in which moral arguments can be pressed by individual citizens to have this punishment abolished. In civil society moral attitudes change; they are able to do so because civility itself is not a moral attitude but a condition of moral choice. The priority of civility does not ensure or require that citizens lead moral lives but it is a guarantee that they may consider different moral criteria in living. Civil statehood does not itself demand lines of internal or external moral conduct in political authorities. It simply ensures that they will be subjected to arguments based on moral criteria over which they have no control whatever. The anti-political sovereign, on the other hand, may be right or wrong or neither, but within its own domain it cannot be openly subjected to moral debate or held to moral account.

The defensive response

It is plainly obvious that the defence of civil statehood is not the defence of morality. It is the defence of the essential conditions of moral argument and choice and these must also be conditions of possible immorality and of innumerable modes of living from which changes of moral sentiment may ensue. The defence of the civil relationship from the supposedly positive moral attacks of sovereigns or their subjects (or their would-be subjects) is a simple one. The sovereign abolishes all moral choices but its own and it therefore abolishes, or attempts to abolish, all criteria whereby its moral claims may be independently judged. Civil statehood ensures the mainten- ance of the conditions of the existence of moral criteria independent of authority and of the conditions in which pressures based on these criteria may be brought to bear on uses of authority.

The generative response

Civility does not rule out all the moral arguments of anti-political sovereigns; it rules out their absolute claims to regulate moral criteria. Thus a moral view pressed by a sovereign to the effect that, say, women should be freed from social and economic pressures tending to restrict them to domestic forms of self-expression may be entirely acceptable to many authorities and citizens in political society. So there is some scope for generative cross- national declarations of a moral character by both sovereigns and civil authorities.

The approximative response

The approximative response takes the form of attempts to expose anti- political sovereigns to something like the conditions of moral argument and criticism that obtain in civil society. But civil governments do not possess morality. If they attempt to use morality as a weapon, an instrument, against

overeigns then they assume the roles of sovereigns themselves. In this case
ivil governments approximate to sovereigns and not the other way round.
f sovereigns actually approximated to civil authorities they would be openly
ubjected to domestic moral argument and criticism, which they clearly are
.ot. In compensation, as it were, for this lack, civil authorities make no kind
f effort to shield the sovereign's affairs from exposure and criticism by
idividuals and organisations in political society. There is no reason why
itizens should not apply to the behaviour of sovereigns the same moral
riteria they apply in their own political affairs. In civil society the sovereign
oes not rank as a special moral case.

Because the sovereign claims to be the source of its own morality any
rrangements made between it and a civil government demands particularly
lose political scrutiny. This is, first, a kind of substitute for the absence of
.oral enquiry in the sovereign's domain. Second, it is a guard against a civil
uthority becoming the sovereign's agent or even itself assuming something
f the sovereign's superiority over morality. Though civil governments are
nder no obligation to be incessantly considering moral principles in their
ctions (being often guided by conceptions of prudence, custom, exigency or
dvantage) they can never legitimately place themselves above moral criticism.
: may conceivably have been prudent in the circumstances for the British and
.merican governments to have agreed with the Soviet Russian sovereign at
'alta to repatriate all Russian subjects coming into their hands as a result
f hostilities in Europe. But this agreement was secret and British authorities
arried out its terms with particular zeal over a lengthy period in ways, and
ith human consequences, that were effectively screened from contemp-
raneous civil enquiry and discussion. They thus assumed the role of agents
f the Soviet sovereign; and by isolating themselves from moral criticism
hey even took on something of the sovereign's moral status.

The sovereign may not, then, participate in civil relations on its own moral
erms, either by means of its official international arrangements or through
he associative relations of its subjects. Now some of the practices of citizens
re indissolubly linked with moral criteria. These are not at the disposal of
overeigns. Thus the cross-national study of psychology and psychological
nedicine is a humane one; wherever knowledge developed in this practice is
ut to inhumane uses a moral issue becomes part of the professional concerns
f psychologists. A sovereign's subject who participates in a cross-national
ssociation is no more excused the autonomous moral commitment intrinsic
o the relevant practice than a citizen is.

The moral point of civil statehood is not so much that it guarantees that
noral criticism will be brought to bear on governments but that it provides
onditions in which moral criticism may be brought to bear on governments.
n approximative moral response of civil governments in their dealings
ith sovereigns thus stresses declarations of human rights and fundamental
eedoms' such as that contained in the Final Act of the Conference on

European Security and Cooperation (1975), not because these directly extend civil statehood (though its extension is not prevented thereby) but because they may have some small effect in defending moral independence within the sovereign's domain. This response is not the same as using, or attempting to use, morality to attack the sovereign's substantive policies.

INTERVENTION

Inside political society authority is constrained by and within jurisdictions. But authority can be misused; an office-holder (a minister, policeman, judge, civil servant, ambassador) can confuse authority with power and subvert the law of the jurisdiction that confers authority on him. An authority that acts illegally in another jurisdiction is no less culpable than it is if it acts illegally in its own jurisdiction. Civil statehood's jurisdictions define illegality in the same general way; consequently illegal behaviour by an authority in another jurisdiction is not in a class of its own. Intervention-as-illegality therefore has no fundamentally distinctive meaning in political society. In the same way, legal behaviour by authorities in a variety of jurisdictions is not interventionary either: French and British authorities do not intervene in the United States when they go through legal processes to obtain landing rights for their supersonic aircraft. No more is the overlapping of different jurisdictions among civil states interventionary: the jurisdiction of the European Community does not intervene in Italy. The same principal applies to the projects and practices of citizens in international political society. A cross-national enterprise is constrained by the various jurisdictions in which it operates. Simply by being cross-national it is not interventionary. Journalistic investigations and discussions across the jurisdictions of civil states are likewise not in themselves a form of intervention. This is simply political journalism. A British newspaper that gives space to the possibility of domestic illegal behaviour on the part of a United States authority is in no conceivable way intervening in a foreign jurisdiction. Such a matter is anyway of concern to citizens wherever they are. If a British newspaper draws attention to the possible illegality of the behaviour of a British authority, then presumably its readers can have a greater role in tackling the problem than they can in resolving similar issues in another jurisdiction. But this a contingent, not a fundamental distinction.

For the anti-political sovereign, intervention in its own domain has a deep significance: it denotes any kind of foreign influence among its subjects that its power does not exactly regulate. Intervention is thus defined by reference to the sovereign's power, which is at its most unfettered domestically. Holding itself to be the master of law in its domain, the sovereign's external influence in political society cannot be expected to be qualified by regard for the priority of civil statehood. The sovereign's conception of itself cannot be made to differ fundamentally according to the site of its activities. In civil society the sovereign may be constrained by legal authority but it cannot be constrained by its own respect for legality, because it has none. For the sovereign, law is its instrument; where law is not its instrument, it must be an external constraint.

The defensive response

When the actions of anti-political sovereigns inside political society are illegal then, clearly, civil authority acts to apply the law. Actions of sovereigns that are not illegal remain interventions because they are not qualified by regard for the priority of civil statehood. Of course this does not mean that civil authority is justified in taking upon itself the mantle of the sovereign and acting illegally to counter interventions that are not themselves illegal. But a number of civil considerations do follow. The defence of the foundations of political argument requires that no citizen or civil authority attempt to gain or to use a sovereign's support in disputes with other citizens or authorities. The crudity of the sovereign's inspiration ought never to be ignored or passed over in silence wherever its influence is felt. Where a sovereign enjoys the ordinary freedoms of civil society to further its influence there is every justification for civil authorities to attempt to obtain something like reciprocation in the sovereign's domain. Thus freedom from interference for Soviet radio broadcasts to civil states can be used in efforts to gain a similar freedom for civil broadcasts to Soviet subjects.

The approximate response

Within political society territorial boundaries may distinguish jurisdictions but they do not distinguish fundamentally different kinds of rule or of statehood. This means that civil boundaries are never a matter of primary importance (when they are, the civil relationship has lost its priority). The approximative civil attitude to an anti-political state cannot thus include the interventionary purpose of extending the power of civil governments therein or of altering such a state's frontiers. If an anti-political state comes to accept civil statehood, the nature of its boundaries changes but not necessarily their position. And the transformation of a body of subjects into a body of citizens frees them from power, whatever its source—it cannot expose them to power. The secure establishment of civil statehood in Spain does not entail any shift in that country's frontiers, nor does it expose Spanish citizens to foreign power—it frees them from domestic power. No influence originating in civil statehood can in itself have the effect of changing the shape of a state or of extending foreign power over its subjects.

The civil relationship is not denied to subjects by civil authority but by their sovereigns. Approximate behaviour towards subjects can thus do no other than proceed as if they were citizens. To treat subjects as anything other than possible citizens would be to admit the legitimacy of sovereignty as a permanent form of rule. If broadcasts to an anti-political state simply propagate the official views of a civil government then the subjects concerned are in effect being treated by civil authority in a way that differs little from the way in which their sovereign treats them. In this event civil authority approximates to sovereignty and not the other way about. So civil opinion that reaches subjects ought to be the diverse opinions of citizens and not official propaganda. And the criteria applied by citizens in criticising sovereigns to their subjects ought to be no different from those they openly apply in criticising one another's governments in international political society. If subjects are possible citizens (from the civil viewpoint they can be nothing else), then civil intervention in a sovereign's domain is simply whatever extension is possible of ordinary cross-national civil contacts. This is only intervention because the sovereign regards it as such; in civil terms it is simply cross-national civil behaviour.

In their ordinary relations civil governments are always making representations to one another on behalf of the interests of their constituents. This is one of the things representative government is about. In just the same way, civil governments may make representations on behalf of their constituents to anti-political sovereigns. But in crossing over the boundary of civil statehood the kinds of civil interests officially represented may be expected to undergo a transformation. Some citizens may be concerned by the effects of the sovereign's domination over its subjects who are their co-religionists, others by the effects of its domination over their professional colleagues. To attempt to bring some kind of influence to bear on the sovereign in matters such as these is a proper approximative activity of civil authorities. The peculiar nature of the interests represented in this way is determined by the sovereign, not by civil authority. If a civil government rejects this kind of representational function, then in effect it allows the sovereign to determine what representation itself is. When this happens civil authority is made to approximate to sovereignty.

There are no necessary limitations on civil states setting up cross-national jurisdictions among themselves to protect individual citizens from abuses of authority—through, say, the investigatory use of torture. The European Court of Human Rights has a jurisdiction against states and it may deal with complaints both from individuals (via the European Commission of Human Rights) and from states on behalf of individuals. From time to time sovereigns may be induced to join with civil states in approximative declarations of vaguely defined individual rights. But a sovereign cannot allow its power over its subjects to be directly qualified by a clarifying cross-national jurisdiction. In these circumstances, approximative behaviour by civil authorities may properly include critical comment on specific infringements of internationally proclaimed rights within the sovereign's domain. This is likely to be the only possible approximation to cross-national legal proceedings. It is of course a form of approximation that can be consistently attempted only by civil states that have themselves accepted a cross-national jurisdiction in such matters.

ECONOMIC PROBLEMS

'wo active components of the economy of the international society of civil
tates are broadly distinguishable: (a) the volatile mass of interconnected
conomic actions and projects undertaken by individuals, companies, govern-
aents and other authorities; (b) the cross-national associations, arrange-
aents, agreements, communications, organisations and institutions through
'hich attempts are made to regulate, moderate and service these substantive
ursuits. Both these parts of the civil economy operate and relate to each
ther through, and by means of, a cross-national language whose assump-
ons, terms, data, concepts, propositions and theories are not at the disposal
f any specific person, group, movement, organisation or authority. The
xistence, adaptability and creativity of this language therefore depends on the
ontinuing priority of civility.

The anti-political sovereign can make no distinction between its economic
rojects and the context, its domain, in which most of them are enacted.
t also claims sole command of the public language of its economic system
nd of the undertakings of its subjects. Yet no ambitious anti-political state
i likely to be able to isolate its economic arrangements entirely from political
ociety's economy, whose technically advanced products are necessary to the
aaintenance of the sovereign's conception of itself as the begetter of progress.
.lso the more commonplace goods and commodities of the civil economy
aay often be needed to cover the deficiencies born of the rigidity of an
conomy that must always be waiting on its sovereign's commands. Trade
'ith political society additionally brings the sovereign into some concomitant
avolvement with foreign financial institutions since imports must be paid
or and temporary or long-term trading deficits covered. The fortunes of its
xports, meanwhile, are subject to the vagaries of civil tastes, incomes and
ommodity supplies. The sovereign thus becomes entangled in many of the
ctivities of the civil economy and may prove adept in the practical pursuit of
s interests therein. But it cannot allow open markets to penetrate directly
ato its domain because they would inevitably undermine its power and
rovide alternatives to, or stimulate spontaneous adaptations of, its officially
aonopolised economic language. Its claim to total control over its domain's
ansactions with the external world together with its jealous possession of
s own economic language invalidate it as a possible participant in the
:cond major component of the civil economy—its cross-national processes
f institutional regulation and development.

he defensive response

'ivil statehood can never be the basis of some sort of conspiracy to keep
eople poor. The economic projects of a sovereign do not as such excite civil
pprehension or ill-will. Its trading activities take an acceptable place in the
ivil perspective because they may bring benefits to the sovereign's subjects
nd because, in the nature of the exchanging relationship, they are of some

advantage to the sovereign's trading partners in political society. But this does not mean that all trade with the sovereign is harmless. Technology of military use assists the sovereign in intimidating its own subjects by its power, in subjugating those states that circumstances allow it to dominate and in menacing civil and other states in the pursuit of what it believes to be its international interests. No part of civil society can legitimately be put to uses such as these. So there is every reason why the civil economy should be prevented (by the use authority if need be) from being the servant of a sovereign acting out its own misconception of rule and foreign policy.

The sovereign has dealings with the civil economy but it is not a part of it. It cannot allow its own economic language to become one of open discourse, argument and enquiry, and it rejects the premises of arrangements founded on the civil relationship. So its role in cross-national economic organisations could be deeply disruptive. There is thus no merit in efforts to incorporate sovereigns or their agents or vassals into regulatory or servicing institutions deeply involved in the civil economy. On the contrary the defensive response guards against such attempts, just as it is unreceptive to the sovereign's seeking advantage in the civil economy in ways that upset rules and arrangements already made between civil authorities. Since the sovereign will not be bound by civility or by the criteria that civil authorities attempt to work out and apply through their economic institutions, and since it is the sole controller of both the economic life and the economic data of its domain, economic relations between it and political society fall into a distinctive, potentially damaging, category. There is a good case, therefore, for the development of special civil rules to regulate economic connections with anti-political sovereigns in such a way as to protect civil interests and arrangements.

The economic language of the sovereign is not in itself necessarily total error. It condemns itself in civil eyes principally by its capacity to maintain and support the power of the sovereign. If it enters civil affairs it does so on civil and not anti-political terms. It contributes to an endless debate; it does not terminate or replace it. The defensive response rejects the propensity of this language that most attracts potential sovereigns: its claims to resolve economic problems of change and conflicting interests by giving an answer that in fact creates a dominating centre of power and thereby annihilates the variety, individuality and spontaneity from which they spring.

The generative response

The anti-political sovereign cannot join in generative efforts by civil authorities to contain and resolve difficulties of the cross-national economy of political society because it is the enemy of civility. But some economic problems of civil states are economic problems of anti-political states too. Dislocative season shifts in commodity supplies and prices is one such.[21] Commodity markets can be stabilised by a number of familiar devices: the pooling of information about prospective yields in different parts of the world; stockpiling in periods of glut; stock depletion at agreed rates in periods of scarcity. A sovereign could enter into, and benefit from, such arrangements. But a characteristic of this kind of market regulation is that it offers exploitative opportunities to those who ignore or bend the rules (by, for instance, de-stocking more rapidly than others at periods of relatively high prices). If sovereigns do not perceive their interests in generative schemes there is no reason at all why civil and other states should delay in making whatever arrangements they can. Nor are they under any duty (rather the reverse) to put up with disruptive or selfish behaviour by sovereigns in such matters. If discrimination against a sovereign is necessary to the operation of generative agreements (relating to commodity markets or anything else), then there is a *prima facie* civil case for undertaking it.

The approximative response

The cross-national economic projects of political society are subject to two kinds of rules: (a) prudential, but not necessarily authoritative, rules particular to categories of economic activity such as banking; (b) formal authoritative rules relating to fair competition and the like that are binding on governments and enterprises of all kinds. In trading relations between civil society and sovereigns, rules of both types cannot be exactly applied. The sovereign cannot be seen to accept civil regulation, and any rules whose applicability depends on free availability of economic data will be regarded by the sovereign as a challenge to its power. Approximative economic relations closely approaching those of political society are thus most likely to be achieved with states, like Poland or Hungary, that are dominated by a sovereign but not totally controlled by it. But in all circumstances something in the nature of approximation can be attempted: information (about production costs for instance) can be sought and, if appropriate, queried; and the negotiation of private or governmental loans should include normal investigations into the capabilities of borrowers to meet interest charges.

The general worth of approximative economic relations lies in their potential: (a) for rendering more complex and practical, and so perhaps less crudely adversarial, the sovereign's connections with, and attitudes towards, political society; (b) for bringing some kind of qualification to the power of the sovereign, at least among some of the states it dominates; and (c) for being of some material benefit to individual subjects who, from the civil viewpoint, are always to be regarded as possible citizens. But the sovereign is not just a slightly eccentric partner in trade, or anything else, and arrangements with it rank for particularly close public examination. Preferential treatment of the sovereign (through, say, the provision of easy finance) inevitably diverts resources that might be put to better civil use and it is therefore always questionable. Less specifically but even more importantly, anything that assists the sovereign, whether preferentially or not, also assists its policies and many of these may be repellent to citizens.

CONCLUSIONS

1.   It is not open to political states to deny the civil relationship to the subjects of anti-political states. This is what sovereigns do. Civil society responds to, it does not create, the rejection of statehood by sovereigns.

2.   The propensities to reject the priority of civility manifest themselves inside political society. They evoke civil responses that may be classified as defensive, generative and approximative.

3.   This categorisation of responses is clearly applicable at the international level.

CHAPTER 10

Outside Political Society: Unpolitical States

This enquiry has distinguished the states outside political society in a negative way. They are states without civil statehood. Among these states it has further distinguished a special case: the state as an unqualified instrument of an anti-political sovereign. In no sense can a plurality of anti-political states comprise a society since what they have in common, total domination by highly structured sovereigns, precludes any such possibility. The anti-political sovereign is an extreme case in relation to statehood, not in terms of its cruelty or rigidity or cunning or of any other such quality. It may be these things but they do not distinguish it. We are thus left with a category of 'unpolitical' states whose individual leaders may be more (or very much less) cruel or rigid or cunning than anti-political sovereigns. Again, this is a category distinguished by negatives: a state in it is neither bound by the conditions of civil statehood nor subject to the total domination of a sovereign conceiving itself to be the coherent historical antithesis of the autonomous civil state.

UNPOLITICAL ATTITUDES TO THE STATE

Civil statehood is a set of conditions that can be met in, among and across any number of states. An appreciation of civil statehood and an acceptance of the priority of the civil relationship do not comprise a doctrine of action but a qualification of action. Civility is categorical in what it excludes, its own replacement. Within the boundaries of civil statehood any number of doctrines can propose different futures. In contrast, the effect of the anti-political annihilation of the autonomy of the state in favour of supposedly implacable social abstractions is to place the future unreservedly in the hands of a sovereign. The anti-political state, thus reduced to an instrumental apparatus, cannot be the basis of conceptual or practical alternatives to the rule of the sovereign. Any number of factors (inter-personal hostility among leaders, social turmoil) could conceivably shake the party structure that is the sovereign of Soviet Russia; but the Soviet state, being an accoutrement

187

of sovereignty, cannot of itself constitute a condition of change. Change in
the unpolitical world is a different matter. Here the state is not autonomous
but it is not indissolubly joined to a determinate historical sovereign either
The nature of such a state must then be determined by the attitudes of those
holding power, or seizing power, over it. Being human, there is nothing
unique or mysterious about these attitudes. They become remarkable when
in the absence of statehood, they are transformed by power into active
characterisations of the nature of particular states. But they are imprecise
the doctrines they generate are little more than justifications of particular
governments; even when widely shared they do not necessarily contain
violent conflict; they cannot be formulated as wholly general conditions of
public conduct. Change is built into the unpolitical state.

The state as a possession

Where the civil relationship is accorded precedence over all other human
associations, personal ambition in governing is held in check by law and
diversely placed authority; by an ambitious leader's need to hold support
among different communities, groups and interests; and by the incessant
pressures and criticisms of legitimate competitors for office. The civil state is
never the actual or possible possession of an interest, community or person
   A country without statehood may be socially diverse but its sections
communities and interests are not constructed on the basis of a general and
impersonal relationship via explicit general rules. The way may thus be clear
for an individual or organisation, by deft use of whatever power comes to
hand, to possess the state. Such a state becomes a tangible object—to be
obtained by violence, subterfuge, conspiracy, bribery, promises, demagogy
personal drive and determination. Government conceived as possession of
the state is tyranny. A tyranny may be erratic and monstrously cruel (as the
current possessor of the state of Uganda is) or it may be relatively circumspect
and humane (in the manner of the present possessor of the state of Tanzania)
Though unhampered by authority a tyranny cannot be sustained by it either
The state is merely an extension of a tyranny's power. If this power collapse
(if a private army breaks up) the state will not protect its ruler from his
enemies. The successfully tyrannised state is put to the service of its master's
enterprises whatever they are. Humane or inhumane, the state has no
categorical bearing on them; as an object it cannot prohibit what is contrary
to its general conditions because it contains none. The tyrant may be con
strained by the nature of his power but the only constraints the state imposes
on him are those resulting from its finite capabilities. Tyranny is not a principle
of rule and it is not a policy. It is a description of a certain attitude to govern
ment that in the absence of a strong fabric of civility may also describe the
nature of a state. When a tyrant dies or is killed or deposed such a state
becomes available to a new tyranny that will put it to uses appropriate to

new structure of power and new ruling temperaments. Other kinds of successors may attempt to transform the tyrannised state from an object into something like a principle. In either case the state itself cannot provide the conditions of ordered change.

As discipline

Civil statehood is a principle of order not of action. It does not direct a mass of citizens towards any end. Leadership in the civil state is politically qualified but the political qualification does not describe leadership. Civility in no way guarantees effective government. Uses and non-uses of civil authority may often seem to be stupid or imprudent. But while its priority lasts the civil relationship ensures that folly, error and indecision may be subject to change; that neither important insights nor interests will for long be overlooked; that citizens will not feel themselves deeply threatened by authority itself and will therefore be able to contemplate its being put to uncongenial uses with distaste rather than panic.

In the absence of civil statehood the functions of government and the notion of order may become deeply confused in the attitudes to the state of those with power, or the possibility of power, over it. Order may thus become instrumental, a means to an end. The state exists to provide government; governing is the achievement of goals; therefore the state is the specific form of order that a government's policies require. By this logic the state becomes discipline. It is a means of tackling specific problems (inflation in the Argentine), of fulfilling the grand ambitions of rulers (the achievement of a version of modernity in Iran) or of regulating a population in such a way as to enable a government to move carefully but independently in the face of external domination (Romania). In some circumstances the conception of the state as a form of discipline may seem to be one to which there are few realistic alternatives. Nor is a state of this kind necessarily put to ends that are themselves foolish or wicked. But this is beside the present point. The state-as-discipline is in fact dependent on discipline, so that a collapse in discipline becomes a collapse of order too. In large populations discipline is unlikely to be maintained indefinitely for a large number of commonplace reasons: goals may turn out to be interminably difficult to achieve, so that discipline comes to seem pointless oppression; or goals may actually be realised, in which case promised relaxation may become breakdown; or the practical instruments of discipline (a party, an army, a police force) may split, nurture a variety of claimants to power, go to war with one another, or decay and become disorderly themselves. Discipline is invariably a limited sort of order. It is specific, unresponsive to social change, intolerant of opposition, self-righteous and probably puritanical. Individual or group opposition to discipline, or to the goals it is claimed to serve, becomes opposition to order. Attacks on government are seen as attacks on the state. The

state-as-discipline often hangs on the brink of disorder. Government become
rigid, prone to panic at the prospect of change. As a form of order, discipline
rejects what is not anticipated by policy. It is thus not a principle of statehood
but a way in which government uses the state.

As community

The individual citizen of civil society may, or may not, find the values of his
life in the sense of community created by a nation, a clan, an organised
religion, a group of artists or some such collectivity that he and others create
Communities often influence civil government. Representatives are invariably
sensitive to the values and interests of large communities among their
constituents and governments commonly assist communities of all sorts
with public subventions (to help preserve a minority language, to maintain
religious schools, to support musical and other societies). But the civil state
as such is not a community. A citizen in Britain is under no compulsion or
obligation to involve himself in the affairs of any particular clan, party,
religion, club or choir or to participate in any sporting, cultural or patriotic
manifestations. A law-observing citizen may pass an unmolested life in total
indifference to the goings-on of all the communities in the society in which he
lives. It may be contended that the civil state cannot survive in harsh external
circumstances unsustained by deep countrywide communal loyalty. No such
necessity exists. It is, and has been, possible for Welshmen, Jews, resident
Poles and Czechs and individualist artists and sheep-farmers to fight in
defence of the British state not as a community but as the civil conditions of a
variety of communities and of solitary individuality as well.

In political society the human tendency to equate the state with a community
is not uncommon. In the absence of civil statehood it may become an official
orthodoxy. An unpolitical state (Libya or Pakistan) may be seen as a quasi-
religious community or (in the case of Uganda) as the servant of a tribe or
(Somalia) as that of a racial community or (South Africa) as a combination
of all these. The state-as-community is almost invariably claimed to be a
justification of arbitrary rule. Virtually no state is in fact geographically
coterminous with any single community. So the community-state becomes
the means of subjugating other, supposedly inferior or disloyal, tribes,
races or religions within its borders. And where its own community or a
community it oppresses overlaps its boundaries into adjacent states it is
likely to add international conflicts to those that exist within it. Law in such a
state becomes a means of preserving an officially defined communal character.
It thus attempts to compel a moral, cultural or religious identity on its
subjects. Since values do not exist in the abstract, these states have a tendency
to enforce definite social institutions—particular forms of education,
marriage and family life, religious observance, public ceremony. A state that
is the instrument of a community has little resistance to a leader who can

effectively claim to be the apotheosis of the communal interest. Entirely general rules constraining authority cannot be born of a community that holds itself to be unique and purposive. The community-state is thus by definition weak. Its strength is that of the community that dominates it. But this community will create internal enemies (and probably external enemies too) by its overbearing claims. And the efforts of a community to resist change by the possession of a state are unlikely to be successful indefinitely. A state that is used to resist social and cultural change cannot also be the general conditions of order. The attempt by a small community to create its own state of Rhodesia inevitably failed to secure stability among a diverse population.

As movement

In the civil state there is one cause that no *political* movement can consistently further: the replacement of the priority of the civil relationship. This is also a condition that ensures the endless beginning, combining, changing, decaying, splitting of movements of all kinds. It is because civil statehood itself is not a movement that a diverse society can express different perceptions of its problems without degenerating into a collection of warring camps. Because the civil relationship is a wholly impersonal one the civil state inevitably tends towards representative forms of government with universal adult suffrage. Impersonality imposes generality and on what other general basis (except the casting of lots) could government possibly be organised? But civil statehood is not democracy and its principles are not those of a popular movement. The regulation of power by authority is an effect of civility that is apt to be resisted by a movement with sweeping aims (the Nazi party) and a large following. In such circumstances, loud claims for the legitimacy of power founded on democracy (usually referred to as 'the will of the people') are likely to be bruited about. These are almost invariably anti-political in purpose. The close connection between civil statehood and democracy does not, therefore, exclude conflict between them. Where the civil state developed historically in advance of democracy (e.g. Britain) it tends to be slightly more secure than where it developed in association with democracy (e.g. Italy). But wherever there is a depth of confusion between democracy and civility the state becomes insecure and the prospect of its being put to the service of unabated power claiming its source in the popular will may be one that constantly threatens. When this begins to happen the nature of order (not simply the nature of what practical action a government should take) becomes the matter of democratic struggle.

Many unpolitical states (Algeria, Pakistan, Indonesia) have been born out of sometimes violent movements. And they have almost all been deeply touched by the language of purely democratic notions of rule. The historical conjunction of this fact with this theory leads often to the perpetration of the doctrine that a particular state is a movement founded on the true interest of its people. Such a view may have practical attractions for hard-pressed leaderships: a combination of a plurality of movements with a weak state may seem an infallible recipe for complete disorder. So order and the language of democracy are conjoined by a single official movement that uses the state to mobilise a population in support of its leaders and their policies. And by these means definite programmes may be instituted; the state-as-movement controls democracy to achieve what may appear to be effective government. Whatever it does (or does not) achieve, rule to this formula cannot infuse strength into the state as a lasting fabric of order. It can give leadership every opportunity to degenerate into tyranny. It can provide the mask (in easten Europe) of foreign domination. It can open a gap between official democratic rhetoric and the unresponsive, if not entirely oppressive, behaviour of the state's rulers. It cannot make contenders for office openly tolerant of one another or adapt the public language of democratic unity to a language of free public debate and doctrinal disunity. It may attempt to direct change but it cannot allow change and stability to play upon each other.

As interests

Being various, civil society engenders large numbers of organised interests that vie with one another in their attempts to influence the use of authority. From time to time an alliance of interests (manufacturing interests, trade union interests, agricultural interests) may achieve relative superiority and succeed in moving policy and law in a preferred direction. But while authority constrains power this process cannot be taken very far. Resistances develop and fresh associations of interests push policy in another direction. Practical government is in fact dependent on the incessant pressures, arguments and protests of interests for its sense of the realities of the society in which it operates and for its information as to the likely, or even actual impact of the measures it proposes and institutes. So formalised are the motions of the universe of civil interests and so intimate its contacts with government that it can be concluded that the civil state is no more than a collection of interests that conduct their conflicts in a way that maintains a fairly stable long-term balance among them.[22] This view is mistaken. It confuses a description of the outcome of civil statehood with an explanation of its nature. The complex rules of the game of interest-relations cannot be the spontaneous creation of interests themselves. In the absence of the civil state there would be no reason why a powerful interest, having won the day, should ever peacefully yield its control of government or why directly opposed interests should not resort to extreme measures against one another. It is because of the civil state that a strong group does not press its interest violently while a relatively dis-advantaged group can show patience in its efforts to sway authority in its own direction. As importantly, the priority of the civil relationship enables individuals both to involve themselves in expressing different, even conflicting, interests at the same time and to alter their group attachments as their personal circumstances change. This individual mobility is possible because interests that are politically qualified do not demand or need the totally undivided loyalty of their supporters. The effect of this individual movement among, and cross-linking between, civil groups is to moderate cleavages and to promote something that may be described as equilibrium among them. But the origins of these effects lie in the limitations that the civil relationship places on interests in the first place. Without civil statehood, ordered change through, and by means of, a shifting equilibrium among a mass of interests would be impossible.

In the absence of civil rule mutually advantageous alliances between interests may be possible. But large-scale peaceful change via a dynamic balance among interests of constantly varying relative strength is far more difficult. Without a strong prior civil relationship, an interest (organised labour in the Argentine, land-owners in Colombia) may become a primary and unshifting loyalty, a matter of their survival even, for its members. The existence of interests without statehood thus intensifies problems of social disequilibrium. A group dominating a government is likely to feel deeply threatened by other interests seeking to exert pressure on it. So it may seem rational for a controlling interest (in, say, Nicaragua) to resist by all available means any growth in the power of its competitors. The state becomes an element in group competition, not a condition of it. An already powerful institutional interest, the army, if it remains relatively undivided, is unlikely to feel inhibited by such a state from using its weight to take on the role of governing and to regulate other interests by the use of force. In an unpolitical country, like the Argentine and other Latin American states, which is swayed by contending interests, the process of government is thus likely to incorporate periods of military rule. But this method of resolving problems of deep instability among groups depends, as a rule, on the suppression of some of them, particularly when, as is often the case, the army itself is intimately associated with a particular interest. In these circumstances a further build-up of social pressures is likely to occur that will eventually disturb an enforced order in radical ways.

RELATIONS AMONG UNPOLITICAL STATES

Attitudes to which unpolitical states are subject are not unfamiliar in civil society: ambitious leaders confuse the offices of civil authority they occupy with personal possessions; those claiming to represent a community may be inclined to use the state to enforce its values on others; from time to time an interest may seem disposed to equate the well-being of the civil state with its own advantage. Unpolitical states are not distinguished by these attitudes but by their inability to contain and qualify them.

The plurality of civil states is described here as a political society. This usage avoids the implication that all civil governments are engaged in a joint project or that all citizens identify with one another in terms of a common concern or movement. They are not and they do not. The political society of civil statehood is one in which any number of cross-national official and unofficial linkages may be forged and any number of practices enjoyed. But it follows that it is open to any particular country, enterprise or citizen to proceed individually. The civil relationship is a complete one because it is impersonal, without necessary boundaries and because it is a condition of other relationships whose nature it does not dictate. Direct relationships (interests, movements, communities, enterprises, practices) are incomplete because each involves relatively few persons and because in each the individual is less than totally engaged (even the most obsessional of artists must enter a market of some kind to sell his works). Being complete, the civil relationship excludes war, which is a consequence of relationships of hostility and not a condition of other relationships of a non-hostile kind.

Because of its inherent weakness the unpolitical state is not as such a sufficient condition of peaceful internal change. Like all other direct relationships, relationships inside the unpolitical state are incomplete; but in this case they are not founded on a complete, impersonal, civil relationship. So the incomplete relationships (interests, movements, communities, even practices) of the subjects of unpolitical states become the elements of possibly extreme conflicts. Politically unqualified rule is apt to deal with such conflicts by attempts at discipline and by tyranny. But these kinds of rule themselves utilise arbitrary violence. They therefore stress the role of power in change (or in resistance to change) and in the containment of actual or latent internal conflicts. Though it may experience static periods, violent change (or violent resistance to change) is thus immanent in the unpolitical state. The same potential exists in relations between unpolitical states. The condition that makes for a possibility of violence between Chile and Bolivia (the absence of civil statehood in both countries) is the same condition that makes for the possibility of violent change within each of them; it is not the property of their longstanding territorial quarrel. The territorial problem relating to Gibraltar between Britain and Spain does not go away simply because civil statehood begins to be established in Spain; what goes away is the possibility of a violent or quasi-violent attempt at its resolution and this removal bring a variety of other solutions within practicable reach.

The potential for violence in some relations among unpolitical states does not mean that all unpolitical relations may be characterised in this way. For one thing, there may be no particular conflicts between states in this category; between, say, the Argentine and Pakistan. For another, there may be no capability for large-scale violence between some such countries; so that the

Argentine and Pakistan could not make war on one another even if their governments were motivated to so engage themselves. More importantly, unpolitical states, in the nature of the category, are deeply diverse. Weak unpolitical government may be wholly preoccupied with internal problems. A conflict-ameliorating sense of identity (of Arab identity or black African identity) may be cross-national. Some of the interests of some unpolitical states (in stable markets for comodities) are in part mutual. Tyrants may be realistically aware of their limited international capabilities; or respectful of cross-national religious ties; or they may simply form friendships with one another. Just as the ways in which different unpolitical states are ruled conform to no single pattern, so the relations among them conform to no single pattern.

Power

Sovereign power is strength (of a movement, an army, a clan, a government), which is implicitly or explicitly held to be unqualified by civil conditions by those with the capability to use it. So in the civil state sovereign power always takes the form of action occurring beyond the (not necessarily spatial) boundaries of civility and it is always a response to violent anti-political challenge. Within the boundaries of civil statehood the authority of a civil executive or judge or police force is not power because in each case it is regulated by explicit laws and precedents that cannot be legitimately changed at the whim and convenience of any one of these authorities and because each civil authority may be held to account by some other civil authority. In the relations of civil states (whatever the influences at play in specific issues) power has no role since, among other factors, no civil authority can act in a sovereign manner towards another civil authority that itself observes the conditions of civility. The United States does not contemplate the use of sovereign power against Norway. Outside the boundaries of civil statehood, no conditions *necessarily* prevent strength from being put to the service of power.

(1) The anti-political state is a special case among unpolitical states; it is the state wholly at the disposal of a sovereign that explicitly and historically rejects civility; the anti-political sovereign, being self-constituted, accepts no prior or exogenous metaphysical or legal or other limitations; its strength is therefore also its power; constraints on its strength are practical and contingent, not constitutional or moral.

The arena of unpolitical states is one in which the anti-political state operates with some freedom, unhampered by the existence of civil conditions. External strength is for the sovereign an end in itself: if the sovereign is power, it needs strength to express itself. The ends to which its strength may be put are in general secondary to its existence. The sovereign has a relatively weak sense of specific interests (in trade or in practical cooperative projects) and a relatively strong sense of its need for strength. Its foreign activities do not therefore always merit analysis by reference to what one might think to be its practical interests. It may simply be crudely motivated to extend the bases of its power.

Because the anti-political sovereign is the total master of its own state and because it cannot acknowledge anything in the nature of autonomous statehood, the state in anything like the civil sense imposes no necessary constraints on its activities and purposes. Whatever the constraints the Soviet sovereign experiences in eastern Europe, a sense of statehood (of wholly general conditions of rule) is not among them. How could a sovereign genuinely accept a kind of legal definition of itself in an area it dominates while denying the validity of any such definition internally? It can for this reason only make contingent distinctions between the internal and the external conditions of its operations. Given the social and linguistic variations among unpolitical states, it is likely that the sovereign will be content to exercise power within them through surrogates—indigenous rulers in receipt of its support and responsive to its wishes. The essential quality it will look for in surrogates is a sense of sovereignty. So the rulers who will seem to be appropriate to this role will be those most given to absolutism, yet lacking the capabilities to make themselves self-sufficient in this manner of governing. A tyranny with substantial capabilities of its own is unlikely to remain for long a submissive or even suggestible client. Surrogates acquired by the anti-political sovereign are thus most likely to be found in otherwise weak unpolitical states. The acquisition of such clients has two kinds of consequences. The strengthening of a tyranny and its association with unqualified anti-political purposes make it a formidable force in any disputes in which it may involve itself. And a disregard for the state as such (of which the anti-political sovereign is the extreme manifestation) is likely to excite apprehension in unpolitical governments whose regimes may be internally vulnerable to the attention of the sovereign or its surrogates. On both scores the presence of the sovereign among unpolitical states accentuates the role of power both internally and internationally.

(2) Regardless of the presence or otherwise of an anti-political sovereign, unpolitical rulers are to be expected to be much concerned with the resources of strength at their command. The absence of strong constitutional supports means that an unpolitical government must maintain its rule in other ways. However large the popular following it is able to attract, some measures taken by such a government will almost certainly be widely uncongenial and if its population is at all diverse there will be some communities or interests whose allegiance will anyway be doubtful. The armed services will thus be closely associated with government or they will dominate it. Even in the relatively easygoing unpolitical state (e.g. Brazil) the distinction between rule and power is not a sharp one.

In its nature, the calculus of power cannot be isolated within the borders of particular unpolitical states. A military capability inside Iraq is also a military capability across the borders of Iraq. Regional systems of power relations among unpolitical states result. The military capabilities of the government of the Argentine concern the governments of adjacent states. To such regional power systems anti-political sovereigns may contribute, directly or indirectly: the Iranian government responds to the strength of Soviet Russia; Sudanese and Egyptian governments respond to the strength of a Soviet surrogate in Ethiopia.

Associations, interests, problems and open diplomacy

Power relations between unpolitical states derive from two sources: first, the active presence among them of anti-political states and their surrogates; second, the important place of power in the internal government of unpolitical states and its possible availability for the prosecution of international quarrels. However, power relations and relations among unpolitical states are not identical. If they were, weak unpolitical states would almost invariably be subject to the domination of their stronger unpolitical neighbours. But large numbers of unpolitical states of varying shades of weakness appear to be able to maintain their independence. No perceptible general trend suggests any imminent revision of this remarkable fact of international relations. During the modern period of the emergence of unpolitical states, the incidence of internal uses of power has exceeded the incidence of the international uses of power between them. And there is no equivalent in the unpolitical world (despite marked concentrations of strength in, for example, Brazil and Nigeria) of the intermittently violent domination of eastern Europe by the Soviet Union.

Unpolitical rule is open to qualification in ways that manifestly moderate the power component of relations among unpolitical states. An explanation of this availability to qualification is apparent from the course of this enquiry. Unpolitical states have been distinguished by two negatives: the absence of civil statehood; and the absence of determinate historical sovereigns. The absence of the first explains the association of power with unpolitical government; the absence of the second explains the generally modest role of power among unpolitical states. An unpolitical government is not, as such, subject to any inherent necessity to revise and control history or to regulate the religious or cultural lives of their subjects, and all these may be redolent of continuing cross-national connections (to think in terms of Latin American history, culture, society and religion is not to give oneself up utterly to woolly illusions). Specific affiliations can also cross many unpolitical frontiers: the subjects of unpolitical states may be Baptists, freemasons, the employees of cross-national corporations. Though individual tyrants (whose passing is assured by their mortality) may become insanely unrealistic, unpolitical rulers as a class are under no metaphysical compulsion to claim infallibility. They may therefore acknowledge the existence within their states of intractable economic and even social problems and seek international support and involvement in tackling them.

Dominant attitudes in each individual unpolitical state are often likely to merge: a ruler may simultaneously regard his state as a possession, a form of discipline, a project and a community. This is a matter of no fundamental importance to this enquiry, which cannot be engaged in an attempt to propound a general theory of unpolitical statehood. Since there is no such thing as unpolitical statehood there can be no theory of it. Unpolitical states are an empirical collection not a theoretical category. So there is nothing intrinsic to the plurality of unpolitical states that is a standing denial of international qualifications of power among them. Again, these qualifications are likely in practice to be mixed. In an empirical collection denoted by negatives it would be absurd to cast about for *a priori* patterns. Some of the ways in which unpolitical power can be qualified internationally are readily classifiable, but classifying is not the same as theorising.

Associations

Links of an associative nature do not easily become common projects: unpolitical Arab rulers more readily denounce an enemy (the community-state of Israel) than they can incorporate themselves in a joint action against it. Associations are not alliances; they are cross-national identities within which both governments and peoples may locate themselves. Associated governments may quarrel about their relative authenticity in relation to this identity and about whether, if at all, their association should support specific policies. The plurality of states within an associative identity means that it is far from easy for a single government or movement to mobilise it to swell its own power. 'Black Africa' does not belong to any one of its identifying elements. But whatever the divisions within it, an association is likely to sustain some sense of fraternity having an inhibiting effect on the degeneration of mutual quarrelling into outright hostilities. The rarity of international war in Latin America is in part the effect of a Latin American associative identity. Though it may affect an organised structure, an association cannot be centralised. The OAU is unlikely to become subservient to its own organisation or to one of its members, and while it remains African it is unlikely to succumb willingly to domination by an outside power. Yet an organised association inevitably draws its members into constant consideration of the practical meaning of their identity. Thus the OAU attempts to formulate general rules about the conduct of inter-African affairs. Unpolitical associations can in these ways have a quasi-civil character: they qualify mutual conflicts but they do not abolish them; and they may have normative influences on their members and even on outsiders.

Interests

Unpolitical states do not fall into a single economic category. They include very poor countries (Pakistan) and rich ones (Saudi Arabia); primary producers (Ghana), industrial producers (South Korea) and mixed primary and industrial producers (Brazil); government-dominated economies (Tanzania) and relatively free economies (Singapore). This diversity generates a complex mass of sometimes conflicting interests and government policies. The interest of some states to secure and maintain high oil prices clashes with the interest of poor agricultural states in low fertiliser costs. The products of poor but industrialising countries (e.g. textiles) may very well be similar and compete in the same markets. Particular interests in an unpolitical state (just as in a civil state) often conflict and so do interests between unpolitical states that otherwise identify with one another. When interests coincide, cross-national organisations of some strength (OPEC most obviously) may be created; yet these may contain mutually suspicious governments. If a general case for preferential economic treatment is to be made in the GATT or the UNCTAD or to the European Community, then many otherwise non-identifying countries may have to find some common ground. The interests of the unpolitical world are not regulated by a sovereign relentlessly manipulating one ideological language. Again this is a quasi-political environment in which criss-crossing connections and tensions are apt to confound crude notions of the centrality of power to international relations, even though power may be central to the domestic affairs of many unpolitical states.

Problems
Interests merge into large-scale problems: attempts to stabilise raw material prices may also be attempts to alleviate dire poverty; and attempts to alleviate poverty merge with efforts to combat poverty-associated diseases. A sense of the existence of world problems (of illiteracy, disease, primitive agriculture and such) has become part of modern civil consciousness. The fact that unpolitical governments have played some part in creating it is more remarkable than it may seem. The notion of world problems is expressly non-national. It invites cross-national concern and assistance; it assumes that in efforts to relieve social problems more is at stake than simply strengthening the hands of unpolitical rulers; even the incessant discussion of world problems at the UN and elsewhere presupposes the state to be something other than the instrument of power. Cross-national assistance to unpolitical states may not induce an attitude of humble gratitude in unpolitical governments (nor should it) but when it is invited, collectively or singly, the state conceived as the exclusive domain of a ruler loses some of its metaphysical gloss. Contrastingly, the anti-political sovereign's consciousness of itself does not include much of a sense (let alone explicit admission) of inadequacy, nor can it easily see its subjects as part of a larger society on anything other than its own terms; little cross-national involvement is invited in world problems as they manifest themselves inside China.

Open diplomacy
The age of open diplomacy has broadly coincided with the acceptance in

constitutional countries of the view that an imperial connection between the civil state and any population extraneous to it cannot in the long run be a proper one. The link between open diplomacy and unpolitical states is close not only in this historical sense but also because the diplomatic stage has, as a matter of fact, been made highly available to them whatever their age, size or relative internal instability. On this stage, *inter alia,* unpolitical states have furthered, or attempted to further, general social causes (the relief of poverty), adaptations of international law (on, for example, the status of sea-bed mineral resources) and specific campaigns of a transnational character (against the domination of the state of South Africa by one of its smaller communities). Public diplomacy put to these uses suggests that the internal affairs of states are a legitimate matter of external attention and comment; that the geographical state as such is not an absolute value and that a language of individual human rights and obligations (however bogus its use may sometimes become in the UN and elsewhere) is a fundamental part of international relations as a whole; that statecraft can simultaneously be concerned with explicit rules and with the pursuit of specific interests; that the interior nature of a state does not exist in isolation from the kinds of international issues it becomes involved in. These working assumptions, however obscured by the noise and hypocrisy of public diplomacy, are far from alien to the nature of civil statehood.

FUNCTIONS OF UNPOLITICAL STATES

The only generalisation that holds for the populations of unpolitical states is a negative one: the civil relationship is not the established foundation of their social and individual experience. The absence of the autonomous state does not mean that unpolitical armies, parties, interests, leaderships, bureau-cracies, and religious or other communities are weak; on the contrary, in each unpolitical state one or more of these is likely to be overweeningly strong. Being itself an outcome of civil conditions, this enquiry is not committed to the unpolitical state as such. These states are facts (not theories or principles) that this enquiry must place in a civil perspective. It therefore understands them collectively as a large international structure that functions in ways that are useful to (or that can be useful to) the maintenance or extension of the civil relationship.

Regulators of power

In the civil state, authority is set against power; in the unpolitical state, authority is submissive to power. Yet it does not follow that the plurality of unpolitical states confers power on rulers. Apart from its possible social and material constraints (poor agricultural countries cannot as a rule support massive armies), the unpolitical state regulates power by virtue of its standing as a geographically delimited domain of rule. Two principal international effects result. First, an autocrat's direct and untrammelled power is likely to be terminated at the geographical frontiers of the state he dominates; this effect is even felt within cross-national associations, so that a powerful Arab ruler cannot blatantly extend his direct rule into any part of another Arab state that is not itself in a condition of collapse. Second, the efforts of an unpolitical government to increase its power are likely to make some of its neighbouring rulers apprehensive; and these adapt themselves accordingly, so that a tendency to use internal power for international purposes is likely to be regulated along traditional balance of power lines by unpolitical states themselves.

Unpolitical states make important contributions to the safety of civil states:

(i) Power is held in the lattice-like structure of the multiplicity of such states. This structure also makes power intelligible, so that it is a fairly easy matter to perceive possibly dangerous trends in sectors of the unpolitical world. Unpolitical states are neither an organised nor an unorganised attack on political society. But if their international instability were as great as their internal instability the resultant world disorder would at least damage the economic interests of civil populations; but much more importantly, it would draw civil authorities into attempts to impose order on so dangerous an environment. This would be damaging to the nature of civil rule (since imperial domination cannot in itself be civil) and it could involve civil states in a variety of possible wars, some of which could be catastrophic to themselves. Unpolitical states as an international structure can contain both power and the instability associated with rule by means of power.

(ii) Unpolitical states are a limitation of sorts to the easy extension of the power of anti-political sovereigns because they supposedly denote populations ruled from within. Anti-political sovereigns must exercise some caution in directing any surrogates they may acquire in unpolitical states. Even in eastern Europe the Soviet sovereign operates with circumspection. In the unpolitical world generally, as a sovereign acquires surrogates and contributes to their power, so counterbalancing effects are produced among other rulers feeling themselves open to direct or indirect challenge.

(iii) The plurality of unpolitical states confers choice on civil authorities in their activities in the unpolitical world. Unpolitical rulers are far from uniformly inhumane. A civil authority involved in African affairs is unlikely to feel obliged to support a savage autocracy. But it may support the African association in a general way and maintain close links with other rulers of relatively open disposition. The plurality of unpolitical states means that civil states do not have to rub shoulders with, and by implication support, power in its most brutal forms.

The individual unpolitical government addresses itself to the external world through its state. But in this international setting the language of the state must be shared among a large variety of states. An interest common to most unpolitical rulers is that this language should stress their right to independence from foreign attack. Other values as well have been injected into the language of open diplomacy, largely as a result of liberal efforts of the past: most obviously, peace is commonly spoken of, and assumed to be, a state of affairs to be maintained or pursued by governments rather than as an effect of a given state of affairs among governments. A public international language of the state that stresses peace and independence places some constraints on a ruler, movement or community that might otherwise regard its possession of a state to be an opportunity of extending its power abroad.

Conditions of self-determination

Judged by criteria derived from simplistic notions of communal or geographical consistency, the land frontiers of most states are arbitrary: Belgium and Switzerland are not more rationally shaped states than Ghana or Kenya, they are simply older; the boundary between the United States and Canada has no more intrinsic sense than the frontiers of Nigeria or Tanzania. The state as such does not depend on some deeper preceding order by reference to which the rationality of its form may be determined. The *civil* state is the conditions of an internal political order and of an international political order too; the boundaries of its jurisdictions are contingent; only its boundary with its environment is fundamental. In marked distinction, the unpolitical state (where its frontiers, for whatever reason, are stable) can provide the framework of an international order; but its internal order is an arbitrary one, driven here and there by the dispositions of those who have power over it. The existence of the boundaries of unpolitical states is thus a matter of very great importance: they place physical limits on the power of any one ruler or ruling group; and in barring outside power they can confer different possibilities of self-determination on each of the populations they delimit.

Self-determination is not self-rule. The population upon which the state of Pakistan confers self-determination is not infrequently the victim of authoritarian military governments. So self-determination is not a protection against tyranny. The difference between Denmark and Uganda is not that one has self-determination while the other does not, but that Denmark has both self-determination and self-rule while Uganda has self-determination only. From the civil viewpoint, the importance of the geographically stable unpolitical state lies in its function of providing for the self-determination of its population. But self-determination is not an end in itself; its merit lies in the possibilities that only it can make available to what in most cases must be arbitrarily demarcated populations.

The possibility of a tradition

No historical law dictates the appearance or non-appearance of civil statehood. But however mixed a state's population, the establishment of civil statehood as its common foundation is likely to be linked to some sense of a common past; only in this way do the misfortunes of unpolitical rule become shared misfortunes. However oppressive unpolitical government may be, its mere occurrence within historically lasting boundaries is likely in the long run to make the problem of achieving stable rule a common one for the population concerned. Though the civil relationship is completely impersonal, its priority manifests itself in part in the non-violent manner in which sometimes bitter conflicts surrounding government policies are conducted. This civil adaptation of public conduct may, for want of a better term, be described as style or tradition. This style differs in some degree from population to population (as between, say, Japan and Sweden). Civil statehood is a constant, but the manner of the tradition that helps to preserve it varies from place to place. The experience of the seriousness of self-determination in a geographically stable state provides the circumstances in which such a tradition can develop. Of course the fact of the self-determining state does not ensure the evolution of a political tradition. But this does not mean that there is any plausible alternative to the state in the performance of this function.

The possibility of choice

Self-determination in the unpolitical state sooner or later means instability of rule (instability, that is, in the practical meaning and application of law) whatever the achievements of a particular unpolitical government may be. The fact of change and the prospect of change (even change at the mercy of power) can implant the sense of the possibility of choice. One way of governing can be chosen in preference to another. Civil statehood is a clear set of conditions that can be chosen; in fact its maintenance means that it is chosen. Again, the possibility of choice conferred by the unpolitical state does not mean that civil statehood becomes an inevitable selection. But without choice in the first place there can be no civil statehood.

The means of international involvement

From the civil viewpoint, all the subjects of unpolitical states are potential citizens. Their interests are not somehow inferior because of the misfortunes they may suffer at the hands of unpolitical rulers. Many such interests (relating to access to world markets for example) are international in the nature of the ends they seek. The state, however oppressive its internal regime, offers a means of furthering interests of this sort. In its international representations, an unpolitical government (of Chile or Ghana or Egypt) has the means to forward interests that would continue to exist, and would still be pressed in much the same way, were it replaced by a political government. In the civil prespective legitimate interests are generated by the problems of the lives of individuals, regardless of whether these are citizens or subjects. That a legitimate interest may have to be expressed by a state in the hands of an unpolitical government is unfortunate but it does not invalidate the interest concerned.

The fact that the state can be (though it may not be) a legitimate international actor even though its government is unpolitical has two additional general functions:

(i) An unpolitical state may be legitimately active in a multilateral context under the auspices of international organisation. Thus the military forces of unpolitical states have participated in UN peacekeeping operations in the Middle East and elsewhere. Though not without its ironies, from the civil standpoint the use of the forces of unpolitical states in this way is a functional effect of their existence as a legitimate international structure even though in many cases the internal autonomy of such states may be less than impressive.

(ii) A state may be unpolitical because it is in the possession of a particular racial or religious or linguistic community. In these circumstances the possessed state is likely to be used to oppress those of its subjects belonging to other communities. A community suffering in this way may be better represented (or those identifying with it may be better represented) in another unpolitical state, in which case the latter may provide an international voice for the otherwise 'stateless' community. Thus African and other unpolitical states may draw attention to the situation of coloured communities in South Africa. All subjects (in the civil view) are potential citizens and a characteristic of a citizen is that the state as such does not debar him from public representation: so there is no reason why one unpolitical state should not be used for the international representation of a community debarred from representation by another unpolitical state in the grip of another community. In some small way unpolitical states as an international structure thus do something to balance the defects of individual unpolitical states as internal forms of government.

Few, if any, unpolitical states are without internal structures in the shape of ministries of health or agriculture or the like. In civil eyes, the projects (the improvement of agriculture and public health) in which official departments of this sort may engage are in no way any less legitimate than those of their equivalents in civil states. There is no *necessary* reason why a tyranny should not be genuinely interested in preventive medicine. Activities like these both create and depend on a large number of cross-national linkages: the developments of public medicine and of scientific farming are transnational in both their character and their effects. The unpolitical state as an internal structure may then be a condition of cross-national projects. Without its own ministry of agriculture an underdeveloped country would not be well placed to benefit from technical advances and from cross-national cooperative assistance that could increase the productivity of its land. In matters like these the state is the condition of all kinds of projects that could not otherwise be undertaken.

CIVIL STATEHOOD AND UNPOLITICAL STATES

Unpolitical states may thus be perceived as a large international structure performing functions of a quasi-political kind. This is true, but it cannot be a complete way of resolving the problems for civil perception created by the unpolitical world. This is not a self-contained entity that may be viewed from afar. It abuts, and may in practice be mixed up with, the society of civil states. Political authorities may act upon, and with, unpolitical states. This being so, the radical differences among such states come to the fore. Though there may be a civil view of the unpolitical world as a whole, a civil authority actually experiences it as a diverse plurality of states. This enquiry must therefore attempt to form a view of the unpolitical state as an individual unit.

Proximity

The distinction between civil states and unpolitical states is not one that separates consistently virtuous governments from consistently wicked governments. A mark of the civil state is that it constrains (and, sometimes, transforms) unpolitical attitudes and tendencies without resort to sovereignty, not that it is altogether free from these attitudes and tendencies. Civility is not just practical arrangements that have this effect, it is as well the basis of explicit criticisms of aspects of life in civil states that seem to infringe or endanger its conditions. Thus attention may be drawn to the tendency for some authorities in the German Federal Republic (by the so-called *Berufsverbot,* the official vetting of applicants for public service appointments) to intrude too far into individual lives. Or some British authorities may be criticised for regarding the problem of the absence of civil conditions from Northern Ireland as reducible to one of policing. Again, a mark of civility is not the absence of such criticisms of the conduct of public affairs but the legitimacy of making them. The individual civil state in its practical arrangements and affairs is not an absolute value.

(1) Just as the nature and existence of civil statehood is not a mystery, so proximity to civil statehood is not a mystery. A tyranny that prevents free foreign travel in the territory of the state it possesses, that monopolises with its own official voice all the means of public communication among its subjects and that disposes of its opponents by secret imprisonment and murder, is further removed from civil statehood than a tyranny that allows travellers fairly free contact with its subjects, does not prohibit the sale and circulation of foreign books and newspapers and attempts to intimidate opposition

largely by open but discriminatory edicts. A military junta that allows freedom of religious practice is likely to be closer to civil statehood than a junta that attempts to compel a single set of religious observances on its subjects. Common sense suggests a number of ways in which the existence of the priority of civility manifests itself: official acceptance of unimpeded travel and enquiry by foreign visitors; the imposition of punishment only as a result of open legal process strictly regulated by known general rules; freedom of publication and debate; and many more. Each criterion can be thought of as a scale; and the proximity of life in any specified unpolitical state to civil conditions can be marked off, as it were, on each of these different scales. The gap between civil statehood and an unpolitical state is not to be measured on one scale but on several and is to be expected to vary over time and from scale to scale.

(2) This method of 'locating' unpolitical states probably articulates the assumptions behind the ordinary approach of citizens to this problem. Its results, however, are far from determinate. It is a relatively simple matter to place an insanely murderous tyrant at the extreme unpolitical poles of almost all the scales that can be imagined. But placing becomes much more complex nearer the boundary of civility. Two problems are prominent. First, the multiplicity of scales (relating to representation, public debate, freedom of publication, open legal process, rigour in the generality of laws ...) necessarily entails overall indeterminacy. Discriminatory laws may be conjoined with open legal procedure; relative freedom of communication with 'fixed' elections. Thus an unpolitical state may be close to civil statehood on a number of scales but relatively far removed from it on others; and if it is impossible (as it is) to weight each scale accurately, the overall placing of such a case must be a rough-and-ready affair. A second difficulty of placing is no less acute than this one. No civil state measures up to all the standards of civility. Obviously most citizens occasionally fall, or nearly fall, victim to anti-political or unpolitical impulses or ambitions. On ·many scales few actual civil institutions could score top marks: judiciaries are rarely wholly independent; most civil executives contain elements that may be apt to ignore the rules constraining their authority; virtually every known electoral system contains a bias of some kind. Given these human and institutional defects it follows: (a) that there can be no single citizen or organisation with sufficient civil authority to determine with complete assurance the weights of scales of civility or the places of unpolitical states on them; and (b) that because civil states are, as it were, relatively virtuous in different directions (one having a more independent judiciary, another having fairer elections) there is legitimate scope for variations in political attitudes towards specific unpolitical states. So the position of an unpolitical state in relation to civility is both actually a variable and interpretatively a variable. No one centre in international political society has sufficient civil stature or knowledge to make final judgements.

Frontiers

International political society's interior frontiers denote different jurisdictions and these can overlap. The frontiers of an unpolitical state cannot denote a jurisdiction in quite the same sense. In this enquiry the term jurisdiction has a civil meaning that cannot be separated from rule through constitutional authority and legal process. But the unpolitical state is without autonomous statehood and is therefore subject (to an indeterminate degree) to the internal whims and exigencies of power. The geographical boundaries of this power are unlikely to be complicated: a 'jurisdiction' overlapping two unpolitical states is likely to become the occasion for a struggle for dominance between their respective rulers. This effect of power on boundaries means that the establishment of autonomous statehood is the necessary condition of stable cross-national jurisdictions. The absence of a civil jurisdiction within the unpolitical state means that its frontiers with political society will tend to vary according to the interests and predilections of its successive governments. A murderous tyranny will close the frontiers of the state it possesses in two ways: first, by directly restricting opportunities for foreigners to witness the misfortunes of its subjects; and, second, by the intimidating hazards to life and property in its territory that are the consequence of its disposition. The impermeability or otherwise of unpolitical frontiers is thus largely determined by the nature and uses of power within them, and these will differ over time and from state to state. All kinds of factors (e.g., diverse and articulate populations, complex cross-national economic linkages) may make for a degree of modesty among unpolitical governments and consequently for some permeability of the frontiers of the states they rule. But though the closure of an unpolitical frontier may be the unilateral effect of internal power, its opening cannot be a single-sided affair. The penetration of private and official aspects of the life of civil society (through, say, direct cross-national investment or official economic or defence assistance) into an unpolitical state inevitably raises the problem of civil support for power. Given that the proximity to civility of any particular instance of unpolitical rule can never be subjected to precisely objective measurement, this problem does not lend itself to fully determinate and authoritative solution. It is a matter of legitimate argument, change and adjustment. But unpolitical rulers who lower their frontiers have no standing in the regulation of civil conduct; in admitting some contacts with political society they cannot also expect to constrain all the comment, enquiry, argument and influence that goes with these contacts.

Equality and ambiguity

In international political society all jurisdictions share an equal validity. The federal jurisdiction of the United States is not in any sense superior to the jurisdiction denoted by the borders of the Irish Republic. It is bigger, but that is all. In just the same way, the jurisdiction of the European Community is not superior as such to the jurisdiction of the Dutch state; the former overlaps the latter, so that in some matters Dutch authorities are liable to legal process at the Community level; but this is not a difference of status, only of competence. Since civil statehood is autonomous conditions, it must follow that all its national and transnational manifestations share in its status and are completely equal in the sense of being part of the same thing. The equality of jurisdictions has nothing whatever to do with their size.

(1) Equality in the acceptance of the priority of civility clearly qualifies a state for involvement in the cross-national jurisdictions of international political society. A state subject to rule by unqualified power, on the other hand, cannot be incorporated into a civil jurisdiction for two reasons: first, it could not be expected to accept civil authority if this clashed with the interests of its rulers; second, its participation in civil institutions would expose citizens touched by their jurisdiction to the possibility of arbitrary regulation from sources outside the boundaries of political society.

The institutions of a civil jurisdiction (whatever its extent) are not only a manifestation of civility, they are its protection too. But it follows from this that though a cross-national jurisdiction cannot incorporate an unpolitical state, it can have the function of protecting hard-won and possibly precarious civil conditions in a state that has lately been freed from rule by power. Since the civil relationship is prior to all other relationships, this protective function also takes priority over any other matters with which such a jurisdiction may be concerned. So if membership of the European Community is likely to protect citizenship in a state in which civil statehood is recently established its application for membership must be seen first in this light and only secondly in the light of all the economic considerations involved.

(2) As a matter of fact, not theory or principle, a state that demarcates a population and assists in its rule by unpolitical governments cannot be the equal of the autonomous civil state. Yet the notion of equality in the world that includes both civil and unpolitical states is not emptied of meaning but becomes rich in ambiguity.

(i) The individuals collected within the boundaries of an unpolitical state can only be ranked in civil eyes as possible citizens who are denied this status by their circumstances. The subjects of unpolitical rule are deprived of an equal relationship to statehood. This deprivation cannot be imposed on them by civil authority. So far as possible, citizens and civil authorities therefore regard subjects as if they too were citizens.

(ii) The unpolitical state whose borders are stable and that is free from foreign domination provides conditions of self-determination for its population. The civil state, on the other hand, confers both self-determination and self-rule. Though self-determination in the unpolitical state may show itself in disorder and tyranny, it remains the essential condition of self-rule. In the civil perspective, therefore, all states, regardless of their size or strength, are equal (or should be equal) in their provision of self-determination. The outcome of self-determination may be judged in terms of proximity to civil rule; but however horrific its results for the subjects of unpolitical rulers, self-determination is still necessary to civility.

(iii) A population denoted by the frontiers of an unpolitical state has interests (in trade and material advancement or in the exclusion of foreign domination from whatever source) that would remain substantially unaltered were the priority of the civil relationship to become established therein. Such interests are in no way inferior to those of actual civil populations; that they may be expressed by an unpolitical government does not alter their status of equality with civil interests. This obviously does not mean that all interests pressed by an unpolitical government fall into this category.

Civil diplomacy

Civil relations with the unpolitical world thus appear to be riven by tensions resulting from conflicts among civil commitments. The civil outlook ascribes a high instrumental value to the plurality of unpolitical states as an international structure that controls and limits power, regulates the effects of the disorders of societies without statehood and constitutes the necessary conditions of self-determination though not of self-rule. The frontiers of the unpolitical world are therefore matters of fundamental importance, essential to the fulfilment of these functions even though the experience of the civil state provides no rational criteria for placing them. The state as a (usually mixed) population in the throes of self-determination cannot exist separately from either the state as a unique territory or the state as the equal in status of all states. The civil emphasis on the role of the state in the unpolitical world may thus seem to be a support of tyrannous government, upon which it seems to confer both internal licence to rule by power and an apparently legitimate equality with political authorities in the conduct of world affairs. Yet all subjects of unpolitical rulers are possible citizens, supposedly deprived of civil conditions by circumstances entirely extraneous to civil statehood.

Tensions like these are not structural defects, to be rectified by radical redesign. They are what distinguishes civil diplomacy from other kinds of diplomacy. No single authority, let alone person, speaks or acts for civil society as a whole. It is a diverse entity and it relates to the unpolitical world in diverse ways. The international institutions that it has created do not all abruptly cease at its boundaries. All unpolitical states need not in fact be treated as if they were identical; their individual proximity to civility is not a matter of indifference to citizens or authorities. Interests expressed by unpolitical governments do not all have equal standing in political society and any unpolitical state seeking to identify with civil states must expect the full weight of civil observation and comment to fall on its affairs. A commitment to self-determination is not a commitment to power; it is a commitment to the possibility of a civil outcome to self-determination.

CONCLUSIONS

1.   The nature of the unpolitical state is determined by the attitudes of those who have power in it. These attitudes have diverse forms and origins. The unpolitical state is thus a condition of unstable change in which power may be expected to play a substantial role.

2.   In the civil perspective the plurality of unpolitical states comprises a structure that can perform quasi-political functions: the international regulation of power, the provision of self-determination, the facilitation of cross-national contact.

3.   Stresses occur in the dual civil commitment to self-determination and to citizenship. Though there can be no method whereby it can be precisely applied, the notion of proximity to civility is central to the resolution of these stresses. Since the frontiers of the unpolitical state are essential to self-determination, internal power can close them to civil contact. It cannot, however, open them to political society entirely on its own terms.

CHAPTER 11

Civil Statehood, Unpolitical States and Issues of Foreign Policy

From the political standpoint, sovereignty is the exercise of power in disregard of the priority of the civil relationship. Civil statehood is this priority. For civil states two general conclusions follow. First, relations across the boundary of civil society should be arranged in such a way as to reduce to a minimum the occasions on which sovereign behaviour on the part of otherwise political authorities may seem to become necessary. Second, the possibility of the occurrence of such occasions can only be expected to disappear when states at large accept the priority of the civil relationship and their subjects become citizens.

CIVILITY AND ITS UNPOLITICAL ENVIRONMENT

The civil relationship is not a plan of action. It is not a defined human identity that can be imposed. And it is not a theory capable of consolidating a movement. It exists as the conditions of the multiplicity of projects and practices in and among civil states. No civil authority either monopolises or directs the civil relationship. The problem this enquiry must now address is that of clarifying the relationship between civility and its unpolitical setting. The civil state does not cease to be itself whenever its authorities and citizens act or consider acting among unpolitical states. But how do seemingly passive civil conditions denote conduct appropriate to circumstances in which they are commonly ignored?

THE FIRST GENERAL CASE

Consider the case of a possible world composed entirely of civil states and unpolitical states.

Neither collectively nor individually could the unpolitical states of this world constitute a physical threat to the existence of civil society, though of course an unpolitical government might use or threaten to use force in, for example, pressing a territorial claim against a particular civil state. Since

211

the generality of civil states themselves comprises a society in which power does not figure in public affairs, they would not be individually motivated to recruit unpolitical military allies in competition with one another; and for just the same reason no civil state would attempt to establish a form of domination over numbers of unpolitical states in order to forestall a military competitor from within civil society. The unpolitical state is both a product and a condition of internal structural instability. There would therefore be no cause to believe that unpolitical governments, themselves subject to the possibility of violent overthrow, could form long-lasting links with one another, least of all that they could create deep military alliances in order to aggress against political statehood. On the other hand, because the internal arena demarcated by the borders of the individual unpolitical state is one in which the distinction between power and authority may have little, if any, meaning, it would always be possible that power might manifest itself violently in the relations between unpolitical governments themselves.

The regulation of power

The system of territorial states can function in two closely related ways: it can hold specific cases of severe structural instability inside the territory of the state in which it occurs; and because of its wide distribution of power this system can restrict the tendencies of unpolitical governments to use force in their foreign enterprises. For these reasons the authorities of civil statehood (which is itself the antithesis of power) would actively support the system of states and would attempt to strengthen its formal rules, prominent among which is the one that requires observance of the integrity of state territoriality. In general terms, civil states would thus favour the territorial *status quo*. But, there being no universal rational determinants of frontiers either in the political or the unpolitical worlds, civil authorities would be disinclined to take dogmatic stands in the detail of border disputes between unpolitical states. For this reason, and because they could not support the violent reconstruction of frontiers either, they would actively further organised international efforts to settle such disputes as peacefully as possible. This might involve the attempted international legitimation of boundaries partially fixed by war. There is no necessary inconsistency here. From the civil standpoint, unpolitical states regulate power, so it would be inconsistent to expect power to play no role whatever in shaping them. Similarly, given that the proper function of balance of power systems in the unpolitical world is to maintain the existence of states, it would not be inconsistent for civil authorities to provide some military assistance to unpolitical governments anxious about the disposition of strength in the unpolitical states around them.

The extension of civility

The only deeply categorical boundary in political eyes is the one that marks the limits of civil statehood, and in the first general case civil states would need some military strength to protect this perimeter. They would also require weapons in order to support international peacekeeping efforts and to pass on to unpolitical states threatened regionally by deteriorating power positions. The regulation of power through the maintenance of the system of states would nevertheless be an instrumental concern on the part of civil authorities. States provide the conditions of self-determination; and self-determination is the necessary, though not sufficient, condition of the extension of civility. Because civility cannot be imposed, its extension could only be served indirectly. Though there would obviously be no certain conviction of ultimate success in this matter, civil states would try numbers of possibilities. They would exert themselves to establish links between the rules of the states system and international organisations of all kinds so that the notion of the state as a world structure might be propagated. They would have a cautious enthusiasm for parliamentary diplomacy so that the activities and pronouncements of national governments, however tyrannical, might occasionally be subject to legitimate debate and criticism in international, if not national, assemblies. Since civil statehood is an entirely general conception, both civil authorities and citizens would lay stress on cross-national enquiries into internal uses of power against individuality, in this way attempting to dissociate self-determination from any notion of the particular state as an absolute value in itself. Such possibilities of extending the civil relationship would not add up to a strategy. Always the innumerable cross-national projects and practices (trade, science, sport, entertainment, gossip) of citizens might be held to be more plausible means to this end.

Indeterminacy
The world of the first general case would clearly be full of practical problems to which there could be no exactly determinate solutions. Providing support of any kind for unpolitical states could not be entirely separated from maintaining their governments in office and some of these might be cruelly tyrannous. Associating unpolitical states with some of the cross-national institutions of political society could provide them with opportunities to hinder and discompose civil governments besides conferring on them the appearance of civil respectability. The history of the European balance of power is no idyll; civil support for regional balance of power systems could result not in peaceful self-determination but in violent international disorder. And so on. Most of these problems would fall into one of three categories. First, there would be those whose handling related to judgements about the proximity of a state to civil conditions. A government in financial difficulties in a state close to acceptance of civil order would be more generously dealt with than a junta primarily devoted to enforcing its own rule. Yet, of course, proximity to civil statehood could never be precisely measured. Second, many interests pressed by unpolitical governments would have a constant, quasi-political validity. Attempts to stabilise commodity prices would merit cooperative civil attention largely irrespective of the standing of the govern-

ments involved. But, again, it would be no simple matter to decide what could be included, and what could not be included, in this category. Third, there would be situations in which numbers of unpolitical states (all linked in a multiplicity of ways with civil society) would be engaged in quarrels of their own. Civil states might now find themselves drawn into problems in which any action (or even inaction) on their part might seem to one of the parties to be an encouragement to the other or to be an infringement of its own self-determination. In these circumstances a civil authority would be motivated to maintain a stable regional international balance, to support states close to acceptance of the priority of statehood and to encourage the parties to move towards their own kind of accommodation. Rarely would these policies be without strong mutual contradictions.

THE SECOND GENERAL CASE

This first case is now changed by the addition to it of anti-political sovereigns.

A world composed exclusively of civil and unpolitical states would not be free of horrors and upsets: poverty, disease, tyranny and war might be familiar to many of its inhabitants. But in such a world there would be no reason to believe civil states generally to be in imminent jeopardy or to fear that disorders among unpolitical states might become worldwide. Though the spread of the civil relationship could not be taken as inevitable, there would be every reason to believe it to be probable in the long term, given common civil prudence, understanding and openness. A number of important changes appear to be wrought in this world of the first general case by the insertion into it of anti-political sovereigns. Most prominently, civil states may doubt their continued existence if sovereigns begin to acquire sufficient strength to act out the crude logic of their own conceptions of themselves. Singly or in groups civil states are therefore moved to increase their strength accordingly. Now there exists a danger that political and anti-political entanglements in unpolitical conflicts may spread to dimensions unimaginable in the previous world. This fear is intensified by the propensity of sovereigns to acquire and support surrogates who are themselves drawn to sovereignty and consequently contemptuous of prior rules, conventions and arrangements regulating international troubles and tensions among unpolitical states. Meanwhile, the strong sovereign, deploying a language entirely uninfluenced by individuality and therefore easily bent to justify all its actions, dominates states near its borders where its power is at its strongest.

The addition of sovereigns to the first general case must intensify its dangers. Whether a complete transformation results must be doubtful. In this enquiry anti-political states have been located as special cases in the more general unpolitical category. But their internal structural stability could in fact be fragile. More importantly, it has been established that sovereigns of comparable strength do not (and cannot over more than short timespan) join in large enterprises, least of all to subvert the unpolitical (or the political) world. Their disposition to associate all conflict in some way with violence is often in evidence in their mutual relations, as in the cases of Soviet Russia and China or of Cambodia and Vietnam. In isolated instances, where foreign domination is resisted (as by Yugoslavia), a sovereign can seem to yield to steady internal amelioration. Even within their spheres of domination, major sovereigns find it virtually impossible to work a total divorce between the state and the principle of self-determination: Poland, Romania, Vietnam and others maintain distinct identities in international relations despite their apparently subordinate situations. And anti-political leaders do not necessarily confuse themselves with their own rhetoric. They may be acutely aware of their limitations and of the dangers to themselves of major disturbances in the states system. So uneasiness about the scale of the effects of possible disturbances originating in the unpolitical world is not restricted to civil society. The sovereign is surrounded by unnerving dangers: by possibilities of resistance to its will among its own subjects; by apparently irresistible tendencies to self-determination among the states it dominates; by the unreliability of surrogates; by the inevitably threatening strength of other sovereigns; by the bewildering many-sidedness of political society as well as its endless technological advances. A sovereign becoming intimately involved in numbers of unpolitical disturbances in areas remote from its immediate domain is likely to feel itself dangerously overstretched. And the physical dangers to itself of violence originating in unpolitical countries escalating to thermonuclear levels of destructiveness are likely to be as vivid to the sovereign as to any other power, authority or individual.

The transformative effects of the second general case on the first are thus problematic. But they may not be perceived as being problematic and can trigger three kinds of reactions in political society that are inimical to civility.

Emulation

In a spirit of desperate competition, strong civil governments may feel themselves drawn to emulate the sovereign: to maintain spheres of domination; to ignore self-determination in order to destroy uncongenial regimes; to cosset tyrants useful to their international purposes. But the emulative tendency is always troublesome to civil society. Because it cannot monopolise a public language of either domestic or foreign affairs, a civil government will have difficulty in disregarding self-determination abroad while itself comprising a manifestation of self-determination in its own state. A more crucial consideration also weighs against emulation. In a civil state the argument that uses an end (international resistance to a sovereign in this case) in justification of almost any means (support for a sadistic tyranny) can never pass unquestioned. Civility is conditions. It makes no distinction between ends and means. This is why civility is the contradiction of rule by a sovereign.

Civil authorities (just like citizens themselves) may be drawn by necessity to step beyond the boundaries of civil statehood in order to defend it; but they do so by way of specific actions, not by taking upon themselves the structural form of the sovereign. To propose that only by becoming a sovereign is it possible to respond to a sovereign transforms a civil description of desperate but necessary defensive reactions into a theory about the plastic nature of the civil state. But the nature of the civil state is the civil relationship. It cannot be something that is not the civil relationship. It is not all plastic.

Simplification

Being the servant of power, the language of the sovereign deals in vast generalisations that can be readily manipulated to suit the sovereign's needs. Civil authorities and citizens may, however, be so impressed by the apparent force of the sovereign's vocabulary as to be drawn to construct their own simplistic images of the world. It may thus come to seem that civil principles should comprise an international entity, a bloc ('the western world'), which should be led into its environment according to simple directions contained in a clear conceptual map. However, any language subject to civil condition is also subject to unregulated complication. Though defence organisation may be very necessary to the defence of civility, it in no way follows that civility is, or ever should be, a bloc, least of all a specifically western one. No assumption could be more contrary to its nature. Strength, however organised, can never in itself maintain, let alone extend, civility as such. Moreover, the nature of the external environment is far from clear. The distinction between anti-political states and unpolitical states is not always an empirically exact one. And proximity to statehood can never be precisely determined in particular unpolitical cases. One of the essential points about civil statehood is that it does not provide a clear map of what lies beyond its boundaries. Citizens and authorities may thus act in this environment in all kinds of different ways. Political society as a whole is not, and can never be a plot. The role of strength in the external world can only reasonably be perceived by civil eyes as an extension of its role in political society: that is, to counter the effects of the strength of sovereigns and to protect the conditions of self-determination. But these are far from precise prescriptions. In some circumstances, arriving at conditions of self-determination (in the Middle East for example) is a central issue. In others, force can have no direct bearing on self-determination, as is the case in eastern Europe. And the problem of scale is always an important one. Massive strength used by political authorities in the unpolitical world can hardly ever, in the nature of the undertaking, actually coincide with local self-determination. Simplification of the external world inevitably distorts the civil perspective.

Incorporation

The existence of a geographical world almost completely covered by states may be confused with the existence of a world system of states similar to that of the first chapter's model. This response to the second general case incorporates all states in terms of a single variable—their relative strength. Thus most unpolitical states are relatively weak, while anti-political sovereigns are for the most part relatively strong. But each state in the world system may be expected to act in the same mode, according to the international disposition of power around it. The relations between civil and anti-political and unpolitical states are thus all subsumed under a fully incorporative model in which governments of all persuasions may be expected to behave similarly. No special problems, it may seem, are created by differences in the nature of states. The defects of the incorporative tendency have already been suggested in the first chapter and elsewhere. It assumes that international relations cannot be *about* anything at all. It denies the existence of political society. Moved by it, a strong civil state would be unable to make any distinction between weak civil states and weak states of other kinds and could make deals at its own level with regard only to its own power position. Nothing could change such a system except massive destruction brought on by a generally manic pursuit of strength and its exertion in the form of power. The incorporative response cannot be integrated into the civil outlook.

FOREIGN POLICY ISSUES

The distinctiveness of the second general case is open to doubt. There must therefore be an element of choice about whether to enter into it in either practical or conceptual terms. These considerations are fundamental to this choice: (i) in the first general case the maintenance of an identifiable civil position, though difficult, is not impossible; (ii) the second general case, on the other hand, evokes responses that are, as indicated, inimical to civility. Consequently, the civil reaction to the second general case must have these components: scepticism as to its accuracy; resistance to the peculiar responses it is prone to stimulate; active preservation of the first general case from the second's transformative effects. So this enquiry now proceeds to review issues of foreign policy in the framework of the first general case. The second general case will be seen as possible effects on this framework that the civil standpoint does not readily accept.

EXECUTIVE DOMINATION

In the third chapter the problems of the executive's role in treaty-making and war-making were surveyed together with those raised by the executive's inclination and need to conduct itself secretly.

The first general case
Civil statehood in this general case would be under no broad external threat. Power would play a greater or lesser part in the internal affairs of unpolitical

states and periodically it would manifest itself violently in their relations with one another. This would be an aspect of the states system's regulation of power at the international level in the unpolitical world. Though this system could not control power in the same way inside state borders, it would provide conditions of internal self-determination. By its nature, the course of self-determination cannot be planned from outside so there could be no determinate civil strategy for bringing about an acceptance of the priority of the civil relationship.

(1) Though a civil executive in this first case might have a specific frontier dispute with an adjacent unpolitical state, it would not feel itself to be under such fundamental threat as to enter into systems of military alliances with unpolitical states to secure its own defence. In efforts to maintain stability in the extra-political environment it is conceivable that a civil executive might be tempted to make specific arrangements with some unpolitical states to guarantee the integrity of their borders. Yet this would be a hazardous policy. Territorial guarantees would only be called for where frontiers were anyway uncertain; but, as has been shown, there exists no fundamental rationale to which the fixing of boundaries anywhere can be categorically referred. Treaties guaranteeing uncertain and disputed unpolitical frontiers would therefore constitute obligations that could draw civil states into attempting to sustain by external force divisions whose functions would relate essentially to the unpolitical world and not to civil society at all. There would be every reason not to enter into such treaties. On the other hand, a generalised commitment on the part of civil governments (in conjunction with unpolitical governments) to an international order founded on the territorial integrity of all states would have much in its favour. It would legitimate all kinds of diplomatic and other civil involvements in disputes among unpolitical states without compelling rigid side-taking. Given the role of power in the relations of numbers of unpolitical states, it would clearly be folly on the part of civil authorities to attempt to act according to clear rules of a supposedly just kind; sooner or later these would have to be imposed (in which case an imperial relationship would be created) or abandoned (in which case justice would have seemed to have been forsaken by civil authority).

Power is arbitrary and cannot, therefore, be clearly distinguished from violence. The prominence of power in them marks unpolitical states as being outside the boundaries of civil statehood. However stable international boundaries in the unpolitical world might become in the first general case, domestic violence would remain an element in the affairs of unpolitical states. Civil authorities would be under no necessity or general obligation to become involved in these troubles. But through ordinary contacts with unpolitical countries, and as a result of the active endeavours and requests of unpolitical governments, some civil involvements in the internal affairs of at least some such states would be inevitable. But, again, rigid commitments would be full of dangers and contradictions. A specific civil obligation to a particular unpolitical government might add immeasurably to its strength without also inculcating any civil sense of moderation in its conception of itself. Thus bolstered, such a government might be encouraged in tyranny. Alternatively, the appearance of dependence on foreign support might further discredit an insecure government among its own population. In general terms, the more foreign help demanded by an unpolitical government, the more unstable its internal situation would probably be. Substantial discontent inside an unpolitical country would be a sure indication of the existence therein of fundamental issues of governmental structure and direction. So, given the civil commitment to self-determination, it would follow that internal unpolitical circumstances of greatest instability would elicit a cautious dis-inclination to direct action on the part of civil states.

(2) In the first general case, then, the weight of argument favouring flexibility in civil approaches to issues touching on both international and domestic instability in the unpolitical world would seem to stress the role of the civil executive. The formalities of legislative control of the executive in foreign affairs would be absent because of the avoidance of rigid civil commitments by way of treaties and declarations of war. Likewise, the fragility of many unpolitical governments and the confused character of the problems often engaging them would together appear to require some delicacy and discretion, which is to say secrecy, by civil states. These apparent effects of unpolitical affairs would again place great emphasis on executives. Two aspects of the first general case would have some effect in relieving civil worries about executive dominance. First, scale would not be a major problem. No ineluctable pressures would drive civil governments into irreversibly large commitments in the unpolitical world. Second, there would be no reason to expect the civil presence in unpolitical issues to be the monopoly of a single executive. The presence of numbers of executives (some acting in combination, others not, but all capable of communicating with one another) could itself be a discreet constraint on any one of them.

But executives free of legislative and other challenge could still have a potential for harm. Circumspection might be pushed aside by the rolling effects of decisions taken in secret. It could also easily happen that the activities of several executives involved in the same issue might have the effect of increasing unpolitical disequilibrium. As important as these practical dangers in their need for exposure would be those problems of judgement on which executives could not claim inherently superior wisdom or knowledge. Civil support for an unpolitical government faced with internal challenge would presumably rest on the case that either it approximated the civil conception of authority more closely than its possible replacements or that, given some assistance with transitory problems, it might be expected to move towards the acceptance of something like civil conditions over a reasonable period. As has been shown, in neither matter can there exist the basis of a fully determinate conclusion. These would therefore be matters on which wide civil enquiry and discussion would be desirable. Indeterminacy would have further ramifications. Neither in the first general case nor in any other can the principal commitments intrinsic to the civil standpoint comprise an ideal unity. The strict maintenance of the territorial integrity of existing states, for example, might not always be conducive to self-determination. Thus an unpolitical state might be the victim of a relatively small internal conspiracy with sufficient power to force its principal opponents to flee abroad; but now the system of states could only serve the cause of self-determination if these expatriates were able to influence affairs inside their own country with a view to bringing down a government dedicated to denying self-rule to its subjects. In these circumstances the principle of self-determination might encourage a civil executive to give some support to expatriates. Yet such an executive's judgement might become entirely warped by its own preferences, which might draw it into supporting violent attacks on a relatively popular internal form of self-determination across otherwise stable international frontiers.

The general problems of relations with the unpolitical world, though complex and stressful, would not be at all mysterious. The civil emphasis on flexibility in the sensitive detail of these relations would not release an executive from the wider constraints of principle. Of course the distinction between matters of detail and matters of overall judgement would be no easier to make in the first general case than in any other. Tension would result between executives and legislatures, and there would be every reason to institutionalise this through foreign affairs and other kinds of enquiring legislative committees. These institutions would be particularly concerned about the scale of involvements in the substance of unpolitical disputes and about the proximity to statehood of parties claiming, or getting, civil support. When principles came into conflict, then intense debate on problems of self-determination and proximity to civility would be called for. Again the question of scale would figure prominently in resulting arguments. This would not be because of mortal dangers created for civil society by large commitments (since in the first general case there could be none) but for three other sorts of reasons: first, because of the likelihood of counter-productive effects in and among unpolitical countries themselves; second, because of the possibility of unfortunate effects for civil society of the expenditure of scarce resources (and even, possibly, of hazarding the lives of some citizens) in situations where civil inactivity would almost always be a tenable option; and, third, because of the conflict of principle contained in the propensity (engendered by scale) to attempt to solve unpolitical problems by enforcing decisions made in civil states. This last failing could afflict legislatures as well as executives. Its occurrence would in fact constitute an effort at imperial rule and the impact of political society on unpolitical conflicts could not consistently take this form. By exclusion, therefore, civil influence would have to make itself felt (if at all) by way of supports for some unpolitical governments rather than others and for some actual or promised performances rather than others; typically these kinds of decisions would manifest themselves as incremental shifts—an increasing tendency to provide support here, a decreasing tendency there.

(3) The point of civil efforts to establish and maintain a stable states system in the unpolitical world would be to provide conditions of self-determination; and the point of self-determination would lie in its being an essential condition of the acceptance of civil self-rule. But civil statehood itself could not be propagated according to a simple table of instructions. So even in the first general case there would be no certainty that the purpose of foreign policy (its abolition as a distinctive arena of public affairs) could ever be achieved. All kinds of suggestions would be made about ways in which self-rule might be furthered: by the integration of unpolitical economies into the international economy of civil states; by unremitting enquiry into, and criticism of, uses of power against individuals in unpolitical states; by the constant open discussion in civil society of the affairs of unpolitical governments; by the absorption of the subjects of unpolitical states into the practices of citizens; by the involvement of unpolitical governments in open international organisations of all kinds in which the habit of criticising power in the context of explicit general rules might become general; and so on, all to be accompanied by the experience of the sometimes horrific processes of government without statehood that self-determination would provide. Notions and assumptions about the spread of self-rule could only derive from political society, so they would not add up to a theory or a plan to be executed by civil governments, secretly or otherwise. This would be political society's strength. Support by civil governments for a particular unpolitical state could never preclude criticism of, and pressure against, uses of power in it. And the projects, practices and campaigns of citizens could be as important to the extension of civility as the doings of executives or, for that matter, of legislatures too.

The second general case

Civil states as a whole may seem in this second general case to be subject to fundamental threats resulting from the intrusive, power-accumulating machinations of sovereigns in the unpolitical world. Numbers of atypical civil responses may therefore seem to be called for: the incorporation of unpolitical states in defence organisations led and sustained by civil governments; vigorous military and other support for well-disposed regimes regardless of their disdain for civility; the maintenance of international regions of domination by strong civil states to ward off hostile sovereigns; firm civil action against surrogates and other unpolitical governments siding with sovereigns; and so on.

The defects in these responses are plain:

(1) If the civil perspective includes a commitment to self-determination,

it must include an acceptance of independent international behaviour on the part of unpolitical states. Attitudes that assume that unpolitical states as a whole are, or can be, or ought to be, under the direction or domination of civil states are thus inconsistent with civility. The sense of choice that sovereigns may contribute to the unpolitical world is, in the civil perspective, no bad thing in itself, so long as its effect is not to shut down choice. But choice would be shut down if civil governments conducted themselves like sovereigns. Then there would only be sovereigns and sovereigns.

(2) If unpolitical states are free internationally, it is to be expected that they will both quarrel with one another and make mutual defence and other arrangements. There can be no categorical case against civil governments providing support for some such associations and organisations, just as there is no categorical case against their supporting individual unpolitical states. But this does not mean that civil authorities can or should take a lead in attempting to construct congenial groupings of these states. This would be to attempt to impose their own concerns on the unpolitical world. Given unpolitical choice, this is, in the first place, impossible. Second, it can all too easily drift towards some form of domination by civil governments or (just as unfortunately) towards the support of specific tyrants in their tyranny. Or, third, it can engage civil states as parties to the unpolitical international disputes that may be the primary preoccupation of these regimes. If civil states have a distinctive character and if a commitment to civility includes a commitment to self-determination, then it follows, in general terms, that the appropriate role of civil authorities in the unpolitical world is one of responding (or of not responding) to the individual or collective requests, pressures and arguments emanating from it.

(3) The international society of civil statehood is neither an alliance nor a crusade. Civil authorities (and citizens) are mindful of the priority of the civil relationship. This mindfulness can never, by definition, be concentrated. No authority can lead civil society as a whole, least of all in efforts to regulate unpolitical affairs. The political inclination to criticism and disagreement must be expected to apply as much to conduct outside civil society as to conduct inside it. This in no way debars executive responses to unpolitical problems. But it does, *ab initio,* rule out grandiose strategies claiming to be the embodiment of civility in its external environment.

(4) In the ninth chapter this enquiry classified (on the basis of internal civil experience) possible responses to anti-political sovereigns. The same responses (by no means exclusive to executives) are as relevant to their surrogates and to their surrogates who manage to elevate themselves to their own versions of sovereignty. There is no reason to believe that sovereigns can band together in long, deeply structured campaigns to master the unpolitical world and there are obvious reasons against pushing them into the appearance of such an enterprise. So the actual variety of civil society's responses to sovereigns and surrogates turns out to be rational in the sense of being

instrumental to the maintenance of civility and to its possible extension.

The effect of all these qualifications of the second general case is that the position of the civil executive outlined in the first general case is left unaltered. No decisive case for massively increased scale is made. Because of wider possibilities of disturbance, an implied need occurs for greater executive flexibility. But at the same time large issues of judgement are also thrown up, to which open debate and enquiry are at least as essential as they are in the first general case, so a legislative–executive balance is still crucial. Similarly, the importance of the role of extra-executive cross-national practices and projects remains unaffected.

INTERNATIONAL ORGANISATION

The third chapter discussed three possible views of international organisation: as a replacement of foreign policy and an essential service to domestic government and administration; as a form of international constitution-building; and as an instrument and a milieu of diplomacy.

The first general case

Because civil statehood would not be directly and constantly threatened in the first general case there would be no call for civil states to create strong defence organisations. Civility would, however, provide the foundation for any number of other official and unofficial cross-national organisations in this society, as explained in chapter 7. Though not directly challenged as a whole, civil states could be damaged as an indirect consequence of disturbances in the unpolitical world and it could even happen that one or more of them might be attacked by a tyranny or a combination of tyrannies. There would thus exist a civil concern for the maintenance of international order among unpolitical states; civil governments would also wish to convey their constant readiness to assist any part of political society that might become at risk of subjection to power. Behind these two practical concerns would lie the civil preoccupation with the extension of the civil relationship. There could be no certain understanding of how this goal could best be served, but it would be agreed that it required self-determination as a condition. So the maintenance of international order would also be conceived as the preservation of self-determination in entities determined by the international grid of unpolitical states. Civil statehood, as has been shown, cannot justify combinations to keep people (whether subjects or citizens) poor, though it does not itself propose definite programmes for making them better off. The economy of civil society would therefore be a broadly open one, merging in many different ways with the economies of unpolitical states. Inevitably, civil organisations intended to secure an evenly growing international economy would have to include these states in their memberships.

(1) The civil commitment to self-determination would be general; deriving

from the potentially universal character of statehood it could not be otherwise. But its generality could not be expressed by a series of explicit defence arrangements between civil states and each unpolitical state, because: (a) this would require civil society as a unit to make treaties in the external world, and this would be neither possible nor desirable; (b) many uncertainties and disputes would focus on unpolitical frontiers, and the commitment to self-determination (among other considerations) would prevent the civil imposition of settlements; (c) numbers of unpolitical states would be in the hands of repressive tyrannies to which no civil state could give any kind of explicit support; (d) the maintenance of self-determination would be an interest of most unpolitical states too and there would be no call to attempt to make a civil monopoly out of it; (e) in the civil perspective, self-determination without civility is a means, not an end, so there would be every reason to attempt to link the civil concern with the maintenance of territorial integrity with explicit unpolitical recognition of the desirability of limiting the power of governments over individuals, yet this would restrict the number of such arrangements that could be made and even in these instances it might constitute an imperial imposition. In the first general case there would thus be an unassailable case for the creation by civil states of a universal organisation containing themselves and attempting to apply the following quasi-civil principles to the unpolitical world: violence not to be used in international disputes (this would be a kind of description of political conflict, but for unpolitical states it would constitute a prescription that they might be expected occasionally to disregard); respect for the territorial integrity of all states regardless of strength or size (which would be a rough counterpart of the civil acceptance of varieties of adjacent and overlapping jurisdictions in political society); and recognition of the importance of limiting the power of governments in terms of human rights (which would be a crude interpretation of the priority of the civil relationship). A universal organisation (like the UN) based on these quasi-civil principles would legitimate any kind of mutual military support among civil states in the event of a threat to any of them, but it would not present political society to the rest of the world as a military bloc. It would also legitimate civil involvement in disequilibrium in the relations of unpolitical states without compelling side-taking and without compelling a scale of involvement that would be contrary to the principle of self-determination. Civil flexibility would thus be preserved. At the same time official and unofficial, explicit and discreet, civil attention to the proximity of unpolitical governments to acceptance of autonomous statehood would be both legitimated and placed at the centre of world affairs.

(2) The multiplicity of cross-national organisations in international political society could link in many ways with the unpolitical world. But an organisation (such as the European Community) with a direct legislative competence in civil society could not take fully into its membership any state itself unbound by statehood, because this civil competence would then

become subject to power in such a state's territory and because citizens could be exposed to the effects of power working through their own constitutional arrangements. But organisations (such as the IMF) designed to contribute to the functioning of cross-national systems generated in the first place in political society (international monetary relations in this example) yet affecting the affairs of unpolitical states would in most instances take them into membership. To deny admission would constitute a contradiction of self-determination since it would prevent such states from being active in matters affecting them deeply. However, civil states could not hand over regulatory authority in their own affairs to the domination of unpolitical governments and formal and informal devices might have to be developed to prevent this from happening. However, the discriminatory effects of these arrangements, if they became necessary, would be limited because the operating principles of such an organisation (in, say, the provision of support for a weak currency) would be much the same for political and unpolitical states. Other kinds of organisations, providing services but making little impact on the policies of civil governments, would be able to incorporate all states on much the same basis.

(3) Civil organisations with direct jurisdictions (like the European Community) would always be disposed to absorb states newly acquiescing in the priority of the civil relationship. In this way political society could act directly to maintain a fragile statehood and this would be the highest priority for citizens.

(4) At the universal or any other level, the organisational links between civil society and unpolitical states would be constitutional in form: assemblies, resolutions, debates, voting and such would be the familiar context of much international contact. No civil authority could be bound, or even necessarily much influenced, by a vote whose outcome depended on the decisions of unpolitical states: but an organisation at the universal level, as indicated, would not be conceived to be a massive international actor in its own right anyway. (For this reason, if no other, organisations could not replace diplomacy; and the often erratic movements of governments in unpolitical states would anyway call for a subtle extra-organisational means of observation and communication on the part of civil states.) The apparent constitutional forms of international organisation would be the inevitable outcome of its usual source in political society and of the civil commitment to self-determination. Its effects would be to familiarise unpolitical governments with the notion, if not the fact, of constitutionality and of its link with the possibility of international society. It would also expose unpolitical rulers to the openly critical comment of civil governments without denying them their own voices or their own possibilities of action.

(5) There would be no deep conflict between international organisation and civil diplomacy since the purposes of the latter would be no different from those of the former. The diplomats of civil states would represent their

own governments and the diverse nature of political society as a whole. There would be sound reasons for the maintenance of as many civil missions as possible in each unpolitical country. Besides conveying the many-sidedness of political society, this multiplicity of embassies in sometimes small countries would have more specific effects as well: it would create the sense of a closely observing world audience of the uses of power; because of the capacity of civil governments to communicate intimately among one another it would provide political society with numbers of interpretations of unpolitical affairs; and it would add to civil flexibility of response because combinations of civil states would be well placed to take cooperative action on some occasions, while on others they might validly react in many different ways to unpolitical crises.

The second general case
The presence in them of anti-political sovereigns may seem to make a charade of international organisations. Being without internal limitation, or any sense of the need for it, a sovereign may be expected to treat international constitutional arrangements as no more than superficial dressings on the inner realities of power. And through its strict command over a language of supposedly absolute social rights, it can easily appear to play havoc with international conventions and structures laying quasi-political stress on individuality. In these circumstances, it may seem, civil states should concentrate on fundamentals: the defence of civility and the counteraction of anti-political power in the unpolitical world. The role of organisation in the latter policy is clear: first, to stress the independence of unpolitical states, so as to limit the impact of sovereigns on them at minimum cost to civil states; and, second, to bind unpolitical states into a complex network of relations with civil states that cannot be broken without cost by any country opting to move into a sovereign's ambit. Civil authorities let their citizens harp on individual rights in the unpolitical world and elsewhere because they cannot prevent them doing so, but official diplomacy can be persistently down-to-earth. It can maintain contact with the facts of power in the unpolitical world and use whatever organisations come to hand to support unpolitical leaderships in ways best designed to forestall the designs of sovereigns.

Four faults are prominent in this view of organisation:

(1) In attempting to resist sovereigns it tends to create more of them. It assumes that political society is a bloc, which it is not. It makes a rigid distinction between anti-political and unpolitical states in disregard of the obvious facts that some unpolitical rulers can be bestially cruel and that some sovereigns (if it seems to strengthen them against other sovereigns) can be relatively well disposed to civil states both inside and outside organisations.

(2) In reacting to the power of sovereigns it ignores the more subtle strengths of political society, among which must be included its capacity to

create large numbers of international organisations and to endure their open and sometimes highly charged presence in its midst. The language of civil statehood cannot be monopolised by any person or authority. This means that political society can relate to the unpolitical world in many different dimensions. In civil society the leaders and subjects of unpolitical states can have an open role in debates about any matter of concern to themselves or to citizens. But this role is assured both by the unregulated nature of the language of civility and by organisations, not by diplomacy, which has of itself little capacity to create a distinctively political environment into which unpolitical states may be drawn.

(3) An open quasi-political emphasis on individual rights (in the UN and elsewhere) is not a highly dispensable civil frill. How else can the civility of civil states identify itself in an external setting? It is also crucial in a more operational sense. It provides a corrective to possibly counterproductive operations that aim to support unpolitical rulers while ignoring their activities as internal oppressors. The manipulation of a vocabulary of social rights by a sovereign is not an adequate excuse for a civil retreat into the crude national rhetoric of power competition. Civility is not abstract and it does not stand to lose in arguments about rights. Its concrete realities (open national and cross-national legal process, explicit constraints on rulers, the expression of individuality in endlessly developing practices) can be contrasted incessantly, in organisations and elsewhere, with anti-political abstractions whose effect is both to create power and to justify all its uses.

(4) A civil world would be one of strong states, not strong powers. Strengthening the fabric of the state in the unpolitical environment of civility is not a task for which any straightforward directions exist nor is it one creative of a sustained sense of civil optimism. But this uncertainty and difficulty means that there is a role here for international organisations. They draw the leaders and officials of unpolitical states into innumerable cross-national structures, which may (what else can?) propagate the notion of the state as a continuing fabric of order that does not cease at national frontiers.

NATIONAL INTEREST

The third chapter surveyed possible sources of the national interest (in geographical circumstances; in the necessity for defence; in the supposed motivation constantly to increase wealth; in the core values of the national community) and in each case found the term deeply wanting in clear substantive reference. The seventh chapter concluded that in the states of political society the multiplicity of official and unofficial interests never in fact fuse into specifically national imperatives. In this political setting the national interest is a symbol whose meaning and functions derive from the context in which it is used. In relations across the boundary of political society with anti-political states, the ninth chapter found that though a compelling governmental response might be evoked by the direct pressures of a strong sovereign conceiving itself to be the embodiment of an absolute value, this kind of national interest cannot have its source in civility itself; it is an effect on civility of the existence of sovereigns.

The first general case

(1) The unpolitical world could throw up a manic tyrant who might feel impelled to attack some part of political society. But unpolitical states generally would pose no fundamental threat to civility such as would provoke a compelling response from authorities and citizens. However deranged individual unpolitical leaders might occasionally become, their capacity to bring disorder to political society would depend on contingent failings among civil states, not on any common quality of unpolitical states. For their part, civil states would approach the unpolitical world with a shared concern to respect the self-determination of its multifarious parts as the necessary condition of the extension of the civil relationship. In a way this would constitute a fundamental civil interest, because a world populated exclusively by citizens would be a safer place than any other possible world. But such an interest would obviously not be specifically national and, as explained in chapter 10, it could not dictate any single strategy of civil conduct, least of all a violent one.

(2) Inside international political society the network of both conflicting and complementary cross-national interests would be infinitely complex and would deeply engage all levels of government. This concrete manifestation of civil statehood would suggest (it could not lay down or guarantee) that the extension of civility would be served in the first general case by the approximative incorporation of the interests and governments of unpolitical states into this network. This might have four quasi-political effects. It could draw unpolitical governments and their subjects into the 'normality' of the cross-national arguments, arrangements and institutions of civil society. It could open, or keep open, the frontiers of unpolitical states (civil awareness of affairs inside South Africa or Zaire is in part an effect of overlapping interests). It could contribute to binding unpolitical rulers into a complex cross-national governmental setting in which crudely extreme internal measures would be materially harmful to their own capabilities (a tyrant of Brazil who might wish to attain total internal domination would have to close national frontiers and would incur considerable costs in doing so, such is the depth and intricacy of the cross-national engagements of large numbers of Brazilian interests). And it could give civil authorities and citizens some leverage on internal unpolitical events in two ways: first, interests based in civil society (cross-national businesses most obviously) could be persuaded or even required to behave liberally in their operations in tyrannised states; second, this cross-national network of interests could provide opportunities

for civil authorities (with the requisite courage to bear costs to themselves) to pressure particular unpolitical governments by the use of their capabilities to interrupt trade, investment, chains of production and other interest-based connections.

(3) Any civil government can claim its policies and intentions to be in the national interest. By this it usually intends to convey its special seriousness and determination in the matter concerned, not that its constituents are solidly united behind it or that successor governments will never do or believe otherwise. In the first general case, it would of course be open to any unpolitical government to use this term in a similar way. Within international political society, national interests in this sense often diverge with no disastrous or even disturbing results because the ways in which different civil governments approach their problems are generally expected to differ. For this reason, if no other, civil governments could be expected to react variously to the expressed national interests of unpolitical governments, so that civil society as a whole would present an accommodative environment for them. Because international political society is not centrally directed, the national interest can put no necessary barrier between it and unpolitical states.

(4) It might still be the case that supposed national interests pursued by unpolitical governments could be highly uncongenial to many civil authorities and citizens. The takeover of local components of cross-national companies; the formation of official cartels to raise commodity prices: such activities could be the cause of deep civil consternation and even material loss. But interest clashes such as these could not occasion violent sovereign behaviour on the part of civil states in the first general case. The pursuit of particular interests would not constitute an attack on civility itself and only this could legitimate large-scale sovereign violence against self-determination on the part of civil authorities. In the civil perspective the interlocking of interests between political society and the unpolitical world (which would inevitably create the possibility of unpolitical action deleterious to sections of civil society) would be an expression of self-determination, not a denial of it. If civility is a condition of the pursuit of self-interest inside political society, it could not reasonably be held to justify violent attacks on its pursuit elsewhere.

The second general case

Domestically, the sovereign is not a condition of a multiplicity of interests. Being a positive value, its own interests are transformed into imperatives that it may enforce by the use of the state it possesses. The inability of the sovereign to distinguish between power, interests and values does not disappear when it becomes active in the unpolitical world. This can have bizarre results. What the sovereign does must also be right; so the Soviet sovereign has assisted 'progressive' governments that have behaved with signal cruelty towards its disciples among their own populations. More significantly in the present context, the sovereign tends to create minor sovereigns where its influence becomes effective (how could it do otherwise? and its constant association of interests with power is apt to manifest itsel in an emphasis on its military strength in its foreign activities.

(1) In their different conceptions of interests the contrast betwee sovereigns and citizens is complete. It follows that in the second general cas there is every reason why the many interest connections between unpolitica states and civil society should be further increased. The second general cas thus emphasises the first; it does not replace it.

(2) Likewise, the presence of sovereigns in the unpolitical world increase the general civil interest in self-determination and in the consequent expressio of varieties of 'national' interests by unpolitical governments. Civility being condition of self-interest, political authorities are well able to appreciate th distinctive, and shifting, concerns of unpolitical governments, even of thos that rule with the support of sovereigns. Civil states are therefore broadl disinclined to shut off trading and other links with such regimes. If self determination is related to the availability of choice there is a strong *prim facie* case for not doing so.

(3) The propensity of sovereigns to merge values, interests and powe does not push civil authorities into the same confusion. But just as direc anti-political pressures on civil states summon up something in the natur of national interests, so do military displays by sovereigns in the unpolitica world require civil counteraction. This is in part a conceptual matter. Th view that international relations comprise an exclusive arena of power i wholly inconsistent with civility. To allow a sovereign to behave unchallenge in such a way as to convey its own sense of the centrality of power both t internal and international affairs in the unpolitical world would be a civi neglect. Complex mutual involvements of civil and unpolitical interests ca have little effect in extending civil conditions if a sense of power monopoly i successfully perpetuated by a sovereign.

WAR

In chapter 3 war was discussed as an instrument of foreign policy; ther foreign policy was considered as a means of regulating war. It was als pointed out that any theory that proposes the state to be a special kind o order is also likely to justify violence against rulers who use a captive stat to impose some other kind of order. In the international order of autonomou civil statehood, the seventh chapter made clear, there could be no war o threat of war because in no way whatever could acts of war be qualifie politically in the sense established by this enquiry. Both internal and externa violence against the civil state must originate in a rejection of civility Chapter 9, in dealing with the relations between civil states and anti-politica states, concluded that the submission of international political society to th military threats of sovereigns would make the world more liable to large scale war, not less so. But countering military challenges from sovereigns did not mean that civil relations with anti-political states (and their subjects) should be conceived or conducted purely in terms of military pressures.

The first general case

(1) Some defence preparation on the part of civil states in this general case would be required by the possibility of attack from unpolitical sources. But these civil capabilities would be modest because many civil states could be counted on to support resistance to any attack from across the boundary of political society; and because unpolitical states, being unstable, (a) would be preoccupied with their own internal and regional international military problems, (b) would for the most part be incapable of developing massive capabilities of their own, (c) would be even more incapable of integrating their capabilities in unified cross-national structures aimed at the destruction of political society, and (d) could have no conceivable common interest in attempting to do so anyway.

(2) In chapter 10 the plurality of unpolitical territorial states was deemed to constitute a structure regulating the power that rules (to a greater or lesser pitch) within each of them. Regional international systems of power balance, it was explained, were a likely manifestation of this regulatory function of unpolitical states and were therefore an unavoidable part of the civil perspective. But a balance of power system is an outcome of conflict in a setting of dispersed military capabilities; and these may vary radically over time and may occasionally express themselves in the form of war.

From the civil standpoint, a balance of power among unpolitical states in the first general case would be seen as an inevitable but not an infallible way of achieving stability; and stability would be generally desirable because nothing much in the way of extending civility could be achieved in circumstances of severe instability. The civil approach to the possibility of unpolitical international war would follow from these premises. Wars of adjustment (that is, wars that might make for greater than existing stability) could not be purposely instigated by civil authorities, because violent relations stand at the opposite pole from political relations. So all sorts of international means would be used by such authorities in attempts to encourage the peaceful settlement of international unpolitical disputes. But the threat of war in all regions could never be abolished by such means and, in the event, a war of adjustment would be preferable to any other kind of war. Three civil reactions to the military realities of unpolitical power would result:

(i) Military material and expertise would be available for purchase from civil sources by parties to balance of power systems. If such systems were conceded to have quasi-political effects, then their maintenance through the acquisition of arms could not reasonably be prevented. Strong specific civil preferences for individual unpolitical states in the matter of military supplies would only be called for where imbalance threatened or where a grossly expansionist tyranny became active. At the same time, given even-handedness, no justification could be found in civility for political states or their citizens to fuel international arms races. Though this would not be a highly probable eventuality in the first general case, because civil states would not themselves be in incessant pursuit of improvements in military technology, it could nevertheless occur. It would be an effect inconsistent with the civil commitment for two compelling reasons: first, an arms race would tend to encourage regional international instability in contradiction of the point of an unpolitical balance of power in the civil understanding (that it should maintain stability through balance); and, second, competitions among civil states to participate in unpolitical international conflict by way of armaments supplies would constitute a species of war by proxy among them and this would be contrary to their own political relations. The civil involvement in trade could nevertheless generate these inconsistencies. In these circumstances, the civil position would suggest that civil authorities (in conjunction with as many unpolitical governments as possible) should enter into understandings or create organisations to regulate their supply of armaments to the unpolitical world.

(ii) Given that the tensions of regional balance of power systems would focus on particular (probably territorial) issues, wars of adjustment might well result. These might be regarded as the unfortunate, but not altogether irrational, consequences of the absence of autonomous statehood. But wars making no contribution to adjustment would, by the same token, be irrational. So limiting actual unpolitical war in the unfortunate case of its occurrence would be a common civil preoccupation. This could be expressed in two ways: by constant diplomatic activity; and by pressing forward with the development of international rules and organisations whose purposes would include the limitation of unpolitical wars. Because many unpolitical states would share a sense of the fragility of their states, the latter course would not be doomed to futility: the broad acceptance of self-determination in a setting of territorial integrity plus institutions adept (in the manner of the UN) at truce appeals, truce supervision, face-saving declarations and such, would be far from impossible to achieve or operate.

(iii) In an unpolitical war where one of the parties became so intemperate in its intentions that little in the way of adjustment could be expected to result, direct civil pressures (through, say, interruptions of military supplies to the stronger and gifts to the weaker) would be entirely in order. There could be no point of any kind in wars whose likely consequences would be further, larger, wars of either an international or internal character.

(3) Internal disturbances would be endemic in unpolitical states and in general there would be no call for civil authorities as such to become actively involved as parties. In states ruled by power, a degree of disorder would be the inevitable consequence of self-determination and it would be inconsistent to attempt to direct self-determination from outside. But deep internal disaffection with a particular set of unpolitical rulers could become an inter-

national issue because of the appeals for support, if nothing else, of anti-government leaders. In the civil frame of reference, as indicated, violence used in an unpolitical state, in the absence of other means of exerting pressure, with the purpose of replacing rule by power with rule by authority, must be just. In the event, it would of course be extremely difficult to determine whether a group in insurrection, or brewing insurrection, were more disposed to the acceptance of the priority of the civil relationship than existing leaders. Though in the civil perspective self-determination would not be an end in itself (but simply a condition of the establishment of statehood) it would provide a crude rule of thumb in these circumstances: a domestically supported unpolitical government would be deemed to be consonant with self-determination, while a deeply rejected government would be deemed to be perverting the course of self-determination. Given that the point of a balance of power system would be the preservation of self-determination, it would follow that a contradiction would arise if a deeply rejected government received military support from civil sources for international purposes, which it then used against self-determination internally. In the first general case nothing could be said for civil assistance in these circumstances unless the existence of the territorial state in question were itself under imminent international threat by a foreign tyranny. But in the first general case, with active civil involvement in international affairs this would be unlikely.

The second general case

Many civil states, singly and in combination, are now heavily armed in order to counter the strength of anti-political sovereigns. But this does not necessarily alter the central feature of the first general case. Still no fundamental threat to civil society emanates from the unpolitical world itself and the quasi-political functions of balance of power systems therein remain the same. However, several transformative influences may seem to be at play: sovereigns become direct parties to some international balance of power systems containing unpolitical states; the general availability of armaments is much greater and the potential scale of both internal and international unpolitical war therefore increases; sovereigns display their strength in the unpolitical world, establish military bases there and contribute to the strength of surrogates and other kinds of tyrannies.

(1) The instigation of unpolitical violence by civil authorities remains inconsistent with their acceptance of the political qualification. Their efforts to encourage the peaceful settlement of disputes and the rapid termination of any hostilities that do occur are therefore undiminished in the second general case. The principles of their sale and supply of military material (that is, the maintenance of international balance as a means both of constraining power and of providing stable conditions of self-determination) are also unchanged. A problem of scale is certainly posed by large outputs of sophisticated weapons and by the propensity of sovereigns (for whom

violence is an intrinsic possibility in all conflict) to supply and deploy military strength in the interests of their sense of power. Yet these factors do not in themselves substantiate a blanket justification in civil terms for the reckless dispersion of advanced military capabilities among unpolitical states. Helping to make wars more destructive than they would otherwise be is no more a political activity than instigating them. Apart from the restraints that civil authorities should exercise over themselves, there is here, as suggested in chapter 9, the possible basis of a generative relationship with at least some sovereigns. If large-scale unpolitical disturbances become potentially global as a result of the scale of weaponry deployed, then anti-political states may well perceive the hazards to themselves in scale and be disposed to enter into some modest understandings and arrangements to regulate the place of more destructive armaments in the unpolitical world. And there is no necessary interest in the perpetuation of arms races among unpolitical governments themselves either; so generative possibilities are in no way restricted to the relations between political and anti-political states.

(2) Political relations, in the sense established by this enquiry, are not the creation of power conflict. It follows that the relations of civil society with unpolitical states are not essentially power relations because the latter are not by nature rigorously opposed to the former and are not inclined (or, for the most part, able) to attack them. These are therefore relations in which citizens and authorities adjust to the existence of power in the unpolitical world, but this adjustment does not describe these relations. Contrastingly, the sovereign, incapable of distinguishing between power and strength in its own domain, cannot do otherwise than place power at the centre of its relations with the rest of the world. This, as already shown, heightens the importance of the many different kinds of relations that civil society is able to maintain with unpolitical states. The relevance of the first general case is increased, not diminished, by the second. But if potentially intimidatory displays of its military strength by a sovereign become a prominent feature of the unpolitical world, then the generalised effect of power there is likely to be increased. The danger now exists that a transformation could actually take place resulting in the displacement of the variety of quasi-civil relations with unpolitical states from a place of importance in the conduct of unpolitical affairs. If civility contains a commitment to self-determination and if self-determination is meaningless without the possibility of choice, then demonstration of the presence of the strength of a sovereign (in the typical shape of substantial naval forces) should be countered by demonstrations of similar strength that is not also in the hands of power. This is not a question of going to war but of acting to protect the first general case from a too easy transformation.

(3) In the civil perspective the plurality of unpolitical states is a structure that maintains conditions of self-determination. But self-determination is not a discrete set of actions rigidly confined within the frontiers of each

unpolitical state. The external relations of unpolitical states are as much a part of self-determination as their internal affairs. The existence of relations between unpolitical states and sovereigns is therefore a part of the civil commitment; as is the possibility that unpolitical states may on occasion go to war with one another. But the civil commitment is not to war itself or to the multiplication of sovereigns. The converse is so. Two rules of international relations, born of the first general case, resolve this ambiguity. The first requires that the existing structure of states be maintained; the effect of this is that all international wars become wars of adjustment. The second asserts the superiority of indigenous rule over all other forms of rule; this ensures that acceptance of foreign support does not become foreign domination. The liberal genius has historically expressed itself in the generation of rules such as these, which are for obvious reasons congenial to almost all unpolitical rulers. And where, as in the Middle East, the conditions necessary to the effectiveness of these rules are lacking, their wide acceptability points to a goal to which both civil and many unpolitical governments may attempt to incline events: that is, the establishment of a regional international order in which these rules could be effective. The sovereign cannot, except cynically, formulate explicit rules constraining its own power in its own domain or elsewhere. It may, however, be sensitive to the dangers of over-extending its limited capabilities or to the disadvantages to itself of exciting widespread disapprobation. So it may come close to accepting quasi-political rules. But it does not do so out of its own nature. The case for the maintenance of civil (and other) military capabilities is thus further supported, as is that for keeping open other possibilities of exerting pressure on sovereigns.

MORALITY

Chapter 3 discussed, *inter alia,* the inadequacy of moral rules conceived as direct guides to the conduct of public affairs. Shifting moral arguments and sentiments, it was suggested, are an ordinary element in large numbers of public issues in civil states. If civil statehood is a condition of individual moral choice, and therefore of interminable moral discourse, no peculiar moral issues, it was explained in the seventh chapter, can be raised by cross-national relations within international political society. The moral contrast between civil statehood and the anti-political state is a complete one (chapter 9). Because the sovereign claims to be the embodiment of a morality, it cannot allow itself to be openly and legitimately subjected to moral criticism in its domain by individuals arguing from independent moral criteria. The civil relationship is not, in itself, a moral one; the relationship between a subject and his anti-political sovereign is the negation of civility because it requires the assumption by the individual, or the imposition on him, of an officially determined moral identity.

The first general case

No moral case need be made for civil statehood, which requires no citizen to abandon, or to adopt, any particular moral code. Civility simply requires morally inspired public or private conduct to be politically qualified; that is, to observe the priority of the civil relationship, which is completely impersonal. A convincing argument for civil statehood can thus proceed along functional lines: it is the only condition in which morality may (or may not) be absorbed into individual and public life without the harmful national and international effects attendant on either the complete merging of power with morality or the complete isolation of power from morality.

Civil authority, being both explicitly limited and responsive to large numbers of contending interests, can never claim to act wholly according to the imperatives of a complete moral system, nor can it ever remove itself from moral arguments over whose criteria it exercises no control. Civil authority becomes self-questioning if it is required to impose morally conditioned decisions on individuals of diverse moral persuasions who are not able to bring either morally based, or interest-based, pressures of their own to bear on public affairs. This is why, in the last analysis, imperialism is the moral antithesis of civility. But self-determination, in civil eyes, is not therefore a moral good. It certainly spares civil authority the moral embarrassment of imperialism; much more importantly, self-determination is necessary to the extension of civil statehood, which is a condition of moral choice. This obviously does not mean that self-determination itself provides conditions of moral or immoral living. It may, for instance, result in absolute government by a religiously committed junta claiming to enforce a complete system of moral rules on its subjects. In civil eyes this is a contingent misfortune of self-determination.

(1) In the first general case a civil state inheriting vestiges of an imperial responsibility would positively and explicitly favour self-determination. But self-determination is not an end in itself, so it would also positively and explicitly favour self-determination in conditions as closely approximating civility as possible. The civil qualification could obviously not be imposed by imperial edict. But the legitimacy of a handover of government to indigenous power would be explicitly located in civility and not in self-determination alone.

(2) Civil statehood is entirely general. In the world of the first case, cross-national organisations would attempt to further quasi-civil notions of rule in unpolitical states. International conventions, commissions and courts of human rights would try to serve individuality and to suggest the importance of general constraints on governments. No subjects of unpolitical rulers could be denied civil conditions by civil states, so no civil authority could combine with an unpolitical government in uses of power against individuality nor could it connive at the concealment of the effects of internal tyranny from citizens or their representatives. From the civil side, the latter would always

be free to enquire and campaign on any matters touching on unpolitical contradictions of civility so far as the circumstances of self-determination
allowed. Within the boundary of civil statehood much stress would be laid
on the role of cross-national courts and on open enquiries into misuses of
authority both for their own merits and as a way of providing a model for
similar arrangements in the unpolitical world.

(3) On occasions (in granting conditional economic assistance say) civil
authorities of either a national or cross-national kind might be obliged to make
important decisions touching the lives of numbers of largely unrepresented
subjects of an unpolitical state. Moral considerations current in civil society
(some version of utilitarianism most typically) would be intrinsic to this sort
of decision-making. It could not be otherwise; civil authority could not, and
could not be expected to, cut itself off from civil influences at any time. But
with self-determination (plus a number of different civil authorities capable
of making different kinds of decisions and thus conferring choice on
unpolitical governments) there would be no question of the direct civil
imposition of morally inspired programmes.

(4) Moral principles attach to many of the practices in which citizens
express their individuality; the study of psychology was an example cited
earlier. All practices would of course be developed cross-nationally in the
first general case and many subjects of unpolitical states would participate
in them. It would be substantially up to citizens involved to protect the moral
criteria of their practices from direct or indirect unpolitical pressures.

The second general case

Though anti-political sovereigns stand at an opposite moral pole from civil
authorities, it does not follow that everything they do or say is therefore
immoral. It is their exclusion of independent moral criteria, sometimes by
the direct use of power, from their domains that distinguishes them, not
invariable immorality. Some unpolitical tyrannies may approximate fairly
closely to civil conditions in allowing much moral diversity (in the form of
different religious and other practices) and even a measure of open moral
criticism and argument; but others may exclude all explicit moral criteria
both from their domains and, effectively, from their own conduct and these
may be more cruel than some anti-political sovereigns.

(1) As explained in chapter 9, generative possibilities (expressed through
the institutions of the UN and elsewhere) occur in the relations of civil
authorities and sovereigns and have resulted in declarations and conventions
of a quasi-civil nature (on, for example, racial equality) and in other pronouncements (about material welfare) morally attractive to many citizens.
Not much in the way of quasi-civil performance is to be expected from a
sovereign because of its total inability to distinguish between its morality,
its power and its interests. But this in no way absolves civil authorities and
citizens from the cross-national moral concerns suggested by the first

general case.

(2) The influence of sovereigns on unpolitical states, even when they support surrogates, is not necessarily highly immoral in itself. It would be difficult to argue conclusively that the current ruler of Cuba is morally inferior to his predecessor. Frantic civil efforts to prevent all involvement by sovereigns in the unpolitical world are not therefore required by some clear moral imperative. From a civil viewpoint the important thing is to preserve the principle of self-determination so that anti-political intrusions can be excluded by indigenous rulers and movements. The kinds of civil conduct suggested by the first general case (and by chapter 9) apply just as much to states ruled by surrogates as to any other outside the boundaries of civil statehood.

(3) The defence of civil society from anti-political rule is a defence of conditions of diverse moral practices, not a defence of a specific system of morality according to some clear rule contained in it. To assist in the defence of some unpolitical state from an anti-political movement or incursion is to defend not civility but self-determination. However, the brand of self-determination in question may include government behaviour widely deemed immoral by citizens of political society. In these circumstances caution in the matter of scale is clearly called for: to support an unpolitical government in such a way as to determine its behaviour clearly cannot be to defend self-determination; to maintain the existence of a government given to ignoring moral opinion is to put civil authority to uncivil use, which, among other things, will almost certainly provoke widespread civil obloquy. Modesty in the scale of support for any specific unpolitical government is of course a characteristic of the first general case.

(4) To contribute in some way to the military strength of an unpolitical state engaged in countering possible external pressure from an anti-political state (South Korea is a convenient example) is to support the maintenance of conditions of self-determination. It is not to approve the domestic actions of specific unpolitical governments. Neither citizens nor their representatives are any more obliged to suspend morally founded criticisms of such governments than they would be in the first general case.

INTERVENTION

The third chapter mentioned two traditional senses of intervention: external involvement in internal affairs; and external involvement in regional international affairs. But large-scale intervention, it suggested, tended to produce a practical intermingling of these categories. The third chapter also surveyed possible intentions of intervention and the possible ways in which these intentions might be achieved. It found goals of intervention so elusive as to conclude that interventions ought always to be approached with extreme caution and flexibility and that, given the delicacy of interventionary issues, almost any means ought to be considered preferable to direct military commit-ment on land. Chapter 7 explained that in international political society intervention has no distinctive meaning; supposedly authoritative conduct that fails to accept the political qualification is pathological regardless of which civil jurisdiction it occurs in. On the other hand, the anti-political sovereign (chapter 9) must hold any extraneous influence on its subjects that its power cannot regulate to constitute an intervention.

The first general case
Given the nature of civility as this enquiry has come to understand it, the intentions of civil states towards the unpolitical world in this general case would be clear: first, to maintain conditions of self-determination; and, second, to facilitate the extension by indirect means of the boundaries of civil statehood. Intervention in unpolitical affairs would have a distinctive meaning for civil states only because of the role of power in them. A world coterminous with civility would, as indicated in chapter 7, be one in which intervention as a special kind of problem would disappear.

(1) Civil states would take a lead in founding international organisations, and in formulating international declarations and conventions, whose intended effect would be to obtain and maintain a stable world structure of states in which self-determination could be enacted. From the civil stand-point, geographical boundaries would always be conditions for the ultimate achievement of citizenship; but for the unpolitical world itself (particularly for overlapping unpolitical communities in it) frontiers as such could become issues of the deepest significance. Nevertheless, the civil interest in achieving conditions of self-determination would sufficiently coincide with unpolitical understandings of the nature of frontiers as to comprise a substantial area of common ground. There would thus exist a basis for the provision of all kinds of cross-national services by both civil and unpolitical states, and for all kinds of diplomatic and other exertions, whose purpose would be to bring all states to an acceptance of a stable pattern of territoriality. Where frontiers were vigorously at issue, a need for truce-maintenance and similar facilities would often exist while efforts to obtain settlements proceeded by diplomatic and other means. The role of brokers in such matters might commonly fall on civil states because of the relative disinterestedness entailed by their own con-ception of the essentially contingent nature of frontiers.

(2) Because of the importance of power in the unpolitical world, violence would inevitably occur from time to time in both internal and international issues. Civil states could be involved (if only negatively through their refusals of support) by appeals and demands from parties directly in conflict. If civil authorities became positively engaged in such troubles, two considerations would be paramount: to relate their actions as precisely as possible to their general commitment to the extension of the civil relationship via self-determination; and to keep a tight rein on the scale of their military actions

and supplies. Limitation of scale would be an important civil preoccupation because over-commitment could have illegitimate consequences. A tendency might be invoked in civil circles to attempt to impose long-term solutions; but imposed solutions to unpolitical problems could not, by definition, be civil solutions. Such impositions would therefore be acts of sovereignty; but civil authorities could only properly act in the role of sovereigns when civility itself was at hazard, and in the first general case this danger could not arise. Slightly differently, civil over-involvement in unpolitical issues (of either the domestic or international varieties) would either have the effect of placing civil strength at the disposal of unpolitical power, which would be beyond the proper competence of civil authority, or it would remove decision from indigenous hands, which would be an infringement of self-determination.

(3) *Internal violence.* The civil predisposition to favour the preservation of order in unpolitical states would not be wholly resistant to suspension. The more oppressive an unpolitical regime, the more citizens would be obliged to view rebellion against it sympathetically as the only means whereby an indigenous population could reasonably be expected to progress in self-determination. No civil authority could directly instigate such a rebellion because this would break the general rule supporting the security of international boundaries. But it would be normal for civil states to shelter expatriates from an oppressed state and for citizens to give them support. And in the first general case there would be no cause whatever for authorities to support in any way a debased tyranny against its rebelling subjects. Civility is a general notion of statehood, and self-determination derives its civil validity from being a necessary condition of it. In civil eyes, violence against internal power that might reasonably seem to be a total contradiction of the point of self-determination would be justified.

Observance of the principle of self-determination within secure international frontiers would require that direct civil engagement in internal violence would almost always depend on the request of an indigenous government. The first problem for a civil authority faced by such a request would be whether to respond at all. Two main factors would weigh in this decision: first, the proximity, or otherwise, of the existing government to the acceptance of civil conditions of rule; second, whether efforts to maintain a specific kind of unpolitical order through intervention would be likely to contribute to the course of self-determination. These two factors could be crucially linked: in many unpolitical circumstances, the closer an existing government to civil moderation, the easier it could be for subversive forces to create the disorder in which they might best increase their power. As explained in the previous chapter, proximity would not be a matter of clear measurement; so different civil authorities could legitimately take different views on whether (and by what methods) to support a specific regime.

Obviously no civil assistance could be given to a government overtaken by a sudden coup. However, a government liable to this fate would be fragile anyway and it would be no part of civil purposes to acquire the dependence of otherwise unsupported governments. Concentrated uses of subversive violence that could not achieve a coup might present appropriate targets for sharp interventions (such as that in Zaire in 1978) by civil strength in the shape, perhaps, of brief airborne operations. The purpose of such efforts would be to bring superior firepower to bear quickly on a force otherwise capable of severely disturbing a reasonably proximate government and of diverting its limited resources into unproductive military uses. It would not be legitimate for a civil force to be made permanently available to an unpolitical government to deal with all its enemies. As indicated above, this would place civil strength at the service of power and it would be an infringement of self-determination.

In the case of an unpolitical government embroiled in long-lasting internal disorders, somewhat different considerations would come into play. There would be a general predisposition among civil authorities against the break-up of existing states (such as the Lebanon) because of the magnitude of attendant troubles and because partition would not necessarily increase possibilities of peaceful self-determination. They would similarly be inclined (given a reasonable degree of proximity) to help prevent government itself from becoming constantly confused with war. There might thus be grounds for some civil involvement in efforts to deal with persistent subversive challenge. Again, actual civil participation would be rigorously limited to brief operations on limited sites. Otherwise assistance would be indirect: gifts of weapons, training in their use and such. Civil authorities would in no circumstances attempt to dominate military campaigns. To do so would be to enforce unpolitical rule or even to take it over, both of which would be infringements of self-determination and of civility. An unpolitical government attempting to stabilise a disturbed population would almost certainly be in general economic difficulties; if civil assistance were forthcoming in these circumstances, it would invariably be accompanied by civil enquiry, criticism, advice, and, sometimes, by conditions.

(4) *International violence.* Much the same principles would apply in the case of international disputes among unpolitical states. From the civil standpoint, unpolitical states would exist to regulate power and to provide stable international conditions of self-determination in which diverse populaces might move to the acceptance of the priority of the civil relationship. Civil authorities would therefore emphasise the maintenance of established frontiers and would be disposed to supply arms for this purpose in a fairly even-handed way. Again, the civil concern would be with the maintenance of states not with the support of all unpolitical rulers, so civil interest in problems of scale and proximity would remain lively. Where the positioning of borders was uncertain and a subject of violence among states, the civil attitude would be more complex. As indicated above, if unpolitical borders were taken to be regulators of power there would be an inconsistency

in attempting to prevent power from playing any part in their location in the first place. In such matters some violence might have functional effects in its indication of the depths of feelings among affected peoples. So there would not necessarily be any inconsistency in civil sources providing military assistance to more than one party in international issues of this sort. This would in no way invalidate, and might enhance, civil efforts to bring settlements forward by diplomatic and institutional means. No civil involvement in any internal or international unpolitical disorder could of course ever be divorced from public civil argument, in which the parties directly in conflict would be free to engage.

(5) Whatever the involvement of civil states with unpolitical troubles, the long-term civil concern with extending the civil relationship would continue and would take all the indirect forms adumbrated in this and previous chapters. Any unpolitical state wishing to identify with civil states, and to receive assistance from them, would have to endure civil attention to their affairs. Civil enquiries, suggestions and criticisms would be endless. Visiting civil statesmen would seek to consult with opposition leaders according to their normal behaviour in international political society. And they would always be making representations on behalf of constituents concerned about the situations of co-religionists, co-artists, co-scientists.

The second general case
Anti-political sovereigns may seem to work parametric changes on the first general case. Again the increased emphasis on armaments among industrialised countries intensifies the general problem of scale. Also the sovereign has no understanding of politically qualified conflict so it cannot make civil distinctions between the state as territory, as government and as general principles. For it, the state is always secondary to power; power is defined in relation to conflict; and conflict is always potentially violent. So the sovereign may seem to be inherently incapable of respect for self-determination and to be totally without disinterestedness in its approach to either internal or international unpolitical disputes. It comprehends all foreign events as contributing to, or detracting from, its own power.

(1) Though the sovereign is not sensitive to civil qualification, it is limited by the consequences of its own outlook. Its own nature creates an environment full of dangers. Its power is central to its relations with its subjects and with the populations it directly dominates. Within its domain it can therefore never be certain of the depth of its unforced support. If it relaxes it may lose control. Vague internal dangers become more specific in the external world. It must always fear the power of other sovereigns. As disturbing is the many-sidedness of civil society, which presents the sovereign with numbers of authorities with which it must deal, each given to shifts of policy and personnel. The life of civil change seems incessantly to be raising the spectre of individuality among the sovereign's subjects and it is forever forcing the

pace of technological change. All in all, the sovereign needs most of its strength close at hand. It has no vast surplus to distribute in the unpolitical world. So it, too, is likely to be aware of the problem of scale in military commitments. As well, the economic conditions it lays on its domain are ever distorting its efforts to increase its wealth. Its own scarcities are often urgent and it cannot be a massive distributor of largesse among unpolitical countries. In the interests of its power, the Soviet sovereign heavily subsidises the Cuban economy; but as a general provider of aid, even to apparently highly congenial regimes such as that of Vietnam, it is parsimonious.

Three other sorts of limitations are created by the sovereign's own nature. First, the leaders it supports are likely to be of tyrannical disposition, though without fully matching capabilities. The sovereign cannot gather to itself highminded constitutionalists. Its power outside its domain is thus apt either to supplement indigenous power or to support puppets. But tyrannical power is notoriously fickle and difficult to regulate; and puppets are not noted for their positive contributions to the purposes of their patrons. So the sovereign's exertions in the unpolitical world may not go far in increasing its own power and may actually diminish it. Second, the sovereign's overtly superior attitude to the state does not endear it to numbers of unpolitical governments that might be adversely affected thereby. Third, the sovereign in fact has a certain affection for frontiers. The walls of its own domain are fundamental to the maintenance of its absolutism within. To throw into question the legitimacy of international frontiers in general might be to loosen its hold on its domain, a chilling prospect.

(2) The sovereign's acceptance of something approaching quasi-civil rules in its conduct in the unpolitical world is thus by no means impossible. Though, to it, self-determination ultimately means responsiveness to its own will, it is generally in no position either to declare or enforce this view. The direct presence of the sovereign or its surrogate in an unpolitical country may therefore be held to depend explicitly on the invitation of an existing government. By the same token, the sovereign or its surrogate should be expected to remove itself when requested to do so. Such a request could be issued in confused local circumstances. If the civil commitment to self-determination is not an empty one, civil strength should be available to encourage the sovereign's compliance. If self-determination depends on choice, civil states have some responsibility for creating international circumstances in which choice is possible. Similarly in the matter of frontier incursions. Though sovereigns may accede to a rule restricting their own efforts, their indirect support for such enterprises could be substantial, in which event self-determination could depend on the availability of civil strength as a counterweight. Neither of these contingencies requires the civil abandonment of flexibility, limited scale and attention to proximity. The existence of sovereigns does not in itself dispose civil authorities to place themselves at the disposition of unpolitical power; but it does not destroy their

commitment to self-determination either. Nothing in this enquiry suggests the inevitability of the preservation of the first general case in the event of total civil inactivity.

ECONOMIC PROBLEMS

International problems of poverty were prominent among the issues reviewed in chapter 3. Though, as a system of creating wealth, the case for the free movement of goods and capital between rich and poor countries was taken to be a telling one, some major flaws were nevertheless detected in it. And as a way of distributing wealth the failings of such a system were seen to be much more pronounced. In chapter 7 it was argued that its relatively wealthy cross-national economy was essentially the creation of political society, not vice versa, and that consequently the preservation of this economy depended first on the maintenance of the civil relationship. Among the things dependent on the priority of this relationship was a complex language, embodying a rich tradition of rational economic discourse, which could not be regulated by any national or cross-national civil authority or movement. The economy of political society as a whole could be conceived as comprising three intimately mixed ingredients: the mass of substantive private and official economic projects and transactions; the autonomously evolving language of economic action, enquiry, explanation and recommendation; and the welter of national and cross-national authoritative rules, institutions, mechanisms and processes whereby attempts were made to modulate levels and trends in economic affairs. Among the merits of this economy were its resistance to any form of centralised domination, its flexibility and adaptability, its capacity to bring authorities and citizens to an appreciation of economic realities, the ease of its extension beyond the boundaries of political society. The anti-political state (chapter 9) could not be integrated into it because of the sovereign's use of power to maintain exclusive control of an economic language and because of its inability to recognise in its domain any valid distinction between its own economic interests and actions and their setting. A positive duty therefore lay on civil authorities and citizens not to allow a sovereign to acquire any control over political society's economy, though this did not mean that there could be no cross-boundary trading links or that all possible cross-boundary authoritative arrangements were ruled out.

The first general case

Being general, civil statehood enjoins democracy. But it also qualifies democracy. Civility denies sovereignty to 'the people' just as it does to any individual, group, interest or institution. In a democracy, governments are to be expected to attempt to regulate levels of economic activity in the interests of large numbers of citizens; governments are also to be expected to embark on substantive economic projects of a general kind (schemes of old age, unemployment and sickness insurance) and of a particular kind (the management of industrial and other enterprises), in part because their efforts at overall regulation will not achieve all the specific results that they and sections of their electorates desire. Government economic performances vary in nature and intensity (and their individual and comparative showings are much analysed and criticised) in different parts of political society, but no democratic government can be expected to be economically inactive. To describe the resultant complexities as 'modern capitalism' or 'the mixed economy' is unnecessary: this is an economy, founded on the civil relationship, with democratic governments and without sovereignty. In other words, it is a political economy. It has an autonomous cross-national language (born of civility) of economic action, comparison, theory, recommendation, argument, enquiry, idealism and self-interest. Because it is without sovereignty, individuals, groups and corporations are active in the large numbers of inter-connected markets that exist in its conditions; because these are also conditions of democracy, authorities of all kinds are also actively absorbed in it.

(1) Given their commitment to self-determination, citizens and authorities would by and large expect and encourage the governments and subjects of unpolitical states in the first general case to pursue their economic goals through the open markets in goods and finance of the economy of political society. Though this would inevitably cause structural economic problems of adaptation in civil states from time to time, it would have a number of quasi-civil merits: it would engage unpolitical governments in a complex cross-national setting that they could not hope to regulate by their power; it could stimulate the growth of diverse centres of economic influence inside unpolitical countries that their governments would have to adapt to in their policies rather than crudely dominate; it would develop numbers of contacts between subjects and citizens that could not be comprehensively manipulated so as to prevent the fairly free cross-national flow of information and opinion; it would propagate skill in the use of the autonomous language of the political economy; while leaving to unpolitical countries themselves decisions on appropriate levels of government economic activity and regulation, it would bring exterior conditions and unregulated criteria of rationality to bear on the practical consequences, so qualifying in some degree the ability of power to rationalise and justify all its behaviour in circumstances purged of independent bases of judgement and criticism.

(2) Unpolitical countries involved in the economy of political society would inevitably be affected by, and might themselves have an impact on, its trends and disturbances. Self-determination would thus be contradicted if such countries were denied a role in the institutions (with all their attendant arguments and pressures) engaged in attempting to regulate and service this economy and its markets. In just the same way, they could expect to benefit from the credit and other facilities provided by international organisations

(like the IMF) and would be as free as civil states to press cases for special treatment. But a number of quasi-civil consequences would follow. No unpolitical government or group of governments would be permitted to attempt to use an international organisation as the instrument of power hostile to civil statehood. The language of economic affairs would be an open one; attempts to replace it with a vocabulary drawn up by power would be firmly resisted. Equally, the kinds of enquiries and recommendations that authorities and international organisations would level at civil states in economic difficulties would also be freely used in dealing with the problems of unpolitical countries.

(3) Just as democratic governments in civil society would attempt both to increase wealth and, from time to time, to redistribute it, so it would be expected that unpolitical governments, particularly in poor countries, would often be similarly engaged. And just as this kind of preoccupation could get civil governments into economic difficulties, so it would be expected that unpolitical governments could find themselves in similar straits. If, in the latter case, the countries affected were poor in the first place, the consequences in human terms might be severe. In the first general case there would thus be much to be said for the provision of particularly generous assistance to unpolitical states with acute balance of payments problems. Here again the civil preference would be for international organisation to be active because then general criteria could be applied that unpolitical states would themselves play a part in formulating and the principle of self-determination would be observed.

From the viewpoint of poor unpolitical countries engaged in the wealth-generating cross-national economy of political society there would be a strong case for some international redistribution in their favour. This would be understandable to citizens themselves recurrently absorbed in problems of redistribution in their own national economies. Any argument used in a national economy would have a similar validity in a cross-national economy. For the reasons already cited, the general civil preference would be for attempting to generate growth in poor countries through the facilitation of trade, by enlightened handling of balance of payments problems, by cooperation in arrangements to stabilise commodity prices, by the provision of investment capital from cross-national public sources, by guaranteeing private investment in poor unpolitical countries and the like. Given the importance of self-determination and the extension of the civil relationship, a preference would also exist for these kinds of arrangements to be made through international organisations in whose management unpolitical states would themselves have a place. The civil relationship is not itself a philanthropic one, and condescension is unknown to it; but from civil conditions spring all kinds of philanthropic movements and opinions and these can obviously influence authorities. So in the first general case many civil states would attempt to make direct wealth transfers of their own to relatively poor unpolitical countries. Apart from the economic difficulties of actually accomplishing this, two non-economic problems would recur. Citizens and authorities in the first general case would properly adjust to, and deal with, power in the unpolitical world; but no citizen or authority would be justified in adding to it. Yet unconditional transfers might in some situations simply increase the personal wealth of tyrants and their cronies or contribute to tightening the hold of such people on their states. On the other hand, transfers made conditional on particular internal performances could infringe self-determination. As well, given the association of poverty with social habits and values, ill-directed conditional civil assistance could be futile and even socially harmful. The case for unconditional transfers to tyrannies would be weak. But so also would be the general case for tightly conditional transfers, particularly in instances of reasonable proximity to civility. All in all, the most rational approach in these circumstances would be pluralist. Different aid-giving authorities could adopt different strategies and be open to different kinds of proposals. Private philanthropy would also be active cross-nationally according to private criteria and to the opportunities and constraints presented by unpolitical environments.

(4) There would clearly be no reason why political states or politically based international organisations should in any way assist unpolitical states bent on direct attacks on civil states. But in the first general case this problem would be a remote one. There would, however, be occasional violent international disputes among unpolitical states. Individual civil states might be involved in some of these and might be expected to use their own economic resources in their efforts to draw the parties to mutual accommodation. But this kind of pressure would not be an orchestrated effort on the part of civil society as a whole. Were it to be so, two fundamental principles would be infringed: political society would have to direct itself like a single bloc in the external world; and self-determination would be contradicted because a massive effort would have been mounted to force the course of unpolitical events from outside. Comprehensive economic sanctions would be undertaken in relation to an unpolitical dispute only through international organisation containing unpolitical states; and the state subjected to these pressures would have had to be shown to have broken an international rule accepted as binding on themselves by the vast majority of unpolitical states themselves. In the ordinary run of unpolitical disputes the services of international economic organisations and of some individual civil states would be available to all the parties. Of course this would not mean that civil resources would be made lavishly available to subsidise the militarist obsessions of particular unpolitical rulers. Autonomous economic criteria would continue to be regarded as applicable to economic affairs.

The second general case
The sovereign is not to be expected to observe rules, relating to tariffs or

anything else, evolved by the economic institutions in which civil and unpolitical states perpetually argue over arrangements appropriate to their economic relations. Nor will the sovereign place any part of its resources at the disposal of such institutions. The economy of its domain is intrinsic to its own power and this the sovereign cannot alienate while it remains a sovereign. Its economy may thus seem to be an unqualified source of strength to the sovereign in its external pursuits. Yet this would only actually be so in a world dominated by sovereigns. In the setting of the first general case, an economy of the sovereign's kind is revealed to be flawed in comparison with the economy of political society. In no deep sense can the sovereign's economy itself add to self-determination in those countries that become linked with it. In its domain the sovereign must regulate the language of economic affairs. It cannot therefore admit unpolitical leaders into open critical discourse with it because to do so would also open it to the possibility of critical examination by its own subjects. Similarly, unpolitical interests cannot appeal for support to active sections of opinion in the sovereign's domain because the sovereign must show itself to the world as undivided and certain of itself. Power claims control of all the important economic relations of the sovereign's domain. Free entry cannot therefore be conferred on unpolitical countries because there is no free economy for them to enter. The sovereign cannot allow its affairs to appear to be regulated by cross-national institutions because this might suggest to its subjects the legitimacy of institutional constraints on power. So there can be little prospect of bodies such as the IMF, or the GATT, in which unpolitical states are active, playing any intimate part in the policies of the anti-political state. The sovereign can bestow gifts on surrogates and other clients. But this is the beneficence of power and displeasing behaviour will lead to its abrupt cessation. No autonomous area of economic affairs touching the sovereign will be available to unpolitical participation regardless of the sovereign's interests. Anyway, the anti-political state is a poor economic performer, unable and unwilling to dispense riches freely.[23] Its interest rates can be high. It is generally unforgiving in the matter of bad debts. It cannot offer the prospect of rapid economic growth, multiple sources of capital and technological dynamism. It does not have them.

Again the second general case increases the significance of the first. In its distinctiveness from the economy of the sovereign, the merits of the cross-national economy of political society become all the more striking. Logically, then, the existence of sovereigns should lead civil states to place increased emphasis on this economy and on all its institutional and other connections with unpolitical states and to all the services and opportunities it can offer them. That these efforts should usually take a pluralist, disjointed form is to be expected because the political economy is not an instrument of any national or ideological campaign. Clearly the existence of sovereigns in the unpolitical world will give civil states strategic concerns there too, and these will sometimes stimulate civil governments to make direct economic transfers with the aim of forestalling sovereigns. When this sort of civil activity occurs it constitutes an effort to preserve the world of the first general case and an inconsistency would occur if it detracted from or replaced it.

CONCLUSIONS

1. The relations between international civil society and unpolitical states can be understood in themselves as a distinctive general case. In the affairs of this general case, citizens and authorities can consistently maintain a civil position. Fundamental to this position is a commitment to self-determination understood as a condition of the establishment of statehood.

2. To approach the unpolitical world as an arena of direct civil struggle with anti-political sovereigns is inherently dangerous to the civil position.

3. Civility therefore requires the maintenance of the relations of the first general case despite the transformative effects created by the active existence of sovereigns. For all its difficulties, nothing in the issues examined by this enquiry shows this to be impossible.

CHAPTER 12

Concluding Remarks

This enquiry began with an examination of principles of foreign policy derived from a model that assumed each state to be like all other states in its external character and behaviour. These principles proved defective because the conception of the world on which they depended could not withstand comparison with the world as it is. Then an attempt was made to get to the heart of the matter through the direct analysis of issues of foreign policy. This method took foreign policy to be a discrete, though complex, set of actions and concerns that could be understood as an entity in its own terms. Any such assumption was quickly disproved by the application of the method itself. Yet it did emerge that the plasticity of foreign policy was not limitless. A fundamental discontinuity existed in the relations of states, on each side of which the issues and structures of foreign policy took different forms. So some understanding of the state was required that could provide the basis of an explanation of this curious frontier. Civil statehood fully matched this task. It was precise yet it could exist in and among any number of geographical states. It established the position of its own boundary in the sense that it was not defined by what was extraneous to it; it thus fully explained the nature of international political society and established a firm link between the internal and external nature of the state. In the sense that civility insisted on the priority of the impersonal civil relationship, it was completely autonomous and this autonomy provided a stable position from which to understand states beyond the boundaries of statehood. It established the meaning of sovereignty and the possible meanings of rule without political qualification. Now the enquiry could return to issues of foreign policy unencumbered by the mistaken assumptions of traditional usage. Foreign policy was not a thing in itself and all its principles were principles of civil statehood or derivations of principles of civil statehood.

It will have been obvious throughout that the procedures, commitment and results of this enquiry contrast markedly with those of orthodox marxism, which reduce the state to an epiphenomenon and which claim both to identify and embody an absolute sovereign. Yet the understanding of autonomous statehood central to this enquiry is not some kind of defensive reaction to marxism. The notion of political relations developed here has origins that far antedate Marx. And the course of the enquiry would have been exactly the same had the contemporary fashion in sovereignty relied on abstractions different from those underpinning communism. Indeed its course would have been essentially unaltered had the environment of political relations been exclusively dominated by miscellaneous tyrants and conspirators. So in the text references to the contrast between the civil understanding and marxism have been made sparingly. Civility defines its negation (the anti-political sovereign), not the other way about; and the paths to sovereignty are by no means exclusively marxist. Another consideration has weighed. It is conceivable that current changes in movements claiming to incorporate a marxist understanding of the state (known generically as 'eurocommunism' in western Europe but lacking a convenient sobriquet in Latin America) may denote an approaching acceptance by them of the priority of the civil relationship and therefore of the absolute character of civil statehood. The imagination suggests a number of theoretical convolutions whereby this conclusion might be reached. However, suspicion of abstraction of the marxist order is intrinsic to the commitment to civility; one such convolution can easily be confounded by another. In the abstract marxist future, the world's population is apparently to be reduced, through struggle, to a single community with one imperative interest. Such a delusion is unlikely to promote modesty in its victims. In the civil perspective only the acceptance of the political qualification is fundamental; civility makes no arbitrary distinctions among human beings, nor does it condemn them to interminable struggle in pursuit of some grey millennium; on the foundation of the civil relationship any number of communities, interests and practices may express themselves; and given the security of statehood the apparatus of individual states may be put to all kinds of national and cross-national purposes. When a marxist movement seizes a state, subjecting it *in toto* to its sovereignty, it appears, as a matter of fact, that abstraction is incapable of constraining power and the future is actually defined by a leadership. In its domain the Soviet Russian sovereign is able to claim and impose a monopoly on the interpretation of Marx and abstractions are duly manipulated to support and excuse power. Thus the export to the Soviet Union of products of advanced technology from constitutional countries can be represented as a clear indicator of their internal weaknesses and contradictions. More seriously, the Soviet sovereign can claim to represent the true interest of the world's populace; so its uses of power can always be claimed to be progressive; and its efforts to achieve military and naval superiority become a universal historical imperative.[24] If civil statehood were abstract it would no doubt lend itself to similar casuistry. But it is not.

Less elementary than its contrast with marxism, this enquiry has developed in a way that pits it against many persuasive views of foreign policy and international relations that are recurrently influential inside political society.

1. In the civil perspective, international relations as a whole cannot be

treated as an arena of power relations. In this enquiry sovereign power has been given a clear meaning: it is the capability and will to move events in disregard of the political qualification and therefore of the absolute standing of civil statehood. No distinction has been drawn between domestic power and international power. There is no place for power at any level inside political society; when it actually occurs in this setting it is invariably an aberration. In international relations as a whole, power thus emanates from anti-political and unpolitical sources. Civil authorities and citizens may be obliged to respond to power but they do not act in terms of power.

2.   Similarly, this enquiry has dismissed crude notions of foreign policy as the perpetual expression or pursuit of the national interest. In political relations the meanings of national interest, of which there are many, are always contextual. In political society the national interest never refers to a sovereign imperative of state. The national interest in this sense is always a response to anti-political challenge and has no direct bearing on other kinds of relations.

3.   The civil understanding developed in this enquiry has rejected the common presumption that a conflict exists between realism and idealism in the perception and conduct of international affairs. The civil relationship is an ideal one. As the condition of all other relations there can never be anything superior to it. This is not to suggest that all the structures, projects and practices that exist inside the boundaries of civil statehood are somehow perfect. This would be absurd. What is ideal at the level of statehood finds expression in the political qualification of what, in almost all cases, is deeply and irremediably imperfect. There is nothing mystical or mythical about the civil relationship and of itself it cannot blind anyone to human failings. At the world level an appreciation of civility actually sharpens the awareness of the nature of power and of its realities and horrors.

4.   Since civility is the antithesis of sovereign power, the civil perspective must include a vision of a world of civil states. The extension of civility cannot be achieved by direct uses of power because power can only resist or overthrow power. The political qualification is not an imposition. But civil authorities may act in ways that delay or discourage the extension of civility or that even retard it. This is why the eleventh chapter refers to the relations of civil states and unpolitical states as a possible world. The point here is that the civil understanding of international relations is critical. It does not deal in large moralistic programmes; but neither does it accept the current international system of states as given. It does not resolve all foreign policy arguments but it does know what they should be about.

Notes

1. For all its simplicity, this model could not have been constructed in the absence of a rigorous academic literature on international and other systems. In the present effort the influence of the following works will be readily detected:
   M. A. Kaplan, *System and Process in International Politics*, Wiley, New York, 1957
   G. Modelski, *A Theory of Foreign Policy*, Pall Mall, London, 1962
   W. Riker, *The Theory of Political Coalitions*, Yale University Press, New Haven, Conn., 1962.

2. This example comes from P. Nettl, 'The State as a Conceptual Variable', *World Politics*, vol. xx, no. 4, July 1968. Reprinted in W. Hanreider (ed.) *Comparative Foreign Policy*, McKay, New York, 1971.

3. Copious evidence to this effect is set out in W. Wallace, *The Foreign Policy Process in Britain*, Allen and Unwin, London, 1976.

4. This general point emerges forcefully from A. Schlesinger, *The Imperial Presidency*, Deutsch, London, 1974.

5. This foreign policy approach to the understanding of international organisation was suggested to me by M. Doxey, 'International Organisation in Foreign Policy Perspective', in G. Keeton and G. Schwartzenberger (eds) *The Year Book of World Affairs*, Stevens, London, 1975.

6. Article 25 (chapter 5), Charter of the United Nations.

7. This argument is developed by J. Narvesou, 'Pacificism: A Philosophical Analysis', *Ethics*, vol. 75, pp. 259–71. Reprinted in R. Wasserstrom (ed) *War and Morality*, Wadsworth, Belmond, California, 1970.

8. This notion of war obviously derives from a reading of Clausewitz. But it is not a representation of Clausewitz. The latest edition of the work in question is M. Howard and P. Paret (eds and trans) *Carl von Clausewitz On War*, Princeton University Press, 1976.

9. The influence of K. R. Popper is evident throughout this chapter but never more so than at this point. Particular acknowledgement must be made of his *Conjectures and Refutations*, Routledge and Kegan Paul, London, 1963.

10. Cf. Martin Wight, 'Why is there no International Theory?' *International Relations*, vol. ii, no. 1, April 1960. Reprinted in H. Butterfield and M. Wight (eds) *Diplomatic Investigations*, Allen and Unwin, London, 1966. This enquiry becomes a kind of rebuttal of Professor Wight.

11. At this point in my journey I took care *not* to consult a dictionary of any kind.

12. See K. R. Popper, 'Towards a Rational Theory of Tradition' in *Conjectures and Refutations, op. cit.*

13. See M. Oakeshott, *On Human Conduct*, Oxford University Press, 1975, particularly the essay 'On the Character of a Modern European State'.

14. See R. Braun, 'Taxation, Sociopolitical Structure, and State-building: Great Britain and Brandenburg-Prussia', and G. Ardant, 'Financial Policy and Economic

Infrastructure of Modern States and Nations', both in C. Tilly (ed.) *The Formation of National States in Western Europe,* Princeton University Press, 1975.

15. This section has distant origins in a sense of disappointment experienced on first reading Kant's *Perpetual Peace,* the latest translation of which is contained in H. Reiss and H. Nisbet (eds and trans) *Kant's Political Writings,* Cambridge University Press, 1971. Oakeshott's comment (*On Human Conduct, op. cit.,* p. 273) gets to the root of Kant's error.

16. See A. Schonfield, 'International Economic Relations of the Western World: An Overall View', in A. Shonfield (ed.) *International Economic Relations of the Western World, 1959–71,* vol. I, Oxford University Press, 1976.

17. The sense of the term 'practices' in this and all subsequent passages derives from (but is not a representation of) Oakeshott, *On Human Conduct, op. cit.,* pp. 55–60.

18. See G. Ardant, 'Financial Policy and Economic Infrastructure of Modern States and Nations', *op. cit.*

19. A suggestion developed by F. A. Hayek, *Denationalisation of Money,* Institute of Economic Affairs, London, 1976.

20. Though the central argument of this chapter is, I think, my own, it clearly could not have been developed in ignorance of the classic writers on totalitarianism— Arendt, Friedrich, Schapiro. I am also aware of an ambiguous indebtedness to Marx.

21. This example comes from C. Hosoy, H. Owen and A. Schonfield, *Collaboration with Communist Countries in Managing Global Problems,* The Trilateral Commission, New York and elsewhere, 1977.

22. The classic statement of the group view of the state that I here refute is A. F. Bentley, *The Process of Government,* University of Chicago Press, 1908.

23. Comparative national income figures have been worked out by I. S. Koropecky; see Z. M. Fallenbuchl (ed.) *Economic Development in the Soviet Union and Eastern Europe,* vol. I, Praegar, New York, 1975, pp. 322–3.

24. See R. J. Mitchell, 'A New Brezhnev Doctrine', *World Politics,* vol. XXX, no. 3, April 1978.

Index

255